D1187936

From Sepoy
to Subedar

'He got up to welcome my uncle'

From Sepoy to Subedar

*being the Life and Adventures
of Subedar Sita Ram,
a Native Officer of
the Bengal Army
written and related by himself*

Edited by James Lunt

Translated and First Published
by Lieutenant-Colonel Norgate,
Bengal Staff Corps at Lahore, 1873

Illustrated by Frank Wilson

Military Book Society

First English edition 1873
This edition published by the Military Book
Society, St Giles House, 49–50 Poland St.,
London, W1A 2LG by arrangement with Routledge
& Kegan Paul Ltd
Printed in Great Britain
by Unwin Brothers Limited
The Gresham Press Old Woking Surrey, England
A member of the Staples Printing Group

This book is dedicated to the

jawan

past and present

with admiration and affection

The Hindi word, *jawan*, meaning village lad, or peasant, has long been used by the officers of the Indian Army as an affectionate description for their soldiers.

Contents

List of Maps

*James Thomas Norgate, 'The Translator', was born in Suffolk in 1824. He joined the Bengal Native Army as an Ensign in 1843, and retired with the honorary rank of Major-General in 1880. He served with the 69th Bengal Native Infantry, which mutinied at Multan in 1858, and he later commanded the 12th Punjab Infantry during the campaign in Bundelkhand in 1859. He died in 1894.

Preface by Translator

I have attempted to render into English the Life and Adventures of this Native Officer, and in so doing have often been obliged to give the general meanings, rather than adhere to a literal translation of many sentences and ideas, the true idiom of which it is almost impossible to transpose into English.

In some parts of the narrative it becomes rather confused, and some of the dates are evidently incorrect, but when it is remembered that this 'life' embraces scenes and events which occurred during a period of half a century, and are related by an old man, these errors are not surprising.

For the opinions contained in the work, I am not responsible.

The narrative without doubt might have been expressed in more elegant language, and there are incidents enough, had one the pen of a 'Grant', to have produced a romantic tale, but as Truth is said to be stranger than Fiction, I have preferred to let it remain in its own unvarnished style and simplicity. For the benefit of those who may wish to criticize the translation, where any idiomatic words are used, the originals are often given, and critics are welcome to put that construction on these as seemeth them best. It is believed that this is one of the first attempts of any native soldier to give his thoughts and ideas to the world, and it took great trouble and a great amount of assurances before the *Subedar* would part with his memoirs; so afraid are the natives (particularly those receiving pensions) of saying a word which might be considered to censure Government.

It is certain that if we were to study this little work, we might obtain a better insight into native modes of thought and character than unfortunately many now possess. This *Life and Adventures* appeared many years ago in an Indian periodical since defunct (alas, the fate of most Indian periodicals) and at the time met with great favour, and excited no little interest.

The Times said in 1863, 'It would be well if all officers whose lot compels them to serve with native troops were to study this life of the old *Subedar*'.

Punjab   The Translator*
1 January 1873

Editorial Note

Sita Ram Pande, the author of these memoirs, was one of the many Indian soldiers who helped the British to conquer India, and thereafter to hold it. He enlisted in 1812 as a *sepoy* into an infantry regiment of the Bengal Native Army, and he remained a soldier until he went on pension in 1860 after forty-eight years' service. During the intervening period he had taken part in the campaigns against the Gurkhas, the Pindaris and Mahrattas, and the Sikhs; he had been present at the storming of Bharatpore; and he had taken part in the ill-fated First Afghan War. He remained true to his salt during the Mutiny. He rose from *Sepoy* to *Subedar*, but only attained the latter rank when he was too old to be able to perform his duties. He claims that he was wounded seven times, taken prisoner once, and was awarded six medals. At the end of this long and interesting career, and at the behest of his last Commanding Officer, he set down in writing the story of his experiences in the service of the always incomprehensible British.

The expansion of British rule in India during the last century is abundantly documented. In addition to State Papers there are numerous memoirs, letters, and diaries of British officers, military and civilian, who played a part, great or small, in extending the frontiers of British India, and in pacifying the interior. Even more humble individuals, such as John Shipp and Private Waterfield, have committed their experiences to writing; but although it may be a mistake to claim for Sita Ram that his memoirs are unique of their kind, it can be said that they are the only account *so far published* of an Indian *sepoy*'s experiences during the first half of the nineteenth century. Other memoirs may come to light in the future; they may be lying in a cupboard in some feudal mansion in Bundelkhand or the Punjab, or be hidden beneath the debris in a humble village home in Madras or Maharashtra. So far as is known, however, Sita Ram was the only Indian soldier of his time to yield to the persuasion of his British Commanding Officer and write the story of his life in the service of the *Sirkar*.

He was reluctant to write his memoirs and for obvious reasons. The *Sirkar*—a Hindi word meaning government or rule but applied in these pages to mean the East India Company—was the fount from which he drew his pension. It was for that pension, small enough in all conscience but sufficient to hold poverty at bay, that Sita Ram underwent so many trials and tribulations. He was fearful lest anything he wrote might offend the Government and result in the termination of his pension. And yet he wrote frankly, giving praise where praise was due, and where criticism was justified he was critical, both of the policies of the East India Company, and of the British officers under whose command he served. There is a great deal of wisdom in the old man's comments, written in the evening of his days, and who of us, with the advantages of hindsight, would quarrel with his observations on the folly of the First Afghan War, or with the causes to which he attributes the mutiny of the Bengal Native Army in 1857?

It is generally accepted that Sita Ram was persuaded to write his memoirs by Lieutenant-Colonel (later Major-General) J. T. Norgate under whom he had served in the 12th Punjab Infantry during the Mutiny. He completed the manuscript in 1861, shortly after his retirement, and sent one copy to Norgate, who was then serving in the Cantonment Magistrates' Department in the Punjab. A second copy may have been presented to the Bajpai family, the landlords of Sita Ram's village in the Rae Bareli district of Uttar Pradesh, between Lucknow and Allahabad. The manuscript is believed to have been written in the dialect known as Awadhi, or western Hindi, and was translated into English by Norgate, assisted by an Indian translator. The first publication, according to Norgate, was in an Indian periodical 'since defunct', and he claims that it received a favourable notice in *The Times* in 1863. However, a search in *The Times* of that year has not discovered the notice. The first extant edition was published in Lahore in 1873, and aroused sufficient interest for an Urdu translation to be made of the English text. There was a second English edition in 1880. Norgate seems to have remained in touch with Sita Ram for some years after 1861, and he makes no reference to the old man's death in the 1873 edition. In the 1880 edition, however, Norgate says that Sita Ram was probably dead. This is more than likely since he would by then have been over eighty, a great age for an Indian in those days.

There was no other edition until 1910, when Lieutenant-Colonel D. A. Phillott, secretary and member of the Board of Examiners in the vernacular languages, decided to use Sita Ram's memoirs as a text-book for the examinations. He translated Norgate's version into simple Urdu, and this version was serialized in *Fauji Akhbar*, the newspaper of the Indian Army until 1947. In 1911 Phillott published Norgate's English version, without alteration, 'for the benefit of candidates', and called this the third edition, regarding Norgate's publications of 1873 and 1880 as the first and second editions. His new Urdu translation of 1910—Part I of the official textbook for the Higher Standard Examination in Urdu—was titled *Kawab-o-Khayal* (*Thoughts and Dreams*). This book was an official publication and successive editions were published in 1914, 1921, 1923, 1931, 1940 and 1943. As a standard textbook it became known to all British officers who served with the Indian Army, and to many officers of the British Army also.

Doubt has been cast on the authenticity of Sita Ram's memoirs by several authorities, and most recently by J. A. B. Palmer in his *The Mutiny Outbreak at Meerut in 1857* (1967). Lord Sidmouth, a military historian of distinction who has closely studied Sita Ram's narrative, found it hard to account for the fact that it has proved impossible to establish with accuracy the regiments in which Sita Ram served. The fact that it has been impossible to trace the original Hindi manuscript, or Norgate's first English translation which he claims to have published in 1863 or thereabouts, has added to the doubts. However, the late Sir Girja Shankar Bajpai, one of India's most distinguished public servants, told Sir George Grierson in 1915 that he had read the Hindi version. Grierson, who was conducting the final examination of probationers for the Indian Civil Service, asked Bajpai to what copy he referred and the candidate replied, 'Sita Ram gave my grandfather a copy of his book, and it is still in our family. I used to read it as a boy and knew it off by heart.' Unfortunately action was not taken to establish whether Bajpai had read Sita Ram's original manuscript, or merely Norgate's translation. His father said later that he did not possess Sita Ram's manuscript. Mr U. S. Bajpai, son of Sir G. S. Bajpai, has similarly denied any knowledge of Sita Ram's manuscript in a letter to me dated 22 August 1968. He went on to say that most of his grandfather's papers had been destroyed, and he could not recollect his father ever having mentioned the book to him.

Sir Patrick Cadell, the historian of the Bombay Army, who devoted many years to a study of Sita Ram's memoirs, came to the conclusion that the memoirs were genuine. 'That the story is absolutely genuine, and Sita Ram's own, cannot, I think, be doubted,' he wrote. 'The little hits at the Mohammedans and the Punjabis, the occasional criticisms, shrewd but friendly, of his officers, the references to Hindu customs, would have required the pen of a Kipling or a Morier to invent, and there is no reason to believe that Norgate possessed this.' Of course Cadell may be regarded as a prejudiced witness, and it is by no means unlikely that Sita Ram embroidered his narrative, and introduced as his own experiences he had been told round the camp fire. 'Unfortunately in old age the memory often finds it hard to distinguish between things seen and things heard,' wrote Sir Charles Oman in his *Wellington's Army* (Edward Arnold). 'It is not uncommon to find a writer who represents himself as having been present at scenes where he cannot have been assisting, and still more frequent to detect him applying to one date perfectly genuine anecdotes which belong to another. One or two of the most readable narratives frankly mix up the sequence of events, with a note that the exact dating can not be reconstructed.'

It is partly on account of Sita Ram's haziness about names and dates that his story rings true for me. He certainly could not have kept a diary from which to refresh his memory, nor is it likely that he wrote many letters, since most of those with whom he might have wished to correspond could not read. His chronology is often at fault; he mentions regiments as participating in a campaign at times when they are still in their peacetime garrisons, but he is correct in so far as they did take part at a later stage in the operations; he confuses the names of his British officers, but gets near enough to the vernacular rendering of the English to make it possible to trace many of them. Even his grouses and complaints ring true; they are those of an old soldier who is convinced that the 'old days were the best days'. Surely most old soldiers think the same? However, there will continue to be doubts about the authenticity of Sita Ram's memoirs until more positive proof of their authorship can be established. I can only say that the longer I have studied them—and this study has extended over twenty years—the more convinced I have become that in essence they are true.

In editing this edition I have had to decide whether to leave Norgate's translation untouched or whether to render it more easily readable. I have decided for the latter. I have also cut out most of the Hindi expressions with which Norgate sprinkled his translation. Since Sita Ram's chronology is often at fault, and also because he rambles a great deal, I have been faced with the choice of either cutting and re-shaping the book completely, or leaving it more or less as it was originally written. I have chosen to leave it because I feel this best represents the way it was written in the original Hindi. Finally, I have had to decide whether or not there should be introductions for each chapter, and footnotes to expand on, or explain, references in the narrative. Although I do not care for footnotes myself, there are unlikely to be many readers who possess a detailed knowledge of British-Indian military history. For those who do, and who find my footnotes irritating glimpses of the obvious, I apologize for the annoyance I may have caused them. However, I hope my notes will be of use for the general reader, who may learn from them something of the Indian *sepoys* who served the British so faithfully in good times and in bad, and who played no small part in the making of modern India.

Mons, Belgium   J.D.L.

Acknowledgements

I must begin by expressing my thanks to my collaborator, Frank Wilson, who has illustrated this book. It is largely as a result of his enthusiasm and encouragement that I have undertaken the editing of these memoirs. He has the advantage over me, having served in the pre-1947 Indian Army, but together we share a deep affection for India and a profound admiration for that splendid fighting man, the Indian soldier.

I have received much assistance from Mr D. W. King and the Staff of the Ministry of Defence Library, the Librarian and Staff of the Royal United Service Institution, and also from Mrs Archer of the India Office Library, Foreign and Commonwealth Office, and Mr W. Y. Carman. I am most grateful to them.

When first I checked through the manuscript to obtain the exact English rendering of the many words in Hindi, I was greatly helped by Captain H. I. S. Kanwar of New Delhi, himself a keen military historian. Major-General K. C. Khanna, Indian Army (retired), a friend of many years' standing, has also assisted me. I am grateful to them both.

I have also to thank Corporal William Davis, RAF, who has spent long hours typing the manuscript, and whose assistance has been invaluable.

This has really been a labour of love, whatever its shortcomings, and I was fortunate in being able to start the writing of it while serving on the staff of the British High Commissioner in India in 1968. My main acknowledgement must therefore be to India, that fascinating land, and to my many Indian friends who made me feel so welcome wherever I went.

A Bombay Grenadier 1800

Khabi sukh aur khabi dukh
Angrez ka naukar.

Sometimes pleasure, sometimes pain,
In the service of the English.

(*marching song of the old Bombay Infantry*)

Introduction

We are still too close to the actual events for an unbiased judgement to be made on British rule in India. When in due course such a judgement can be made, one aspect of British rule is certain to surprise historians. This is that so vast a country, containing so many warlike people, could have been conquered by so few soldiers, and thereafter have been held in subjection by a military garrison composed chiefly of natives of the country. Indeed, the chief danger to the continuance of British rule lay in the spreading of disaffection in the native army, as was noted by Sir Thomas Munro, Governor of the Madras Presidency from 1820 to 1827. '. . . The spirit of independence will spring up in this army long before it is ever thought of among the people,' he wrote. 'The army will not wait for the slow operation of the instruction of the people, and the growth of liberty among them, but will hasten to execute their own measures for the overthrow of the Government.' The native army was in fact the key to British security, and the accuracy of Munro's prediction was proved correct thirty years later when the Bengal Native Army rose in revolt; had the Madras and Bombay Armies thrown in their lot with Bengal, all India would almost certainly have been lost.

The British went to India to trade—not to conquer. The Honourable East India Company traced its origins to the charter granted by Queen Elizabeth I on 31 December 1599, to 'the Governor and Company of the Merchants of London, trading unto the East Indies'. The Company's first factory, or trading settlement, was established in 1612 at Surat, on the west coast of India, and in 1640 another settlement was established at Madras on the east coast. In that same year the first expedition was sent to Bengal, and was so well received by the Nawab of Bengal that the Company decided to establish a trading post on the river Hooghly, which has since grown into the great city of Calcutta. Bombay, which came into British possession as part of the dowry of Catherine of Braganza, was ceded by Charles II to the Company in 1668.

The Company, during its early years in India, did its utmost to avoid becoming embroiled in the affairs of the various Indian potentates from whom it had received concessions to trade. Its attitude towards military expenditure did not differ from any other commercial enterprise's. War was basically unprofitable and hindered economic growth, and therefore the Company's servants were strictly charged to confine themselves to commerce. However, this was not as easy for the men on the spot as it was for their masters in London. The fact that the hinterland was seldom at peace, the various rajahs and nawabs warring continually with each other, forced the Company to take steps to defend their settlements against attack. Fort St George was built at Madras, Fort William at Calcutta, and permission was reluctantly given for the recruitment of small numbers of European soldiers and half-caste Portuguese, known as Topasses, who provided guards and escorts on ceremonial occasions, and acted as a police force within the settlements' boundaries. Their military value was negligible.

It was, however, the struggle between the British and French for the control of southern India and Bengal that compelled the Company to revise its military policy at the expense of its profits. War broke out between the two countries in 1744, and the French captured Fort St George after only four days' siege. The principal reason for the French success was the lack of an adequate force with which to oppose them, the Company preferring to economize in soldiers and to rely instead on its Indian allies. But when help was needed the allies were found wanting. Having reduced Fort St George, the French then moved farther south to Fort St David which was weakly defended. The garrison consisted of about 200 Europeans and 100 Topasses, together with some ill-equipped levies. Energetic efforts were made to raise and equip 2,000 Indian irregulars under their own officers but led by European commanders. It was from this disorderly mob that the senior regiments of the Company's Madras Native Army traced their descent. This force would certainly not have been strong enough to withstand the French but the Nawab of Arcot intervened on the side of the Company and the French withdrew. When the assault was renewed, in 1747, the arrival of a British fleet bringing reinforcements saved the day.

Among those reinforcements was a certain Major Stringer Lawrence, later to be known as the 'Father of the Indian Army'. A portrait of this stout and rubicund officer hangs in Fort St George, and one wonders how he managed to endure the hot and humid climate of Madras in his thick scarlet coat, tight-fitting waistcoat and breeches, not to mention his wig. Lawrence can claim the credit for being the first British officer to form native or *sepoy* regiments on the European model. He provided them with British officers and non-commissioned officers, and a proper code of pay and discipline, as well as ensuring that in discipline and training they were fit to take their place alongside European battalions in the field. The Hindi word *sepoy* is derived from the Persian *sipahi*, meaning soldier, and the East India Company's Indian regiments were always referred to as native, or *sepoy*, until 1885, when the word native, which the events of the Mutiny had somehow made derogatory, was dropped. *Sepoy* went out of use some time later.

Robert Clive, who had originally gone out to India as a civilian 'writer' in the Company's service, soon discovered his military talents in the wars against the French and he became Lawrence's ablest lieutenant. When he was sent from Madras at the end of 1756 to restore the Company's fortunes in Bengal, he emulated Lawrence's example by raising a battalion of carefully selected *sepoys*, clothing them on the British pattern, and appointing a British officer to instruct and command them. This, the earliest Bengal Native regiment, was known for many years as the *Lal Paltan* (the Red Regiment) from the colour of its tunics, but later it went by the name of *Gillis-ki-Paltan* from Captain Primrose Galliez who commanded it for many years. It was the 1st Bengal Native Infantry (1st BNI) when it mutinied at Cawnpore in 1857, and was thereafter disbanded. The word *paltan* is derived from the English platoon, which is itself a corruption of the French *peloton*. In Indian terms it came to mean a regiment, or battalion, of infantry, while *rissalah* denoted a troop or regiment of horse.

Many years were to pass before the Company's Native Army was established on regular lines but from the first it was divided between the Presidencies of Bengal, Madras, and Bombay. The different circumstances existing in each Presidency resulted in each Presidency Army being virtually autonomous under its own Commander-in-Chief, although the Governor-General in Calcutta, who was also Commander-in-Chief until 1833, exercised supreme control. At first the main expansion of the Company's territories took place in the south, involving the Madras, or 'Coast', Army, and the Bombay Army to a lesser extent. However, as the Company's control over southern India was consolidated with the defeat of Tippu Sultan towards the end of the eighteenth century, the centre of interest moved first to the Deccan and Central India, and then towards Sind, the Punjab, and the North-West. The Bengal Native Army then became the largest and most important of the Presidency Armies, and its Commander-in-Chief took precedence over his Madras and Bombay colleagues as Commander-in-Chief in India. This situation lasted until 1895 when the offices of Commander-in-Chief of the Madras and Bombay Armies were abolished and all the troops in India were placed under the direct command of the Commander-in-Chief in India, and under the control of the Government of India.

The Company had from its earliest days in India maintained an establishment of European troops. These were originally recruited from various nationalities, of which the Germans proved the steadiest; by the beginning of the eighteenth century the composition was mainly British. The 1st Bombay European Regiment was the senior of the Company's European regiments, and Clive formed the Bengal European Regiment in 1756. This regiment ended its existence in 1922 as the Royal Munster Fusiliers, while the British Army's link with the East India Company's Army has ended even more recently with the disappearance of the Durham Light Infantry from the Army List. The second battalion of that very distinguished regiment was descended from the 2nd Bombay European Regiment. All these European regiments had distinguished records, but the Bengal Horse Artillery was probably the *corps d'élite* of the Company's European troops and had nothing to fear by comparison with the Royal, or King's, Troops. The latter were provided by the British Government at the Company's expense and were costly to maintain. The Company therefore endeavoured to keep their numbers to a minimum and in 1824, for example, there were only four British cavalry regiments and seventeen infantry battalions in India. This amounted to less than 30,000 men, and they were widely dispersed throughout the sub-continent. In that same year the Bengal Native Army alone contained sixty-nine infantry battalions, and the strength of the three Presidency Armies amounted to upwards of 200,000. For the security of its possessions in India, and for their further extension, the Company relied mainly on its *sepoy* regiments.

Although the organization of these regiments was slightly different in each Presidency, depending on the types of *sepoys* enlisted and the whims of the individual Commanders-in-Chief, there was not a great deal of difference between a Madras, Bombay, and Bengal battalion. There were twenty-three British officers in each battalion establishment, but there would seldom be more than nine or ten present at any one time; the remainder would be absent on the staff, on leave, or in other kinds of military and civilian employment. These officers held the Company's, not the King's, commission, and there was bitter rivalry between the Company's officers and those officers of the British Army serving in India; nor was this rivalry diminished by the fact that the Commanders-in-Chief of the Presidency Armies were usually found from the British Army. In each battalion there was a small *cadre* of a dozen or so British non-commissioned officers, who had either enlisted directly into the Company's European regiments, or who had transferred to them from the British Army.

The remainder of the battalion was composed of the natives of India, amounting in all to about 1,000 men, but strengths tended to fluctuate in accordance with the Company's financial policies. There were from eight to ten companies in each battalion, nominally commanded by a British officer, but often a native officer would be in command. The Grenadier and Light companies consisted of picked men, and it was not unusual to form 'Flank' battalions from the Grenadier or Light companies of several regiments in order to provide a stiffening for some particular operation or campaign. Since there were few British officers present with a battalion at any one time, most of the administration and training was carried out by the native officers. The senior of these in an infantry battalion was the *Subedar-Major* (*Rissaldar-Major* in the cavalry). There were ten *Subedars* in each battalion, one per company, and rather fewer *Rissaldars* in a cavalry regiment. The junior native officers were called *Jemadars* and normally commanded platoons. This name has now been dropped in the Indian Army and *Naib-Subedar* has been substituted; the word *jemadar* is also used to describe a sweeper, of menial caste, and it was never a popular title. Sergeants were called *Havildars*, and Corporals were *Naiks*.

Each Presidency Army recruited mainly from within the borders of its Presidency, but all three armies recruited from other areas as well. It is wrong to assume that the Bengal Army was mainly composed of Bengalis, as has sometimes been suggested in the correspondence columns of Indian newspapers; comparatively few Bengalis were in fact enlisted, as much on account of the Bengalis' reluctance to enlist as for any other reason. The bulk of the Bengal Army was recruited from Oudh, in what is now Uttar Pradesh, and from Bihar. Both Hindus and Mahommedans were enlisted, although high-caste Hindus made up the majority. The Bombay Army also recruited quite large numbers of *Purbias* (men from the east), which was the general name for men, and particularly for Brahmin and Rajput soldiers, from Oudh and UP. These sturdy peasants made smart soldiers but religious scruples, due to their high caste, made them difficult to handle at times. They had, for example, an aversion for serving beyond the sea, or even beyond the river Indus, or in Sind. The Madras and Bombay Armies, containing as they did a much smaller proportion of high-caste Hindus, gave much less trouble, and were relatively unaffected by the Mutiny in 1857.

The profession of arms was, and still is, a very honourable one in India. Therefore there was never any shortage of recruits. But promotion was slow, because discharge was seldom requested, and a man might expect to serve thirty or forty years before he became a native officer. Promotion was equally slow for the Company's British officers, and Colonels of over sixty, and Generals of over seventy, were not uncommon. Long service in the trying climate of India, without any of the amenities that today make it bearable for the European, must inevitably have sapped both physique and mental faculties. Training was mostly restricted to the parade ground and the musketry range; manoeuvres involving more than a few companies hardly ever took place; battalions were often split up into small detachments over wide areas, escorting treasure, acting as police, and so on. It was on the whole a dull and stultifying existence, in which home leaves were few and far between, and some British officers spent thirty years in India without returning to England. British officers with any ambition soon tired of regimental duty and sought alternative employment of which there was plenty to be had. Those with a gift for languages joined the Political Department, the high road to advancement in the Company's service, while others joined the Public Works Department, Customs and Excise, or other civil departments. Those who were content to remain at regimental duty can hardly be blamed if they became fossilized by the dull routine of cantonment life, but by no means all the Company's officers come into this category. Some of them managed to retain their vigour and keenness, and had a remarkable hold over their men.

By today's standards the Company's soldiers were ill-trained and inefficient, and yet they were incomparably superior to the undisciplined Indian levies which took the field against them. In particular, the superior handling of the Company's artillery more often than not guaranteed the victory, and the nearest the British ever came to defeat in India was against the Sikhs, whose artillery was equally well-trained and well-served. When one remembers that battles in those days were fought at close quarters, often reduced to the hundred yards or so that a musket ball would carry, it is not difficult to visualize the devastating effect of a discharge of grapeshot delivered at point-blank range. It needed highly disciplined troops to stand up to such fire, and to the bayonet charge that invariably followed through the billowing cannon smoke, and few of the Company's enemies were capable of doing this. Usually they left the field as fast as their legs, or their horses, could carry them.

The author of these memoirs took part in no less than seven major campaigns in the course of his forty-eight years' service, and this gives us some idea of the amount of fighting that took place before the British consolidated their rule over India. Most of these campaigns were internal and were fought to establish British predominance in the sub-continent. The wars against the Gurkhas in Nepal, the Pindaris and the Mahrattas in central India, and against the Sikhs in the Punjab, were all part and parcel of the extension of the East India Company's rule until it embraced the whole of India. The fighting that followed the Mutiny of the Bengal Native Army in 1857 comes into a slightly different category since it was, from the British point of view, basically an internal security operation and would doubtless be described as a counter-insurgency operation today. However, the campaign in Afghanistan from 1838 to 1842 was an entirely different campaign from all the others in which Sita Ram took part, and for this reason it requires some explanation here.

From times immemorial the classic invasion route into India has lain through the passes in the north-west, and indeed it was only as recently as 1962 that the Indian Government was made uncomfortably aware that there were also other invasion routes in the north and north-east. Napoleon's invasion of Egypt in 1798 caused great alarm in Calcutta, where the Governor-General and his Council believed that it presaged an overland invasion of India via Persia and Afghanistan. The alarm petered out with the return of Napoleon to France in 1799 but it revived again later. This time it was the Russians who seemed to be menacing Britain's empire in India. They had defeated the Persians in 1827 and had begun to thrust out into Central Asia. Both the British and the Russians endeavoured to establish their influence in Persia, and with a variety of other Central Asian potentates, such as the Amir of Bokhara, and the activities of their agents in these areas was described by Captain Arthur Conolly, who was one of the British agents, as the 'Great Game'.

Russophobia was rampant in Calcutta by 1830 and there were many in London who also suffered from the complaint. It was believed that Russia had ambitions to extend her rule across Central Asia to embrace Afghanistan, and that once her frontier lay along the Hindu Kush an invasion of India was inevitable. The men who believed this were not irresponsible scaremongers but sober-minded statesmen, politicians, and civil servants, and they concluded that the British must establish their influence in Afghanistan before the Russians could get there. This could be done in one of two ways: either Afghanistan could be annexed and administered as a possession of the Crown, or a ruler who was friendly with the British could be established on the throne and be supported by British subsidies.

It so happened that at the time there was an Afghan king living in exile in the Company's territories in India. He was Shah Shujah-ul-Mulk who had been driven from his throne in 1809. Anarchy had followed his departure and ten years were to pass before Dost Mahommed emerged as the strong man of Afghanistan. Even Dost Mahommed, however, could not claim to control the whole of Afghanistan, and moreover he was engaged in a deadly feud with Maharajah Runjeet Singh of the Punjab, who was the Company's ally. Despite the advice of Captain Alexander Burnes, who led a mission to Kabul in 1837, that the British should support Dost Mahommed on condition he guaranteed to have no truck with the Russians, opinion in the Governor-General's Council was inclined to favour the cause of Shah Shujah-ul-Mulk. A treaty was entered into with the latter, as well as with Maharajah Runjeet Singh, whereby Shah Shujah was to be restored to the throne. The British hoped that most of the military support for Shah Shujah would be provided by the Sikhs, but Runjeet Singh was far too wise to allow his soldiers to become embroiled in the mountains of Afghanistan. It therefore became necessary to provide a British expeditionary force to escort Shah Shujah to Kabul and restore him to the throne. Once this had been done, the British intended to withdraw, leaving Shah Shujah to be protected by his own troops which had been raised and equipped in India. Thus the First Afghan War, misconceived from the outset, started as a military promenade and ended in a military disaster.

Sita Ram's account of this campaign, and of the other campaigns in which he participated, provides an excellent example of the attitude of the Indian *sepoys* towards their master, the great Company *Bahadur*, and the British officers who led them. When all was going well they considered themselves to be invincible, but once things began to go wrong, they became first bewildered and then dispirited. They found it hard to comprehend that the English were as fallible as other men, and they soon lost confidence in their leaders and themselves. An army of mercenaries, as the Bengal Native Army was, needs to be successful for most of the time, if not for all of the time, and there can be no doubt that the disastrous campaign in Afghanistan played an important part in damaging the *sepoys'* trust in their British officers. That Sita Ram appears to have retained that trust until the end of his long service is one of the most remarkable aspects of these memoirs, and it redounds greatly to his credit. Loyalty is after all one of the principal requirements of a soldier, and is second only to courage.

Foreword by Sita Ram

FROM SEPOY TO SUBEDAR
Being the Autobiography of a Sepoy

*Defender of the poor!—obedience, etc., etc.—*I have, by the fatherly kindness of the Government, been granted my pension, and according to your desire, I now send your Lordship, by the hands of my son, the papers containing all I can remember of my life during the forty-eight years I have been in the service of the English Nation in which I have suffered seven severe wounds, and received six medals, which I am proud to wear. I trust what I have now written, and what I have before at different times related to your Honour, may prove that there were some who remained faithful, and were not affected by the Wind of Madness which lately blew over Hindustan; for my belief is, it was this which blighted the army. My Lord knows I am not much of a Munshi, although I have been taught Persian; therefore my language must be excused. And without doubt, I have forgotten the English years in some instances; but what I have related to you, and what I have here written, it is true. To say more would be overstepping the bounds of propriety.

> May prosperity ever attend your footsteps!
> Your slave,

(signed) *Sita Ram*, Subedar

Tilowee, Oudh, 1861   Pensioner

India

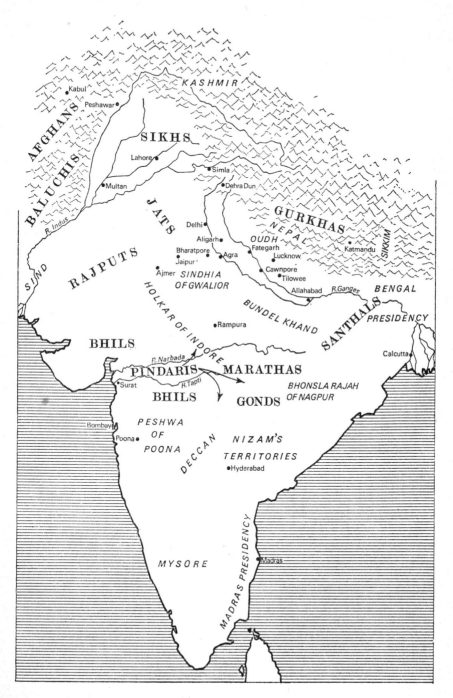

'. . . and relate the wonders of the world he had seen'

1   *The Beginning*

The Beginning

In this chapter, which in the Hindi version began with a long invocation to the Hindu gods, Sita Ram tells of how he became a soldier, despite the opposition of his mother and the family priest, Pandit Duleep Ram. It was his mother's brother, Hanuman, who fired him with ideas of military glory. Hanuman was a native officer (Jemadar[1]) in the East India Company's Bengal Army, and Sita Ram mentions the gold beads worn by his uncle in uniform. These were a mark of distinction, native officers wearing one row of gold beads, and the sepoys three rows of white beads. Sita Ram refers to the East India Company as the Company Bahadur, meaning all-powerful. He also refers to it sometimes as the Sirkar, or government.

Sita Ram was a Brahmin, the highest Hindu caste, and he was therefore subject to the strictest religious observances which, as will be seen later, greatly complicated his life as a soldier. His father was a yeoman farmer of comfortable circumstances who lived in the village of Tilowee, in the Rae Bareli district of Oudh, in what is now the State of Uttar Pradesh (UP). Tilowee lies roughly midway between the cities of Lucknow and Allahabad in the very heart of Hindustan.

At the time of Sita Ram's birth, Oudh was an independent kingdom with its capital at Lucknow, and it was from Oudh that the East India Company recruited the bulk of its soldiers for the Bengal Army, and a lesser number for the Bombay Army. It had originally been a Mughul province, ruled by a Nawab appointed by the Emperor, but the Mughul empire was fast disintegrating by 1797, when Sita Ram was born, and viceroys of provinces had set themselves up as independent princes. The notorious misgovernment of Oudh led to its annexation in 1856 by the East India Company, resulting in much discontent among the soldiers enlisted from Oudh who lost under the Company the valued privileges they had formerly enjoyed in the civil courts when Oudh was independent. The annexation of Oudh by Lord Dalhousie was one of the contributory causes for the Indian Mutiny in 1857.

I was born in the village of Tilowee, in Oudh, in the year 1797. My father was a yeoman farmer, by name Gangadin Pande. He possessed about 150 acres of land which he cultivated himself. My family when I was young were in easy circumstances, and my father was considered a man of importance in our village. I was about six years old when I was placed under the care of our family priest, Duleep Ram, in whom my

---

[1] There were three grades of native officer. The junior was *Jemadar*; the next was *Subedar*, or *Rissaldar* in the Cavalry. The senior was *Subedar-* or *Rissaldar-*Major, of which there was only one in each infantry battalion or cavalry regiment.

father and mother placed implicit confidence, and they never did anything of importance without his advice and consent.

By him I was taught to write and read our own language; also a slight knowledge of figures was imparted to me. After I had acquired this I considered myself far superior in knowledge to all the other boys of my age whom I knew, and held up my head accordingly. All other castes were far below my notice. In fact I fancied myself more clever than my preceptor Duleep himself, and if it had not been for the high respect he was held in by my father, I should on some occasions have even dared to tell him so. Until I was seventeen years of age I attended my father in the management of his land, and was entrusted to give the corn to the coolies he sometimes employed in cutting his crops, drawing water, and so on.

My mother had a brother, by name Hanuman, who was in the service of the Company *Bahadur*, and was a *Jemadar* in an infantry battalion. He had come home on leave for six months, and on his way to his own home, he stayed with my father. My uncle was a very handsome man, and of great personal strength. He used of an evening to sit on the seat before our house, and relate the wonders of the world he had seen, and the prosperity of the great Company *Bahadur* he served, to a crowd of eager listeners, who with open mouths and staring eyes took in all his marvels as undoubted truths. None of his hearers were more attentive than myself, and from these recitals I imbibed a strong desire to enter the world, and try the fortune of a soldier.

Nothing else could I think of, day or night. The rank of *Jemadar* I looked on as quite equal to that of Ghazidin Hydar, the King of Oudh himself; in fact, never having seen the latter, I naturally considered my uncle as of even more importance. He had such a splendid necklace of gold beads, and a curious bright red coat, covered with gold buttons; and, above all, he appeared to have an unlimited supply of gold *mohurs*.[2] I longed for the time when I might possess the same, which I then thought would be directly I became the Company *Bahadur*'s servant.

My uncle had observed how attentive I was to all his stories, and how military ardour had inflamed my breast, and certainly he did all in his power to encourage me. He never said anything about it before my father and mother, or the priest; still, he repeatedly told me privately that if I wished to be a soldier, he would take me back with him on his return to the regiment. How I longed to mention this to my mother, but dared not for I well knew her dearest wish was for me to become a priest. However, one day when I had been reading with Duleep Ram about the mighty battles fought by the gods, I fairly told him my wish to

[2] Gold *mohurs* were part of the coinage of the Mughul Empire.

become a soldier. How horrified he seemed! How he reproached me, declaring that all the instruction he had so laboured to impart to me was thrown away, and that half the stories my uncle had told me were false; that I might be flogged, and certainly should be defiled by entering the Company's service. A hundred other terrors he conjured up, but these had no effect on me.

The priest immediately went to my parents and informed them of my determination, and thus broke to them the subject I had not the courage to tell. To my great surprise my father made no objections; these all came from my mother, who wept, scolded, entreated, and threatened me, ending by imploring me to give up the idea, and abused my father for not preventing such a catastrophe. At this particular period of which I now write a lawsuit was impending over my father, about his right to a mango grove of some 400 trees, and he thought that having a son in the Company *Bahadur*'s service would be the means of getting his case attended to in the law courts of Lucknow; for it was well known that a petition sent by a soldier, through his commanding officer, who forwarded it on to the Resident *sahib*[3] in Lucknow, generally had prompt attention paid to it, and carried more weight than even the bribes and party interest of a mere subject of the King of Oudh.

Shortly after my parents had been informed of my desire to take service with Company *Bahadur* my uncle left them to proceed to his own home fifty miles away. Although my mother never expressed any wish for him to pay another visit when he was about to return to his regiment on the expiration of his leave, he told her that he intended to do so, and that he should take me with him if I were still of the same mind. I walked the first few miles with him on his journey, and made him tell me all about the service I wished to enter, over and over again.

Upon my return home I had to sustain the united attacks of the priest and my mother. They tried every inducement to make me give up the idea. My mother even cursed the day her brother had set foot in our house, but all they could get from me was a promise that I would think over the matter. This I did, and every day became more and more determined to follow my uncle. I now felt idle, and did very little else than learn to wrestle or play with sword-sticks, and consequently neglected my father's fields, which caused me to fall under his displeasure. However a threat from him that I should never be allowed to see my uncle again had

---

[3] The East India Company was represented at the court of the King of Oudh by a Resident, who was a senior civil or military officer of the Company's service. His duties were supposedly advisory, but in fact the King knew that behind the advice lay the ultimate sanction of force.

the effect of bringing me a little to my senses, and my father had no occasion to find fault with me afterwards.

The months passed away, and the rainy season had ended. I was engaged in cutting sugar-cane, with my back towards the road, when I was called by name by someone on a pony. I soon recognized my uncle and flew to his embrace. After inquiries for my father and mother, he asked me if I wished to be a soldier still, and looked pleased when I answered so decidedly, 'Yes'. He told me I was a fine young fellow and that I should go with him.

My uncle remained a few days at our house, during which time, having my father to back him up, he in a measure succeeded in bringing my mother to think it was my destiny to be a soldier, and her fate to part with her son. The priest was requested to look at my horoscope and discover the lucky day for my departure, which he informed us, in the evening, would be at six o'clock in the morning of the fourth day from that day, if no thunder was heard during the period. How anxiously I watched the clouds during those days! How I prayed to the gods of the rain and clouds! And in the evening of the third day, when some dark clouds came up, I was in despair lest rain should fall, and fate be against me.

Duleep, the priest, who really loved me, gave me lots of advice, and made me promise never to disgrace my brahminical thread.[4] He also gave me a charm in which was some dust a thousand Brahmins had trod at holy Allahabad, and he assured me that this charm was so powerful that as long as I kept it no harm could ever befall me. He bestowed on me likewise a book of our holy poems. My father bought me a pony, but gave me no money, as he considered I was now under my uncle's care, and that he could well support me.

The morning came unclouded. It was 10 October 1812,[5] and at six o'clock in the morning I and my uncle left my home to enter what for me was an unknown world. Just before starting, my mother violently kissed me, and gave me six gold *mohurs* sewn in a cloth bag, but being convinced that it was her fate to part with me, she uttered no words but moaned piteously. My worldly baggage when I left home consisted of my pony, my bag of gold *mohurs*, a small brass bowl and string,[6] three

[4] This thread is worn next to the skin, hanging loosely across the body from the shoulder, and is never removed, not even for bathing. It is one of the distinguishing marks of an orthodox Brahmin.

[5] Sita Ram is inclined to be hazy over dates, which is not surprising in view of his age when he was writing his memoirs, and the fact that the Christian calendar differs from the Hindu. He probably means 1814, not 1812, since he says he was seventeen years old when he set off to join the army.

[6] None but a Brahmin can cook for a Brahmin, or draw water for a Brahmin. Hence the small brass bowl with a string to let down into a well to draw water.

brass dishes, one iron dish and spoon, two changes of clothes, a smart turban, a small axe (for self-protection), and a pair of shoes. My uncle's baggage greatly exceeded mine; it was rolled up in a large bundle and carried by a coolie from village to village. This poor man considered himself amply rewarded for his day's work by our giving him whatever bread was left over after the daily meal.

'*He bestowed on me likewise a book of our holy poems*'

'. . . bandits and thugs who then infested the roads'

2   *Joining the Regiment*

Sita Ram describes his journey to Agra, or Akbarabad as it was then called, where his uncle's regiment formed part of the garrison. He also tells of his enlistment into the Army.

Travel in India during the break-up of the Mughul empire was a hazardous business. Bands of armed robbers roamed the countryside and highway robbery was commonplace—'In those days only the strong man armed could guard his goods, and then only until a stronger than he should come.'[1] But perhaps the greatest hazard came from the thugs, or stranglers, who murdered partly for religious motives, and partly for gain. The thugs travelled in bands, posing as innocent travellers, and joined up with other travellers until the moment had come to strike. They believed themselves to be servants of the goddess Kali, wife of Siva, who had taught them their craft in return for her protection, and the yellow scarf, knotted at one end, with which they strangled their victims, represented the hem of Kali's robe. Murder by strangulation was therefore a divine mission, while the booty obtained thereby was the thugs' earthly reward.

Their secrets were so closely kept that it was many years before the British stumbled on the truth about thuggee, and it took a great deal longer before the evil was eradicated. Some of the bands operated under the patronage of powerful landowners, and there was in any case a conspiracy of silence which was hard to penetrate. A special department was set up to stamp out Thuggee, and for much of its existence it was headed by Sir William Sleeman, an officer of the Bengal Army, whose determination and patience largely contributed to the defeat of Thuggee. Over 3,000 Thugs were convicted between 1831 and 1837, and some of them boasted of 700 or more murders. Sita Ram's party had a narrow escape from a band of thugs who fell in with them on their way to Agra. He gives a good description of how the thugs operated, and of how one of his companions was strangled.

The story of his first encounter, as a credulous Indian village boy, with the almost mythical British, rings true to life. It is also descriptive of the almost paternal relationships between officers and sepoys which then existed in the Bengal Army. Later in his memoirs Sita Ram laments the weakening of this relationship, but it is only fair to say that British officers of the Madras and Bombay Armies were critical of their colleagues in the Bengal Army, believing that they paid far too much attention to the religious scruples and susceptibilities of their high-caste sepoys, which in turn led to a weakening of discipline.

[1] *Twilight of the Mughuls* by Percival Spear, Cambridge University Press, 1951.

My uncle and I went one march in the morning. We rested during the heat of the day under a tree, and in the evening we marched the same distance as we had in the morning. For the night we always put up at a *serai*[2] whenever this was possible. On the third day we arrived at a village called Dersungpor where two *sepoys* of my uncle's regiment, whose leave had finished, joined us. One was called Tillukdaree Gheer, and the other Deonarain. They appeared delighted to meet my uncle and treated him with great respect. Deonarain was accompanied by his younger brother, who was hoping to enlist. They were all carrying swords, and Tillukdaree also had a blunderbuss, called a 'young tiger'. We looked a rather formidable party, and felt secure against the bandits and thugs who then infested the roads.

After about three or four days a party of itinerant musicians came up with us and begged that we should join forces for the sake of protection. They consisted of two men with drums, four men with *sitars*,[3] two men with cymbals, and one with a kind of trumpet. They told us that they were on their way to attend a marriage festival at a town which lay on our way.

For several days everything went smoothly, and the musicians enlivened our march by playing pretty airs. But during the night of the fourth day my uncle, happening to be awake, discovered that all the musicians had collected together and were in some earnest debate, speaking in a low tone of voice and in a tongue[4] which he could not understand. Alarmed at what he saw, he immediately aroused the other *sepoys* and told them he believed that the musicians were in reality thugs. He then appointed one of our party to watch them while the rest of us again laid down to sleep.

The next morning my uncle told the musicians that he was obliged to make long marches, and that therefore they would be unable to keep up with us. They, however, begged to be allowed to accompany us, and at the same time expressed great fear of being robbed on the road. Nevertheless my uncle marched very early the next morning, leaving them behind. We went some eight miles on the high road, and then branched off by a side path, intending to join the road again some thirty miles farther on.

The next four days passed without incident. At the evening's halting-place on the fourth day we were joined by a party of about

[2] A resting place for travellers where stabling was usually provided for animals.

[3] A *sitar* is a kind of violin which has recently become popularized by The Beatles.

[4] India is, of course, a land of many languages, and of even more dialects.

twelve men, carrying bundles of bamboos which are used for making pipe-stems. These men begged to be allowed to join us for protection, as the musicians had done. In the morning, when it was light, I fancied that one of these men was remarkably like one of the former party, and mentioned this to my uncle who went to them and entered into conversation. But their language was different from that of the musicians, their clothes were very dirty, and they looked like coolies. Still he was on his guard, and appointed one of the *sepoys* to keep awake and watch the movements of these people.

During the night, after we had halted, I could not go to sleep for a long time, as I believed these men were also thugs. However, in spite of my endeavours to keep awake, I fell asleep eventually, but was shortly afterwards awakened by a noise like a cock crowing close by.[5] I sat up, and in a moment one or two of these men were by the side of the sleepers. I shouted loudly, and my uncle jumped up with his sword drawn, and rushed at them. Although this was the work of a moment, the fiends had managed to strangle the brother of Deonarain with a silk cord, and had rendered Tillukdaree senseless. He was just saved by my uncle who cut down the thug standing over him. The others disappeared immediately, leaving their bundles of sticks behind them. However, in this short space, the thugs had managed to steal my uncle's gold beads, worth 250 rupees,[6] and Tillukdaree's blunderbuss. He had fallen asleep when he was supposed to be on watch.

After all this had happened, we went to the village nearby and roused the entire population, but no-one showed the slightest inclination to pursue the blood-thirsty murders. We passed the remainder of the night on the outskirts of the village, having carried with us the dead body of Deonarain's brother. In the morning we found the bamboos still at our

[5] The tactics adopted by the thugs (more properly *thags*, meaning deceivers) seldom varied. They began by winning the confidence of those to whom they had attached themselves, and would if necessary travel many miles and for several days until any suspicion of their real intentions had been dispelled. Then, when the leader of the band judged that the moment had come to strike, they would prepare their victims' graves, and each select a victim to strangle. The signal to strike was usually the cry 'Bring the tobacco!', but this was sometimes varied by the sound of a cock crowing. The actual strangling was the work of a moment, the handkerchief, or silken cord, having a knot at one end to assist the stranglers' grip. Once the deed was done, the bodies were searched and then buried, the booty shared, and the thugs moved on in search of other victims. At the end of the expedition, which might last several months, the band dispersed to their own homes, and returned to their peaceful avocations, until they were summoned by their leader to assemble for another foray. Few thugs showed any remorse for the murders they had committed, believing they were serving a religious end, and many of them were respected members of society. The ramifications of Thuggee ran deep and many a landowner, or minor rajah, was in receipt of 'hush-money' from the gangs.

[6] The rupee at this time was worth about two shillings.

former camping place, and my uncle sold them to a tobacco merchant for 46 rupees, but not without an altercation with the village headman who claimed that they belonged to him, by right of their having been left on his ground. We stayed a complete day at the village in order to perform the funeral rites for Deonarain's unfortunate brother. Fortunately for Deonarain's comfort we were only a few miles from the holy Ganges, and he had the satisfaction of seeing the priest cast his brother's ashes into the stream, thus securing his brother rest in our Hindu heaven. Tillukdaree was so weak from the effect of the thug's cord round his throat that he was obliged to hire a pony cart, and we proceeded, now a mournful party, on our way.

My uncle now allowed no parties of any kind to join us, although several begged hard to do so since they saw we were armed. Nothing of any consequence took place during the rest of the journey so far as I can remember, until we arrived at Agra, where my uncle's regiment was then stationed.[7] We arrived there on 14 November, and when we came near the lines we met several *sepoys* of the regiment going down to the Jumna to bathe. They all embraced my uncle, and, before we came to the lines, some thirty men of his Company came running out to meet him and asked a thousand questions. My uncle went to his own house, which had been kept neat and clean by a havildar who had lived in it during my uncle's absence.

After bathing, and eating the morning meal, my uncle put on full regimentals and went to pay his respects to the Adjutant *sahib*,[8] and Commanding Officer. He took me with him. I was rather dreading this because I had never yet seen a *sahib* and imagined they were terrible to look on and of great stature—at least seven feet tall! In those days there were only a few *sahibs* in Oudh; only one or two *sahib* Residents in Lucknow, where I had never been.[9] In the villages of my country the most extraordinary ideas existed about them, and any one who had chanced to see a *sahib* told the most curious stories. In fact nothing was too far-

[7] Agra, which stands on the banks of the River Jumna, about three hours' drive from Delhi, was the capital of India during the reign of the great Akbar, and is of course famed for the exquisite Taj Mahal, built by Akbar's son, the Emperor Shah Jehan. It had become an important British military garrison by the time Sita Ram arrived there in 1814.

[8] The addition of the word *sahib* to a title, rank, or name, signifies respect, but during British rule in India it came to represent the British, or *gora log*, i.e. the white people, or Europeans.

[9] The East India Company's Resident at the court of the King of Oudh had a numerous staff, as well as a substantial escort of troops, commanded by British officers. It would be to these *sahibs* that Sita Ram is referring, although he had never seen them himself.

fetched to be believed. It was said that they were born from an egg which grew on a tree, and this idea still exists in remote villages. Had a *memsahib*[10] come suddenly into some of our villages, she would, if young and hand-some, have been considered to be some kind of fairy, and would probably have been worshipped; but should she have been old and ugly, the whole village would have run away to hide in the jungle, believing her to be a witch. It is therefore hardly surprising that I should have been so terrified at the prospect of seeing a *sahib* for the first time in my life.

I remember once, when I was attending a fair at the Taj Mahal in Agra, an old woman said she had always believed that *sahibs* came from eggs which grew on a tree; but that morning she had seen a *sahib* with a fairy by his side. The fairy was covered with feathers of the most beautiful colours, her face was as white as milk, and the *sahib* had to keep his hand on her shoulders to prevent her from flying away. All this the old woman had seen with her own eyes, and she swore it was true. I am not so ignorant now, of course, but I would have believed it when first I arrived at Agra. I afterwards often saw that *sahib* driving out with his lady. She wore a tippet made from peacock feathers, and the old woman had mistaken this for wings.

We went to the Adjutant's house, which was four times the size of the headman's house in my village. He was on the verandah, with a long stick, measuring young men who were recruits. He was very young, not as tall as myself, and had no whiskers nor moustache. His face was quite smooth and looked more like a woman's than a man's. This was the first *sahib* I had ever seen, and he did not fill me with much awe. I did not believe he could be much of a warrior with a face as smooth as that since among us it is considered a disgrace to be clean-shaven; in fact a smooth-faced soldier is usually the butt for many jokes. However he banged those young recruits' heads against the wall in a manner which showed he had no fear, and they looked as if they thought he was about to kill them.

After he had finished with the measuring, the Adjutant took notice of my uncle, and to my surprise spoke to him in my own language. He seemed glad to see him, asked after his welfare, and touched his sword.[11] He then asked who I was, and on being informed that I had come to enlist and was my uncle's nephew, he told my uncle to take me to the Doctor *sahib*, to whom he wrote a letter. I was astonished at the speed

[10] *Memsahib*, the female equivalent of *sahib*, was usually taken to mean the wife of a European. I am not aware that it was much used by Indians to signify an Indian lady of rank.

[11] Sita Ram's uncle, as a mark of respect, would have handed the Adjutant the hilt of his sword to touch. This custom was followed in the Indian Cavalry until 1940, or later.

of his writing; in less time than I could have put water to the ink and written one line, he had filled a page, which he then doubled up and gave to my uncle, and we went to the Doctor *sahib*'s house.

This was even bigger than the Adjutant's. My uncle told me that the Doctor was married and had several children. He was at home and we were ordered into his presence. A chair was provided for my uncle, but no notice was taken of me so I squatted on the ground. My uncle made me stand up, and told me afterwards that it was bad manners to sit down in the presence of a *sahib*. After reading the note, the Doctor ordered me to strip, but I was so ashamed I could not move, for there was a *memsahib* in the room. She was sitting at a table covered with a sheet, and feeding two children with eggs—those unclean things![12] I began to regret having followed my uncle, and remembered the priest's warning about being defiled. However I was ordered sharply to take off my clothes, and both the children began calling out—'Papa says you are to take your clothes off! Don't you understand? Donkey, pig, owl!'—and the Doctor joined in, saying I was a fool and an ignorant villager. Then the children cried out—'Oh, mamma, is he covered with hair?' I was so ashamed that I ran out onto the verandah, but my uncle came out and told me not to be afraid. No harm would be done to me. The Doctor then pushed me into an empty room and examined me, by thrusting his hand against my stomach, which nearly made me vomit. Then he opened my eyelids with such violence that tears came into my eyes, and he thumped my chest. After this he pronounced me fit and ceased tormenting me—to my great relief.

My uncle next went to pay his respects to the Colonel *sahib*. We were kept outside for an hour, and then ordered to approach. I was now in such a state of terror, not knowing what horror might next befall me, that my legs knocked together. I imagined that the Colonel *sahib* must be terrible to gaze upon—he commanded one thousand men—his wish was law! Judge my surprise when I saw an old man, very short and stout, without a hair on his head or face, and with a skin of a bright red colour. He was smoking a magnificent *hookah*.[13] He got up to welcome my uncle, and after I was introduced spoke very kindly to me, telling me to be a good boy and imitate my uncle in everything.

I have said this was the first time in my life I had ever seen

---

[12] Sita Ram, as a Brahmin, would have been a strict vegetarian, for whom even eggs would be tabu.

[13] The smoking of *hookahs*, or hubble-bubbles, or water-pipes, was part of British social life in India until about the middle of the nineteenth century when for some reason it died out. There were even some women who smoked *hookahs*, and the spacious Anglo-Indian household of those days usually included a servant whose sole task was looking after the *sahib*'s *hookahs* and providing the tobacco. These servants were known as *hookahbadars*.

any *sahibs*. I had now seen three, and how different they were to my ideas of them. I could not believe they were so brave as they were reputed to be; they were all smaller than my uncle and did not look half as strong. And what a number of curious things they had in their houses. I could not imagine what they did with them. In one corner of the Colonel's room was a table full of glass cups of all sorts and sizes, and in another corner a stand with seven or eight guns. The walls were hung with the heads of animals —tigers, stags, antelope, and other deer. The *sahib* was wearing a tight blue coat, buttoned up to the throat with big brass buttons, and with two lumps of what I then thought was gold on his shoulders.[14] He wore white pantaloons, and long black boots with golden tassels on either side. Although I was not struck with his size or strength, still there was something in his eyes which I shall never forget; they were like the eyes of a hawk and seemed to look through and through one. After we had left, my uncle told me that the Colonel was a renowned sportsman who had killed as many as nine tigers.

In a few days I was sent to begin my drill. It is a day I shall always remember, for is it not impressed for ever on my mind? The parade-ground was covered by parties of six or eight men, performing the most extraordinary movements I had ever seen, and these to orders in a language of which I did not understand a single word.[15] I felt inclined to laugh, and stood astonished at the sight. However a violent wrench of my ear by the drill *havildar* [sergeant] soon brought me to my senses. I had to attend drill for many months, and one day I happened to forget how to do something and was so severely cuffed on the head by the drill *havildar* that I fell down senseless. I complained to my uncle who was very angry with the drill *havildar*. Although he never dared to strike me again, from that day on he bullied me in every other way and used to abuse me at every opportunity. As I had gone to great pains to learn my duties, I resented this treatment very much and had almost made up my mind to run away. The drill *havildar* told the Adjutant that I was obstinate and stupid, and would never make a soldier.

I told my uncle of the treatment I was receiving, and said I repented of ever having come with him. But he encouraged me, and one day the Colonel *sahib* came to inspect the recruits and I managed to do my drill to his satisfaction. He ordered the Adjutant to test me in the whole of my drill, and the Adjutant told the Colonel that I was fit to join the ranks. I so longed to wear a red coat, and to have a musket of my own. Besides

[14] Sita Ram is here referring to the gold-lace epaulettes of a field officer.
[15] It is only within the last three years that the Indian Army has adopted Hindi words of command in place of English.

which, I had only been eight months at my drill, and out of a party of seventy-eight recruits, many of whom had enlisted before me, I was the only one selected to join the ranks. Few were ever sent to do this, unless in war-time, until they had been at drill for a year, and often for even longer periods.

'*My uncle next went to pay his respects to the Colonel* sahib'

'At first I found it very disagreeable wearing the red coat'

3   *The Gurkha War:
1814-1816*

Sita Ram devotes part of this chapter to a description of his British officers, and their relations with the sepoys, and he also touches on the relationship which existed between certain British regiments he knew and the Bengal Native regiments. He then goes on to tell of his experiences in the war against the Gurkhas which began in 1814 and lasted nearly two years.

There is considerable obscurity regarding the regiments in which Sita Ram served. Lord Sidmouth devoted forty-five years' study to this and concluded that Sita Ram was either continually changing his unit, or through deliberate intent, or loss of memory, embroidered his story.[1] Quite apart from Sita Ram's haziness over dates, he never mentions any of his regiments by their numbers. This is not altogether surprising since the Bengal Army underwent several reorganizations in the course of his service, and in 1824, in particular, the numbering of regiments was completely changed. Moreover the sepoys usually referred to their regiments by their popular names, as a soldier from the Middlesex Regiment might have referred to his unit as the 'Die Hards'.[2] Most sepoy regiments were known by the names of the British officers who had originally raised them, but Sita Ram does not use even this method to identify his regiments, although he does refer later in his narrative by their popular names to three regiments which took part in the First Afghan War (1838–42). His memory may have been failing him, as Lord Sidmouth suggests, or he may have felt this was a matter of no concern. However, the most likely explanation is that he was anxious to cover his traces for fear lest his frank comments should incur the displeasure of the all-powerful Company and endanger his precious pension. His translator, Norgate, may have entered with him into this conspiracy of silence in order to overcome Sita Ram's initial reluctance to write his memoirs.

We can be fairly certain, however, that Sita Ram's first regiment was the 2nd Battalion of the 26th Bengal Native Infantry.[3] It was the only sepoy regiment stationed at Agra at the time when Sita Ram says he enlisted, and moreover he tells us that his first commanding officer was 'Estuart' sahib. 'Estuart' is a common rendering of Stewart in the vernacular, and there was a Major Benjamin Stewart serving with the 2/26th BNI at Agra. Although he was only the third major in order of seniority, the other two

[1] *Journal of the Society for Army Historical Research*, Vol. XXXVIII, No. 154, June 1960.

[2] From the celebrated incident at the battle of Albuhera, 1811, when their dying commanding officer, Lieutenant-Colonel Inglis, cheered them on, with 'Die hard, 57th! Die hard!'

[3] The 26th Bengal Native Infantry was raised in Cawnpore in 1804. It consisted of two battalions, of which the 2nd was known as *Hindri-ki-Paltan* from Captain R. Henry who was appointed to the battalion in 1805 and who for some time commanded it. In the reorganization of 1824, when two battalion regiments were abolished, 2/26th became 52nd BNI. It mutinied in 1857 at Jubbulpore and was disbanded.

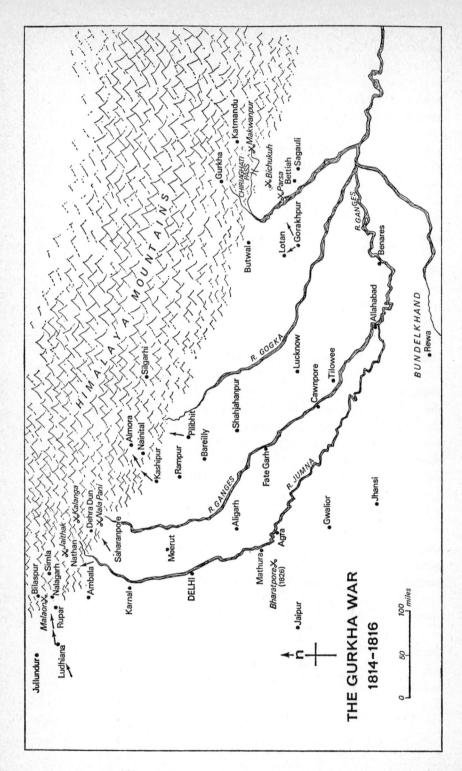

THE GURKHA WAR
1814–1816

Jullundur
Ludhiana
Malaon
Bilaspur
Simla
Nalagarh
Rupar
Nathan
Jaithak
Kalanga
Ambala
Dehra Dun
Nala Pani
Saharanpore
Karnal
Meerut
DELHI
Aligarh
Mathura
Bharatpore
(1826)
Agra
Jaipur
Gwalior
Jhansi

HIMALAYA MOUNTAINS

Almora
Nainital
Silgarhi
Kashipur
Rampur
Pilibhit
Bareilly
Shahjahanpur
Fate Garh
R. GANGES
R. JUMNA

Gurkha
Katmandu
Makwanpur
CHIRIAGHATI
PASS
Bichukuh
Parsa
Bettiah
Sagauli
Butwal
Lotan
Gorakhpur
R. GOGKA
R. GANGES
Lucknow
Tilowee
Cawnpore
Benares
Allahabad

BUNDELKHAND
Rewa

N

0   50   100
miles

majors were employed elsewhere, and Stewart was probably acting as
Commanding Officer.

Sita Ram's great hero was his first company commander
whom he calls 'Burrumpeel'. Like any other young soldier, his company
commander meant a great deal more to him than his Commanding Officer, and
'Burrumpeel' certainly seems to have been an officer of character. He was
wounded during the Gurkha War, and again later. By the time Sita Ram came
to write his memoirs 'Burrumpeel' had become the paragon of all military
virtues. This is hardly surprising. I can remember my first company commander,
who did not rise above the rank of Lieutenant-Colonel, far better than my
first Commanding Officer who became a very distinguished General. Attempts to
identify 'Burrumpeel' have unfortunately failed. It is probable that it was a
nickname. Sita Ram says that he was wounded at the storming of Kalanga
during the Gurkha War, but the officer commanding the company of the
2/26th BNI in that action was Thomas Thackeray, uncle of the novelist, and he
was killed shortly afterwards at Jaithak. Whereas 'Burrumpeel', according to
Sita Ram, recovered from his wound after sick leave in England, and
returned, only to be wounded again in the operations against the Mahrattas.
'Burrumpeel' must therefore remain a mystery.

The East India Company, after patiently enduring frontier
skirmishes with the Nepalese for many years, went to war with them in 1814;
the campaign which followed is usually known as the Gurkha War. The ruling
class in Nepal is of Indian origin, being Rajputs who took refuge in Nepal
from Moslem persecution early in the fourteenth century. They first established
themselves in the little town of Gurkha from where they eventually conquered the
whole of Nepal as we know it today. By the end of the eighteenth century they
had extended Nepal's boundaries to include Simla in the north-west and
Sikkim in the east and their expansionist policies had brought them into conflict
with the Company. Gurkha rule was not popular among the hill people
who said of them, 'They had no law to guide them, nor did they care for
peace and prosperity'; but they were formidable soldiers and the British thought
hard and long before it was decided to bring the Gurkhas to heel.

Four columns of British and Indian troops took part in the
operations; there was also a fifth, or subsidiary, column composed mostly of
irregular troops under Gardner and Hearsey. The northern column was
directed against the Gurkha strongholds in the mountains around Simla, and it
was commanded by David Ochterlony, as fine a soldier as ever served Britain
in India. The centre column marched from Meerut to assault the fortress of
Kalanga and to cut the Gurkha communications with Nepal. It was
commanded by Sir Rollo Gillespie, a name to conjure with in India at that time.
The third and fourth columns operated farther to the east with the aim of forcing
the passes into central Nepal and seizing the capital, Kathmandu.

Only Ochterlony's column was successful. Gillespie was killed while leading the storm of Kalanga; he was buried in Meerut cemetery where his obelisk rises high above the jungle surrounding over a century's worth of British graves. Kalanga eventually fell, but not before its ninety surviving defenders had made their escape; while at Jaithak, the next fort to be attacked, there was a complete reversal. Sita Ram was present at both these actions. There was similar failure in the east, but Ochterlony's success had alarmed the Nepalese. Their general, Amar Singh Thapa, and the Nepalese Government, asked for terms.

Several months of negotiations followed, and this respite was utilized by the Gurkhas to strengthen their defences covering Kathmandu. They then refused to ratify the peace treaty. War broke out again and Ochterlony was given command of all the Company's troops. He out-manoeuvred the Gurkhas, capturing their supposedly impregnable fortress at Chiriaghati after a daring night approach-march which could equally easily have resulted in disaster. The Gurkhas capitulated in order to avoid the occupation of Kathmandu. A peace treaty was signed at Sagauli in 1816. By this the Nepalese lost Simla, Dehra Dun, parts of the Terai, and Sikkim, but retained their independence. They agreed to accept a British Resident in Kathmandu[4] and allowed the Company to recruit Gurkhas for the Bengal Army.

I took my place as a regular *sepoy* in my uncle's company, Number 2,[5] eight months from the day I had entered the *Sirkar's* service. But my annoyances did not cease here. Through some influence of the drill *havildar*, the European sergeant of my company took a dislike to me and was continually finding fault and getting me punished. I discovered that I had never given the usual present to the drill *havildar* when I had passed my drill, and I determined never to do so after his bad treatment of me. This fee was sixteen rupees, of which five or six went to the European

[4] There was a British Resident in Kathmandu, with a personal escort of troops, from the end of the Gurkha War until India became independent in 1947, but for almost all the time his movements were restricted to the valley of Kathmandu. The Nepalese would not allow him to visit outlying areas, even though it was from these areas that the British recruited their Gurkha soldiers, and it is only within the last fifteen years or so that Nepal has been opened up to tourists. It is a land of singular charm and beauty.

[5] Number 2 was always the Light Company. These were introduced in India as a result of the British Army's experience in the Peninsular War. There was a Grenadier and a Light company in each battalion, consisting of picked men, and it was common practice to take the Grenadier and Light companies from several battalions to form an *ad hoc* Light Battalion, or 'Flank' Battalion. Sita Ram appears to have served in such a unit for part of the Gurkha war.

sergeant of the company to which the recruit was posted. At this time there was a European sergeant with each company of *sepoys*.[6] Some of them knew the language quite well, and on the whole were kind to us, but others did not know our language, or could not make us understand their meaning, and instead resorted to low abuse. Numerous complaints were made to the Adjutant, but he nearly always took the side of the European sergeant, and we could obtain very little or no redress.

At first I found it very disagreeable wearing the red coat; although this was open in front, it was very tight under the arms. The shako[7] was very heavy and hurt my head, but of course it was very smart. I grew accustomed to all this after a time, but I always found it a great relief when I could wear my own loose dress. The uniform of the British was always very tight and prevented the free use of arms and legs. I also found the musket very heavy, and for a long time my shoulder ached when carrying it.[8] The pouch-belt and knapsack were a load for a coolie.

There were eight[9] English officers in my regiment, and the Captain of my company was a real *sahib*—just as I had imagined all *sahibs* to be. His name was 'Burrumpeel'. He was six feet three inches tall, his chest as broad as the monkey god's,[10] and he was tremendously strong. He often used to wrestle with the *sepoys* and won universal admiration when he was in the wrestling arena. He had learnt all the throws and no *sepoy* could defeat him. This officer was always known among ourselves as the 'Wrestler'. Nearly all our officers had nicknames by which we knew them. One was the 'Prince' *sahib*, and another was known as the 'Camel' because he had a long neck. Another we called 'Damn' *sahib* because he always said that word when he gave an order. Some of the officers were very young, mere boys, and when they were not on duty they were always hunting and shooting.

---

[6] There was a small cadre of British non-commissioned officers in each *sepoy* unit, consisting usually of a sergeant-major, one sergeant per company, and a quarter-master sergeant, who usually retired rich if he did not die of drink. These NCOs were mostly men who had gone out to India originally with a British regiment, but who had elected to transfer to the Company's service (where the pay was better and the perquisites considerable) either on discharge or when their British regiments left the Indian Establishment.

[7] This smart but not very practicable headdress had been copied from the British Army, as indeed had most of the uniforms of the Company's Army. Very little concession was made to the climate and the thick and tight-fitting uniform must have been particularly trying for Indians, whose normal dress is cotton, and both light and loose.

[8] This would be the smooth-bored musket 'Brown Bess', weighing 9 pounds and with an effective range of 300 yards. It was only accurate up to 100 yards.

[9] The establishment was 23 British officers, but of these at least two-thirds would be absent on leave, or in staff or other employment.

[10] Hanuman, the monkey god, is one of the better-known gods of the Hindu pantheon.

The Colonel *sahib* owned four elephants and often organized tiger hunts. At the time I am writing about there were tigers in abundance in the jungles around Agra, near Bharatpore, and on the road to Mutthura.[11] These jungles have since been cleared away and there is not a tiger to be seen, but Colonel 'Estuart' *sahib* seldom returned from a hunt without two tigers. He was well-known all around and the villagers came from as far as thirty miles away to inform him where the game was; they were certain of receiving a good reward. Nowadays the *sahibs* do not go out all day during the hot weather, but formerly they bore the heat just as well as we do, and sometimes even better.

Most of our officers had Indian women living with them, and these had great influence in the regiment. They always pretended to have more influence than was probably the case in order that they might be bribed to ask the *sahibs* for favours on our behalf. The *sepoys* themselves were sometimes instrumental in persuading the officers to take their female relations into their service, but such men were usually of low caste, or else Mahommedans.[12] In those days the *sahibs* could speak our language much better than they do now, and they mixed more with us. Although officers today have to pass the language examination, and have to read books, they do not understand our language. I have seldom met a *sahib* who could really read a book or letter although he had been passed by the examining board. The only language they learn is that of the lower orders, which they pick up from their servants, and which is unsuitable to be used in polite conversation. The *sahibs* often used to give *nautches*[13] for the regiment, and they attended all the men's games. They also took us with them when they went out hunting, or at least all those of us who wanted to go.

Nowadays they seldom attend *nautches* because their Padre *sahibs* have told them it is wrong. These *sahibs* have done, and are still doing, many things to estrange the British officers from the *sepoys*.[14] When I was a *sepoy* the Captain of my company would have some of the

---

[11] There are still tigers near Bharatpore, but they are few and strictly preserved.

[12] Although Sita Ram does not appear to approve of his officers keeping Indian mistresses, he does seem to favour 'sleeping dictionaries'! By no means all British officers kept Indian mistresses; many married Indian wives in the normal fashion, and some of these were ladies of high birth.

[13] *Nautches* were entertainments provided by troupes of professional dancers, both men and women. Although the dances were mainly classical, many were highly erotic, and often, but by no means always, the dancers were also prostitutes. *Nautches* might last all night and were an acquired taste so far as the Europeans were concerned, but the *sepoys* loved them.

[14] Sita Ram is here expressing a belief widely held by the *sepoys* that British chaplains were coming between the officers and their men. The *sepoys* also feared that the chaplains were seeking to convert them to Christianity, as some of them undoubtedly tried to do, and this was another of the many causes of the Mutiny.

men at his house all day long and he talked with them. Of course many went with the intention of gaining something—to persuade the company commander to recommend them to the Colonel for promotion, or to obtain this or that appointment in the regiment—but far more of us went because we liked the *sahib* who always treated us as if we were his children. I am a very old man now and my words are true. I have lived to see great changes in the *sahibs'* attitude towards us. I know that many officers nowadays only speak to their men when obliged to do so, and they show that the business is irksome and try to get rid of the *sepoys* as quickly as possible. One *sahib* told us that he never knew what to say to us. The *sahibs* always knew what to say, and how to say it, when I was a young soldier. If I am speaking too boldly, your Honour must forgive me!

The officers of the Royal Army[15] since the Mutiny do not treat us in the same fashion as they used to do. I am fully aware of the execration my unworthy brethren deserve for their brutal conduct during the Mutiny, but surely this should come from their own officers, and not from officers of the Royal Army. Even when it was known that I had served with the force which relieved Lucknow, I can nevertheless remember being called 'a damned black pig' by more than one officer of the Royal Army. And yet I can recall that officers of the 13th and 41st Foot,[16] when I made *chappatis*[17] for them in Kabul, told me, 'Jack *sepoy* is a damned good fellow!' I have not served forty-eight years with English officers without knowing the meaning of all this. It can largely be attributed to hastiness of temper, and who can struggle against fate? I always was good friends with the English soldiers, and they used to treat the *sepoy* with great kindness. And why not—did we not do all their work? We performed all their guard duties in the heat. We stood sentry over their rum-casks. We gave them our own food.[18] Well, English soldiers are a different breed nowadays. They are neither as fine nor as tall as they used to be. They can seldom speak one word of our language except to abuse us, and if they could learn polite expressions as quickly as they can learn abusive ones, they would indeed be apt scholars.

I have noticed that a regiment new to India, both officers

[15] Regiments of the British Army, serving on the Indian Establishment (and paid for by the East India Company), were usually referred to as the Royal Army, or as King's Troops, or (under Victoria) Queen's Troops.

[16] Sita Ram is here referring to the British Regiments he met during the First Afghan War. 13th Foot are now the 1st Battalion, The Light Infantry; 41st Foot are now the 1st Battalion, Royal Regiment of Wales; 16th Lancers are now 16th/5th The Queen's Royal Lancers; and the 17th Foot are the 4th Battalion, Royal Anglian Regiment.

[17] *Chappatis*: the flat, baked wheaten cake which is the bread of northern India.

[18] During the siege of Jellalabad (1841-2), the *sepoys* of the 35th BNI gave up their rations to HM 13th Foot.

and men, always abuse us Indians more than an old regiment. The 17th
Foot always called us brothers; the 16th Lancers never walked near our
cooking places nor spat on our food, and we served with them for years.[19]
I have heard it said, and once I asked a Colonel *sahib* who could understand
me a little whether it was true that the *Sirkar's* best soldiers were all killed
by the Russian cannon [in the Crimean War]. He told me that very few
were killed, but that thousands died of cold and sickness as they did in
Kabul. However, it was thought during the Mutiny that the Russians had
killed all the *Sirkar's* soldiers and that only boys could be recruited in
Britain. Some of this must be true because I have seen only boys in many
red-coated regiments in recent years.[20]

A short time after I became a regular *sepoy* it was
rumoured that the Company was going to take Nepal from Amar Singh
Thapa,[21] and our officers were full of hopes of going with the army which
was being assembled at Mutthura. Orders soon arrived and we marched
from Agra to Mutthura in two days. There we were attached to General
'Gilspy's' force.[22] There was also another force under General 'Loneyackty'.[23] We marched until we came to Dehra Dun, near the mountains,
without seeing any of the enemy, but we heard they were all collected at
Nala Pani,[24] which was a fort on a hill. The Gurkhas were always considered

---

[19] This reference may seem obscure to those unacquainted with the
strict religious observances of Hindu Brahmins. If even the shadow of a non-Brahmin falls
across the cooking place, or the dish, the food is defiled and cannot be eaten.

[20] There was probably a great deal of truth in Sita Ram's criticism
of the changed attitude of the British troops, but it must be remembered that he is writing
in the immediate aftermath of the Indian Mutiny, when such incidents as the massacre of
women and children at Cawnpore had aroused an ugly spirit of revenge. No one struggled
harder against this than the Governor-General, Lord Canning, who was rewarded for his
efforts by the contemptuous nickname, 'Clemency Canning'. It is much to be regretted, but
not for that reason to be glossed over, that events which occurred during the Mutiny—on
both sides—coloured British and Indian attitudes for many, many years afterwards.

[21] Amar Singh Thapa was the leading Nepalese general.

[22] 'Gilspy' is the vernacular rendering for Gillespie. Major-General
Sir Rollo Gillespie (1766-1814) had played a prominent part in putting down the mutiny at
Vellore in 1806. It was said of him that 'he was not only the bravest man that ever wore a
red coat, but also extremely capable and resourceful' (Fortescue).

[23] 'Loneyackty' is the vernacular rendering for Ochterlony, whom
even British troops found easier to call Malone! Major-General Sir David Ochterlony
(1758-1825) ended his distinguished career as Resident at Delhi where he is said to have
maintained even greater state than the Mughul emperor himself. He resigned after having
his policy abruptly overruled by the Governor-General, Lord Amherst, and settled in
Meerut where he is supposed to have died of a broken heart.

[24] Nala Pani was near Kalanga, which the Gurkhas were fortifying.
Kalanga was described by Gillespie: '... as stiff and strong a position as ever I saw: garrisoned
by men who are fighting *pro aris et focis* in my front, and who have decidedly the resolution
to dispute the fort so long as a man is alive. The fort stands on the summit of an almost

to be brave soldiers, and their knives were much dreaded.[25] A touch from them meant certain death. Our force was ordered to march on the fort. The approach road ran through thick jungle and several of my comrades were wounded by arrows. These came from the jungle without making any sound and we saw no-one. Many of the *sepoys* said it was magic and the work of demons. We fired volleys of musketry when the arrows came thick, but the jungle was so dense that we never knew whether any of the enemy were killed.

As we approached the fort, the General *sahib* ordered four columns for the attack. These were to approach the fort from different directions, but the paths were so bad and steep that one column arrived before the others. It was exposed to such heavy fire that it had to retreat, leaving behind many dead.[26] This disheartened the *sepoys* very much, and seeing the European soldiers running back made it worse. At this moment General 'Gilspy' led a European regiment[27] to the attack, but despite all his bravery (and he was a veritable lion), he was beaten back two or three times. He was on foot, cheering on his men, when he suddenly fell dead. Then we retreated again, and my regiment covered the withdrawal.

We retreated about one mile, and then halted for four or five days until the big guns could arrive from Delhi under Captain 'Hallow' *sahib*.[28] The walls of the fort were not very high, and the officers of my regiment wanted to try scaling ladders which we soon made from the jungle trees. But General 'Maulay' *sahib*[29] would not allow the attempt to be made because our losses had already been so terrible. In my regiment forty-eight men had been killed. The British regiment had lost nearly two companies,[30] but they never lost heart and went into the attack again and again. They were like young fighting cocks. The *sepoys* were rather

---

inaccessible mountain covered with an impenetrable jungle; the only approaches stockaded, and stiffly stockaded.' It was held by about 600 Gurkhas under Balbahadur Singh.

[25] The Gurkha *kukri*.

[26] Sita Ram must be referring to the assault on the first stockade by about 100 dismounted men of the 8th Light Dragoons (today, Queen's Royal Irish Hussars). They were inadequately supported and had to withdraw.

[27] Three companies of the 53rd Foot (later King's Shropshire Light Infantry, and now 3rd battalion, The Light Infantry).

[28] This is an example of Sita Ram's retentive memory for names and places, if not for dates. The artillery train was in fact commanded by Captain-Lieutenant Bettine, but the howitzers and mortars had been previously ordered up under Lieutenant Hall, whose name must have stuck in Sita Ram's memory.

[29] This would be Colonel Mawbey of the 53rd Foot who took temporary command after Gillespie's death. He should not be confused with Major-General Bennet Marley who also commanded a column during the Gurkha War.

[30] The 53rd Foot had lost ninety-eight killed and wounded, or about a third of their number. 8th Light Dragoons had five officers and fifty-eight men killed and wounded out of about one hundred present at Kalanga.

dispirited, but their spirits revived when the guns came up. The walls were battered and breaches were made. Another assault was then mounted, but although we pushed forward as hard as we could, the British actually running up the breaches, we were still driven back. No-one succeeded in entering the fort. It was the sight of the arrows filling the air which frightened many of the men, rather than the sound of the matchlock balls which we could not see. The Mahommedans in the ranks were the most disheartened; as three attempts had failed, they said that Allah must be against them.[31]

However, next morning, when a grand attack was launched on the fort from all sides, we advanced nearer and nearer without an arrow or a shot being fired at us. A drummer boy ran up the breach and then called out that the fort was deserted.[32] The Nepalese had all escaped through the jungle without our knowing anything of it, or hearing a sound. It was now the turn of the British soldiers to be down-hearted because they were angry that the enemy had tricked them.[33] I escaped without a wound, but my Captain *sahib* received an arrow in the chest. It was difficult to remove on account of its broad point and the Doctor *sahib* said that the Captain would die if the arrow was extracted. However, the *sahib* suffered great pain and was in such agony that he pulled out the arrowhead himself. Blood and froth gushed from the wound and he nearly bled to death. I never expected to see my Captain *sahib* recover. He was so loved by the men of his company, and was such a universal favourite in the regiment, that his absence was hard to bear. But 'Burrumpeel' *sahib* was sent to England, and the regiment lost its champion.

At this time a new General came, 'Martindale' *sahib*,[34] to take command. The enemy had collected at another fort, Jaithak, and our army was ordered to march against it. Here again the British troops attacked like tigers and fought like madmen, but we were all driven back with considerable loss. My uncle was wounded in the knee by a matchlock

[31] Sita Ram, as a high-caste Hindu, seldom loses an opportunity to have a dig at his Mahommedan comrades.

[32] The Gurkhas evacuated the fort on 30 November 1814. The place was full of dead and wounded, and the surviving defenders had been forced out by the stench of corpses and lack of water.

[33] It is pleasant to be able to record that this resentment did not last long. I visited Kalanga in 1968 and not far from the foot of the hill are two whitewashed obelisks within a walled enclosure. One obelisk commemorates General Gillespie, while the other bears the following inscription:

'As a tribute of respect for our gallant adversary BULBUDDER Commander of the Fort AND HIS BRAVE GOORKAS who were afterwards while in the service of Runjeet Singh shot down in their ranks to the last man by Afghan Artillery.'

[34] This would be Major-General Gabriel Martindell who took over soon after Gillespie's death, and who made the unsuccessful attack on Jaithak. This was another fort, not far from Kalanga, covering the approaches from the plains.

ball which caused him great pain. I was permitted to look after him in the hospital tent. All the Mahommedan *sepoys* now said that the war was an unlucky one, and that it would never succeed, but my uncle said that the *sahibs* and their British soldiers always fought the better for being beaten at the outset of a campaign.

The next day we heard that the *Sirkar*'s army which had advanced by way of Gorakhpur and Bettiah had been destroyed by the Nepalese.[35] The *sahibs* began to look anxious, although our General told us that only several companies had been cut off, but the entire army had not been destroyed. Nevertheless most of us believed the rumour, and my uncle was the only one who believed the General's story. The army was now in a sad state and not much fit for fighting. Most of the wounded men died from green fever.[36] The local people thought the Company's good fortune had vanished, and several local potentates, taking advantage of this, began to collect soldiers to use against the Government. Our column retired to Dehra Dun to rest the soldiers. The enemy did not harass us; being hillmen, they were afraid to venture out into the open plains.

Within a few weeks we received news that 'Loneyackty' *sahib* had beaten Amar Thapa and that peace had been made.[37] Our force then marched to Saharanpore [near Meerut] where there was a large fort. The *Sirkar* permitted Amar Thapa to go back to his own country because of his bravery. The English respect brave men and do not kill them. This is curious, for is not a brave man the most dangerous enemy? Indeed, as we all expected, as a result of the *Sirkar*'s letting Amar Thapa go free, war broke out again after a few months. I was never able to understand the *sahibs*. I have seen them spare the lives of their enemies when these were wounded. I have seen an officer spare the life of a wounded man who shot him in the back as he turned away.[38] I saw another *sahib* spare the life of a wounded Afghan, and even offer him some water to drink, but the man cut at him with his curved sword and lamed him for life. 'The wounded snake can kill as long as life remains,' says the proverb, and if your enemy is not worth killing, surely he is not worth fighting against?

[35] This must refer to the attack on two posts of Marley's column on New Year's Day, 1815. Three companies of the 2/15th BNI under Captain Sibley were overwhelmed at Parsa after a gallant resistance.

[36] 'Green fever'? Could it have been gangrene, or was it malaria, which was then endemic in the foothills of the Himalayas? The Indians' success in gaining control over malaria is one of the most remarkable events in the history of India since Independence.

[37] Ochterlony's successful operations around Simla which alarmed the Gurkhas and ended the first phase of the war.

[38] This almost certainly refers to the wounding of Captain Hopper, 31st BNI, at Kalat on 13 November 1839, during the First Afghan War.

My regiment was now ordered to join General 'Loneyack-ty's' force by forced marches. One night, when we were near a place called Peithan, the alarm was sounded. A dreadful uproar took place in the camp and at first we could not account for it. A herd of wild elephants had entered the camp and were attacking our transport elephants,[39] which had broken their chains and were running wild. They ran among the tents, screaming and roaring, upsetting tents, and trampling to death a European soldier and two officers' servants. The European soldiers wanted to open fire on the elephants, but in the dark it was impossible to tell which were wild, and which were the Commissariat elephants. The officers had great difficulty in preventing their men from opening fire. Had the soldiers done so, no-one can say what damage would have been done; the musket balls would doubtless have killed some of our own men. After a while the wild elephants moved off and quiet was somewhat restored. The *mahouts*[40] succeeded in recovering all their elephants except two, and these were never seen again.

I was on sentry duty that night and never shall I forget it. I had never been so frightened before. I expected to be trampled on at every moment and yet I dared not leave my post. Even my uncle admitted to being afraid because he had not yet recovered from his wound and was unable to run. The guyropes of one tent became entangled with an elephant's feet and the tent was torn down before the occupants could get out. They were enfolded in the tent like fish in a net and were dragged for some distance. The sides of the tent saved them from being seriously injured, but they were frightened as I had never seen men frightened before. They were greatly laughed at the following morning when the new way they had chosen to strike their tent became known. I saw the European who had been killed. His chest was stove in, his face was black, and his eyes nearly started out of his face. It was an awful sight.

Our column joined the rest of the army near Chiriaghati[41] where the enemy had taken up position. We marched round towards Makwanpur, and two battles were fought in which the Gurkhas were severely beaten and the village of Bichukuh[41] was taken by storm. The

---

[39] This was not an uncommon occurrence when wild elephants came into contact with tame ones. Large numbers of elephants were employed in the Company's Army. They carried the heavy baggage and pulled the siege guns. There are still herds of wild elephant in the Terai on the border of India and Nepal.

[40] *Mahout:* elephant driver.

[41] Chiriaghati and Bichukuh were fortified passes leading into the plain of Khatmandu. Ochterlony out-flanked them before launching an assault. His tactics were exceedingly daring, and the more so because the morale of his troops was poor at the beginning of these operations. There is an interesting account of this very daring march in *The Path of Glory* (The Memoirs of John Shipp), edited by C. J. Stranks and recently published by Chatto & Windus.

Gurkhas thought that Kathmandu would be captured as we were not more than thirty miles away from their capital. They sent envoys with flags of truce and peace was proclaimed. The terms of this peace were very hard.[42] The Company *Bahadur* took large provinces from the Gurkhas for security, but they also returned some small places the enemy seemed to value. This part of the war had only lasted a few weeks.

[42] This is not entirely true. The Nepalese certainly lost their previous conquests, but they retained their independence. Had Lord Dalhousie been Governor-General, they would probably have been annexed.

'. . . and their knives were much dreaded'

'. . . a set of mounted robbers'

4 *The Pindari War*

The emperor Aurungzebe died in 1707, and his death was followed by anarchy for more than a century. There were many contestants to succeed the Mughuls, some of whom came from within India like the Mahrattas, while others came from across the mountains like the Afghans, or from beyond the seas like the British and the French. The viceroys of great provinces, such as Hyderabad, made themselves independent monarchs, while all over India lesser feudatories of the Mughuls carved out for themselves large or small principalities. Ordinary folk were at the mercy of bands of freebooters, and none of these were more feared, nor were more rapacious, than the Pindaris. In this chapter Sita Ram describes his experiences during the operations carried out against them in 1817 and 1818.

It is said that the Pindaris acquired their name from a fondness for a liquor called pinda. They consisted of numerous bands of robbers of from two to three thousand strong whose area of operations extended throughout Central India and the Deccan. The Mahratta chiefs, smarting under their defeat by Lake[1] and Wellesley[2] in the war that had lasted from 1803 to 1805, made use of the Pindaris to serve their own tortuous ends, as did the chiefs of Rajasthan who had not as yet crossed swords with the Company, and it was to the deserts and jungles of Rajasthan that the Pindaris usually retired after carrying out their raids.

They swept through the countryside during the raiding season like locusts, devouring all in their path, but they would melt away in the face of resolute opposition. 'When they set out on an expedition,' wrote Sir John Malcolm,[3] 'they were neither encumbered by tents nor baggage; each horseman carried a few cakes of bread for his own subsistence and some feeds of grain for his horses. The party, usually consisting of two or three thousand good horse, with a proportion of mounted followers, advanced (as secretly as they could and without plundering) at the rapid rate of forty or fifty miles a day, turning neither to the right nor left till they arrived at the country meant to be attacked. They then divided and made a sweep of all the cattle and property they could find; committing at the same time the most horrid atrocities and destroying what they could not carry away. They trusted to the secrecy and suddenness of the irruption for avoiding the troops who guarded the frontiers of the countries they invaded, and before a force could be brought against them, they were on their return. If pursued they made marches of extraordinary length (sometimes upwards of sixty miles) by roads almost impracticable for regular troops. If overtaken they dispersed and reassembled at an appointed rendezvous; if

[1] General Viscount Lake (1744–1808). One of the best of the British generals who commanded in India.
[2] Later the Duke of Wellington, who was contemptuously described by Napoleon as being 'only a *sepoy* general'.
[3] Major-General Sir John Malcolm (1769–1833); soldier, administrator, diplomat and writer. A great servant of India who ended his career as Governor of Bombay.

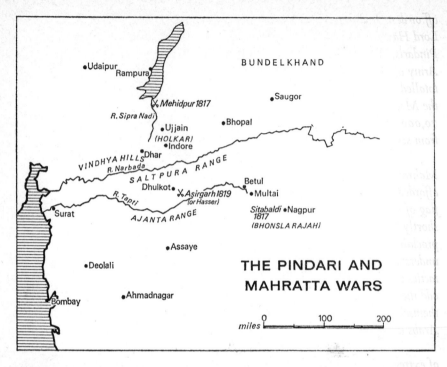

Map labels:
- •Udaipur
- Rampura
- ✗ Mehidpur 1817
- R. Sipra Nadi
- •Ujjain
- (HOLKAR)
- •Indore
- VINDHYA HILLS
- •Dhar
- R. Narbada
- S A L T P U R A   R A N G E
- Dhulkot•
- R. Tapti
- ✗ Asirgarh 1819
- (or Hasser)
- •Surat
- A J A N T A   R A N G E
- B U N D E L K H A N D
- •Saugor
- •Bhopal
- Betul
- •Multai
- Sitabaldi •Nagpur
- 1817
- (BHONSLA RAJAH)
- •Assaye
- •Deolali
- Bombay
- •Ahmadnagar

THE PINDARI AND MAHRATTA WARS

miles 0   100   200

followed to the country from where they had issued, they scattered into small parties, and nowhere presented any point of attack.'

Some idea of the havoc they wrought can be gained from the record of one of these bands that killed 182 peasants, wounded 505, and tortured 3,033 in the space of an eight days' foray. A favourite form of torture was to 'tie a bag of hot ashes over a man's mouth and nose and thump his back; this not only made him divulge without further waste of his tormentor's time, where he had hidden his belongings, but subsequently caused his lungs to rot'.[4] Sita Ram laments the devastation caused by these bandits, and it was indeed incredible. Malcolm records that 315 of the 351 villages in the state of Dhar had been abandoned, while 1,663 out of 3,710 villages in Indore lay in ruins. The Pindaris recruited their ranks from all over India, but they mainly consisted of discharged soldiers, escaped criminals, and vagabonds who offered their swords to such acknowledged leaders as Chitu (a Hindu) and Karim Khan (a Mahommedan).

From 1812 onwards the Pindaris, aided and abetted by the Mahratta chiefs, extended their raids into the Company's territory. A particularly savage raid was made in March 1816. A Pindari band swept right across central India and penetrated deep into the Madras Presidency. They returned to their base unmolested, having plundered over 300 villages, and carried

---

[4] *Honourable Company* by M. Bellasis, Hollis & Carter, 1953.

off or destroyed property to the value of £100,000. The Governor-General, Lord Hastings,[5] was himself a soldier, and he was determined to destroy the Pindaris. A large force for those days was assembled for the task. The Grand Army of Bengal was concentrated in the north under Hastings' own command; it totalled some 43,000 troops. The Army of the Deccan, consisting of troops from the Madras and Bombay Armies, was formed in the south; it contained about 70,000 regular and irregular troops. The plan was to sweep through central India from south to north and rid the land of the Pindaris.

This design was to some extent frustrated by the conduct of the Mahratta chiefs, and also by the terrain. The Mahrattas seized the opportunity afforded them by the Company's involvement with the Pindaris to raise the flag of revolt yet again. Holkar of Indore was the first to take the field, followed shortly by the Peshwa of Poona. They were joined by Apa Sahib after he had proclaimed himself the Bhonsla of Nagpur in February 1817. This understandably complicated Hastings' plan of campaign; to the Pindaris, whose tactics were tip and run with the emphasis on the latter, Hastings had now to add the Mahrattas and their Arab mercenaries. Although the ordinary Mahrattas themselves had little stomach left for the fight, the same was not true of the Arabs who fought fiercely until the last man and the last round.

The area of operations covered more than 150,000 square miles of extremely difficult terrain. Roads were virtually non-existent and the tracks were infamous. The rivers were only fordable during the dry season. Vast tracts of jungle were inhabited by aboriginal tribes like the Bhils and Gonds who murdered any straggler. Disease was endemic and cholera put in an appearance for the first time in the history of the British Army.[6] Hill forts crowned every inaccessible crag, and the villagers were cowed and sullen after years of intimidation by the Pindaris. The problem of co-ordinating operations in such terrain, and over such great distances, was a formidable one. The only means of communication was by mounted dispatch-rider, while some idea of the logistical problem can be judged from John Shipp's description of his task as Baggage Master of the Left Division of the Grand Army. Although this Division amounted to no more than 8,000 soldiers, it was accompanied by 80,000 men, women and children, 50 elephants, 600 camels, 11,000 bullocks, horses, mules and pack ponies, 500 goats, sheep and dogs, 250 palanquins, and vehicles of every kind and description. The imagination boggles at the thought of having to move such a conglomeration of people and animals through a virtually trackless and foodless wilderness in pursuit of a mobile and elusive enemy, but it was done, and the operations ended in success.

[5] Hastings was Governor-General from 1813 to 1823. As Lord Rawdon he won the battle of Hobkirk's Hill in the American War of Independence. He went out to India as the Earl of Moira but was created Marquis of Hastings after the Gurkha War.

[6] Cholera had moved up the Ganges from Calcutta during the monsoon and first struck the Grand Army at Rewa in October 1817.

The part played by Sita Ram was not a particularly distinguished one, but he was honourably wounded and behaved throughout in a soldierly fashion. He has some interesting theories to account for the fighting qualities of his British comrades which are as likely as not to be true of their time.

My regiment[7] was ordered to return to Mutthura after the Gurkha War, but we had not been there long before we were sent to join the large army which was assembling under the personal command of the Governor-General, Lord Hastings. We were to take the field against the Pindaris. These were a set of mounted robbers who seldom fought a battle if they could by any means avoid it, but who marched about the Deccan and other provinces, plundering helpless towns, exacting large sums of money from the bankers, carrying off the best looking women, and attacking and maiming people without regard to their age or sex. No place or person was safe. On one day this village would be looted, and on the next another as much as eighty miles away. Sometimes a thousand horsemen would appear before a town and hold it to ransom; in this fashion as much as two *lakhs*[8] of rupees has been carried off. If the robbers imagined from the way this money was paid that it was obtained without much difficulty, they would then assume that the town was rich and contained even more booty. They would leave at a gallop, halt twenty miles away, and return at night to loot the place of everything of value which could possibly be carried off. They would kill any man, woman or child who offered the least resistance, and often carried off with them the headman, or the richest citizen, in the hopes of extorting a large ransom. An exorbitant sum was usually demanded, and the anxieties of the victim's relatives would be aroused by accompanying the demands with his ears, fingers, or hands, coupled with threats that if the ransom was not paid, the victim's head would be the next to follow.

Hindustan was at this time tormented by demons from the lowest hell. I cannot describe the horrors of those days—may the Gods grant that they never return! The very word Pindari, and the name of Chitu, their Chief, was accursed. Merchants trembled when they heard it; maidens wept; no-one felt safe. These robber bands were made up from many kinds of people, and young men of noble family but of no wealth

[7] The Flank, or *ad hoc*, battalion in which Sita Ram had taken part in the Gurkha War had not been dispersed; it was retained for the campaign against the Pindaris. It consisted of the Light Companies of the 1/1st, 1/5th, 1/6th, 1/7th, 2/16th, 1/17th, 2/26th, and 1/27th BNI. It formed part of the Centre Division assembled at Cawnpore.

[8] One *lakh*: 100,000 rupees; about £10,000 at that time.

joined them. However they were chiefly men from southern India.[9] The Pindaris always bribed the big Rajahs or Nawabs[10] who often shared in the loot, although this might well be plunder from the rajah's own towns and villages. The robbers could therefore always find a refuge in friendly territory whenever they were sore pressed.

I now considered myself an experienced soldier, for I had suffered defeats and had helped to win victories. I had served with *sahibs* and with European soldiers. In my opinion the reason why the English are invincible is because they do not worry about defeat. Four times have I seen a European regiment driven back with terrible slaughter, and yet their fifth attempt was as fierce as their first. It is astonishing that they do not become confused if their leader is killed; another officer will take his place and will be obeyed in just the same fashion. Now in an Indian army, if the general or leader is killed, the whole army falls into confusion and generally takes to flight; the men will not follow the next leader. The principal reason for this is because Rajahs or Nawabs generally fight for their own benefit. They collect all the plunder into their own treasuries and spend it only on themselves and their favourites. They do not use the treasure for the good of their subjects. The result is that people do not care for war, other than for the opportunity it gives them for plunder, or for seizing power. Then again, few Princes of Hindustan ever pay their troops regularly. However brave the individual soldiers may be, there can be no real discipline if an army is allowed to pay itself by plunder. Princes seldom grant pensions to the families of soldiers killed in their service, and care little for the soldier when he is disabled and can be of no further use to them.

The Company's officers fight, but plunder is not their sole object. The strict rules of the army prevent this to a great extent. They are paid regularly, and know they will continue to be. Also they know that if it is their fate to be wounded, they will still be cared for, and often rewarded. As for the European soldiers—I hardly know why they love fighting as much as they do, unless it is for grog. They would fight ten battles in succession for one bowl of spirits. Their pay is negligible, so it cannot be for that. They also love looting, but I have seen them give a cap full of rupees for one bottle of brandy. I have been told that the English doctors have discovered some kind of essence which is mixed with the soldiers' grog. Great care has to be taken not to mix too much, since otherwise the

[9] This is probably incorrect. The hard core of the bands were men from northern India, with a fair sprinkling of Afghans, Pathans, and Baluchis.

[10] Rajahs (Hindu) and Nawabs (Mahommedan) might rule states the size of Wales or only a few villages.

men would all kill themselves in battle by their rashness. I know that water has always to be mixed with their spirits, although they do not realize this. Whenever I have seen them discouraged, or fighting half-heartedly, it has always been on occasions when they were deprived of their usual ration spirit. Sikh soldiers,[11] who drink English liquor, say they have no fear when they can get ration rum, but country liquor burns up their livers and makes them fools instead of heroes. I am sure there must be some kind of elixir of life in ration rum; I have seen wounded men, all but dead, come to life after having some rum given to them. Be this as it may, I am convinced there is something very extraordinary about it. I know European soldiers worship liquor, give their lives for it, and often lose their lives trying to get it. I have spoken to Doctor *sahibs* about this subject and they have told me that in their own language it is called water of fire, water of life, etc.[12]

My regiment was ordered to join the headquarters of the Governor-General and we proceeded by forced marches into Bundelkhand. There was a very large army—at least 100,000 soldiers.[13] The work we had to perform was very arduous, marching and countermarching in a country where there were no roads. News came of a body of Pindaris being here one day, and there the next. Detachments were sent after them but seldom with any success. The movements of an army can best be compared with the game of chess, but one day we accidentally came upon a large body of the enemy. They had only just dismounted and were as ignorant of our approach as we were of their presence. We managed to get close enough to fire several volleys at them but they were soon off at a full gallop down slopes where even foot soldiers dare not venture. Some thirty or forty were killed and wounded, and we captured several horses.

My company was sent in pursuit of some of the enemy who had been dismounted. While chasing one of them, my foot caught in a bush and I was thrown headlong into a deep ravine. I lay at the bottom stunned for a while, and when I recovered I saw a man with a matchlock taking aim at me from a range of less than twelve yards. I covered him with my musket, but unfortunately the flint had been knocked out during my fall and naturally the musket would not fire. The Pindari got round behind me and fired from above, hitting me in the back near the left shoulder. I rolled farther down into the ravine and remember nothing

[11] The Sikhs probably possess the hardest heads in Asia.

[12] The British soldier's existence in India at this time was hard, brutish, and more often than not, short. Drinking one's self into a state of oblivion was as good a way as any of forgetting the miseries of the present.

[13] Rather exaggerated: the Grand Army of Bengal totalled rather less than 50,000 and was widely dispersed.

until it was dark. Then I awoke with a burning thirst to find myself covered with blood, not only from my wound, but also from the thorns that had lacerated me. My face and hands were dreadfully cut. I was unable to move and lay there till dawn in terrible pain. I then managed to crawl up the bank, but was so exhausted by the effort that I fell back into the ravine.

This made my wound start bleeding again, but the loss of blood did not weaken me as much as I had expected. I dragged myself a little farther, and now began to think that death must be near as I had a raging thirst. I had just about given up all hope of life when I heard the tinkle of a cattle-bell, and this sign of life in such a wilderness gave me fresh vigour. In about an hour or so I came across a herd of buffaloes under the care of a boy and girl. Although I called to them in the name of God to give me some water, they disappeared into the jungle as soon as they saw me. After about an hour the girl reappeared, and seeing I could not walk approached nearer to me. I spoke to her, but all she would answer was, 'yes! yes!' I could not understand her, nor she me. I tried by every sign I knew to make her understand that I wanted water, and at last she seemed to understand. She pointed to a tree, and I crawled towards it to find a small earth-walled well from which they drew water for the cattle. She drew me some, and I drank it, although it was warm and tasted bitter like medicine. However it put life back into me and I washed my wound as well as I could.

It was no use talking to the girl because we could not understand each other. I then tried explaining my situation by sign language, but this frightened her and she ran off again into the jungle. I lay near the well all day, and in the evening four men arrived. They had evidently been sent by the girl since they approached me with great caution. After a great deal of jabbering they led me to their village which consisted of a few huts made of branches and thatched with broad leaves. They were not unkind, but I could not eat their food as they were men of low caste; they seemed to be iron smelters. I managed to make one of them point out the direction of the road, and I enquired where the *Sirkar*'s army was. I understood him to reply that it had moved off a long way, but was unable to discover in which direction. I remained with these people for two days, existing on some dry *chappatis* I had in my knapsack and some milk which I was permitted to draw myself.

On the third day one of the men led me to a beaten track. He pointed to a large tree about two miles away, and also to both sides of the track, at the same time going through the motions of an arrow flying from a bow. I took this to be a warning to look out for my life. I found a thin piece of white stone which gave out sparks, and fixed this to my musket in place of the flint. However, I was much too weak to have fired it, and despite my weapon I was quite defenceless. I offered the man some money, but he shook his head and pointed to his stomach, indicating by signs that I took to mean that money was useless in that country. I think, from what I subsequently learnt, that these men were afraid of being found with any of the government's money in their possession. Had this been discovered at that time, it would have been quite sufficient to bring down the Pindaris' wrath on their heads, and this was so frightful to contemplate that these miserable wretches, in that remote jungle, dared not do anything that might offend the Pindaris.

The men left me by the roadside, and I made for a large tree, using my musket to help me along. However, I moved very slowly because the pain in my chest was so bad. I had an attack of coughing, during which I coughed up clots of blood, and this frightened me so much that I gave up all hopes of life. Towards evening I reached the tree, and found underneath it a tomb with its attendant holy man.[14] He spoke to me in my own language, much to my delight, although it was only to tell me to go away and not cause him any trouble. I lay down close by, related my sad story, and his heart began to soften; but he told me that if the Pindaris found me, or knew that he had rendered a *sepoy* of the *Sirkar*'s army any assistance, they would spear both him and myself. He then made me a poultice of neem leaves[15] and bathed my wounds which gave me great relief. The fact that I was a Brahmin had a great effect on him. He hid my uniform and musket in the jungle and sprinkled me with red ochre dust. [Presumably to disguise Sita Ram as his disciple.]

From the position he had chosen for his seat, he was able to see a good way up and down the road, and therefore, whenever anyone approached, I had time to hide. No-one came near the place for five days, other than a few herds of cattle and their drovers, and I was now able to move a little. However the musket ball had lodged in the muscles of my back, and the wound began to suppurate, giving me great pain.

On the sixth day we saw a cloud of dust in the distance which was moving more rapidly than dust raised by a herd of cattle. The holy man told me to hide inside the tomb which had a large slab of stone covering the entrance; this slab was also smeared with red ochre. I crept in and was nearly suffocated, despite the small openings on either side of the

---

[14] The Indian sub-continent is dotted with tens of thousands of shrines and tombs, many of them with an attendant. The attendant may be following a hereditary occupation, as is frequently the case with Mahommedan holy places, or may be a wandering hermit, or *saddu*, who has chosen to attach himself to the shrine. Sita Ram does not specify the religion of his rescuer, but he was probably a Hindu.

[15] Neem: a common Indian tree, the leaves of which are believed to have a therapeutic value.

tomb, but my life depended upon my remaining perfectly still. Within a few minutes a party of about thirty horsemen rode up and asked for water. They then asked the holy man whether he had seen any Europeans, or their *sepoys*, or any of their own people. His answers appeared to satisfy them. They dismounted and started to prepare some food they had brought with them. They began to talk with the holy man, telling him how they were hemmed in on every side and chased hither and thither like partridges. They had come eighty miles since the previous day and intended to join their leader, Karim Khan, who was proposing to seek refuge in Gwalior territory.[16] They also said their numbers were much reduced; whereas formerly they had amounted to nearly 200,000, they had now dwindled to a few thousand. They complained that their leaders had deserted them, and that Chitu and Karim were both seeking their own safety in flight.

Two of them lay down to rest on the shady side of the tomb, and I was terrified lest they should hear me move or breathe. As the sun rose higher, the inside of the tomb was like a bread oven, and my sufferings were nearly as bad as death. However, about midday, they mounted their horses and told the holy man that '*Teekur Garh*' was the password to give any of their party who might come that way. They then disappeared into the jungle. I waited for half an hour and emerged from my living tomb, more dead than alive. How I thanked the great Siva[17] for preserving my life!

Two more days elapsed and we saw another cloud of dust coming from the opposite direction. I ran into the tomb once again, but this time they were cavalry troopers from the Company's army. When I heard them talking about the Governor-General and General 'Esmith' *sahib*,[18] I knew I was safe. I came out of the tomb and made myself known to the *Rissaldar* commanding the party. He would not believe my story at first, but the holy man brought my musket and uniform from where he had concealed them in the jungle. They gave me a pony to ride, and after bidding farewell to my kind protector, and leaving three rupees in his bowl, I went off with them. It chanced that this party belonged to a cavalry unit which was with my column, and within three days I was in the arms of my uncle who had given me up for dead. I had been absent thirteen days and no-one in my company knew anything about me. Some said they had

[16] Gwalior's ruler was the great Mahratta prince, Scindiah. Although his sympathies were undoubtedly on the side of the Pindaris, the presence of a considerable British force on his territory, under the command of the Governor-General in person, greatly limited his freedom of action.

[17] Siva: The principal Hindu deity.

[18] This could refer to Brigadier-General Lionel Smith of the Madras Army who commanded one of the columns in the campaign, but he was operating far to the south.

seen my dead body, while others said I had been taken prisoner by the Pindaris.

I was so weak, thin and exhausted that I had to go to hospital. The Colonel *sahib* came often to see me and hear my story, and the other officers were equally kind. The Doctor *sahib* cut the ball out of my back, and I vomited a quantity of blood which gave me great relief. I now began to get better and stronger each day, but I could not bear the recoil of a musket and was therefore no use in the ranks. I was appointed orderly to the Colonel until such time as I could be sent home. I therefore avoided having to carry a musket or take my turn as sentry. The Adjutant *sahib*, who had never been very friendly before, now became very kind to me. He told me that he was very pleased that I had retained my musket and ammunition, despite my injuries, and had brought them back safely. I suppose this may have been the reason for his changed attitude towards me, but I think the notice taken of me by the Colonel *sahib* and the other officers also had something to do with it.

'. . . but this time they were cavalry troopers from the Company's army'

'*When my mother came out to draw water I called to her*'

5   *Return to the Village*

*Sita Ram's wound was so severe that he had to be sent home
on sick leave before he was again fit for service, and in this chapter he
tells of his return to the village. Soon after his arrival there he discovered
that his family had 'arranged' a marriage for him, as is still the custom
throughout most of India, although nowadays more and more educated young
Indians are insisting on choosing their own bridegrooms or brides. We are also
given some insight into the problems of caste in India, for Sita Ram was for
some time declared an outcaste because of the help he had received when
wounded from 'untouchables'.*

*He is never very accurate where chronology is concerned,
although he is correct in mentioning the defeat of Holkar by General Hislop at
Mehidpur on 21 December 1817. However, he is wrong when he ascribes the
death of Chitu, one of the leading Pindari chieftains, to a bite from a snake.
Chitu was in fact present during the fighting at Asirgarh, described in the
next chapter, but escaped and roamed the jungles until he was killed and eaten
by tigers. According to Fortescue, 'he had very narrowly missed capture by the
17th Light Dragoons in March 1818, escaping only through the speed of his
black horse, an animal with hoofs so abnormally large that his tracks could
always be recognized. Since that time Chitu had roamed far and wide, living
the life of a hunted beast, until soon after the fall of Asirgarh he disappeared
into the jungle and was seen no more. The black horse was, however,
tracked, and was found grazing, still saddled and bridled; and search in the
jungle revealed first mangled remains which could not be identified, and at last
the head of the once famous chieftain.'[1] The fate of the other famous Pindari
chieftain, Karim Khan, was less spectacular. He surrendered to Sir John
Malcolm on 16 February 1818.*

*After his purification to restore his caste, Sita Ram married
and soon thereafter returned to his regiment. This seems to have been a
leisurely journey, but it was probably difficult to ascertain exactly where his
unit was located in the vast distances of central India. He travelled by way of
Jaipur in Rajasthan and was greatly impressed by the lay-out of the city;
Jaipur is in fact the only city in India, other than New Delhi, which has been
built to a plan, and of course Jaipur preceded New Delhi by 200 years. While
there Sita Ram visited the Maharajah's zoo and saw for the first time a giraffe
and an ostrich. These had been presented by Nasiruddin, Nawab of Surat on
the west coast, whose vessels traded throughout the Indian Ocean. The East
India Company had assumed control of Surat since 1800, and the Nawab, who
had previously been subject to the Mahrattas, became a pensioner. The titular
dignity continued until the death of Nasiruddin in 1821, and it is this kind of
information which lends authenticity to Sita Ram's story.*

'Burrumpeel' also makes a reappearance in this chapter,

[1] *History of the British Army,* Vol. xi, by Sir John Fortescue (Macmillan).

*having apparently recovered from the wounds he received in the Gurkha War.
Attempts have been made to identify him with William Pickersgill, who was
an officer in the 2/15th Bengal Native Infantry which Sita Ram is presumed to
have joined on the break-up of the 'Flank' battalion. However, the Army
Lists show no officer serving with the 2/15th in 1818 who was serving with
the 2/26th in 1812, although Pickersgill was severely wounded in the Gurkha
War and was sent to Mauritius to convalesce. We are therefore no wiser
concerning the mysterious 'Burrumpeel' but this does not necessarily imply that
he did not exist. During a campaign of the kind fought against the Pindaris,
there must have been a good deal of coming and going within units, as well as
many temporary attachments to units which were under-officered, and
'Burrumpeel' may come into this category.*

It is noteworthy that during the Pindari War the enemy
always had much better information about our movements than we did of
theirs. Any movements on our part, even if conducted with the utmost
secrecy, were immediately known to the enemy. Large numbers of spies
were employed by us, and were permitted to help themselves from a large
bag of rupees whenever they gave us accurate information, but this was
very rare. I am sure they always informed the enemy of our activities, and
only told of a party of Pindaris being near after they had warned them of
the approach of our force. Therefore the enemy always had time to escape.
Our troops would march as quickly as possible to the place where the
Pindaris were reported to be, and it is perfectly true that they had been
there, for the villagers bore witness to the fact. The spies got the credit for
being very good, but one thing is certain—the enemy never were there at
the time when the *Sirkar*'s troops arrived. Whenever our army did fall in
with the enemy, it was purely by chance, when no information about
their presence had been received, or when the spies claimed that there
were no Pindaris within forty miles.

I would have thought that everyone would have been
glad to assist the Government to exterminate these ill-bred dogs, but such
was not the case. Numbers of rajahs and princes gave them assistance, some
quite openly, and others by stealth. All the folk in Bundelkhand[2] were on
their side, but this is hardly surprising. If they had possessed horses, they
would have been Pindaris as well, since an inhabitant of Bundelkhand is a
greater villain and lover of plunder than a Mahratta, if that be possible. It

[2] Bundelkhand is a hilly and heavily forested area lying due south of
Cawnpore and the River Jumna. It had a bad reputation for lawlessness, and was one of the
areas where Thuggee was rampant.

used to puzzle the Generals and Colonels when they heard that a party of these robbers had taken refuge in the territory of some rajah whose towns had themselves been looted, but I have already explained the reasons for this.

Detachments marched at all hours of the night without knowing which direction to take, and guides were then ordered to show the way to such and such a place. But these guides, unless they were watched like hawks, usually managed to fade away like wild animals into some dense piece of jungle. When a *sahib*, cleverer than others, ordered the guides to be tied with ropes, they either selected the wrong road, or pretended not to understand what was said to them. Shooting them had no effect—they sympathized with the Pindaris and hated the *Sirkar*. I have also heard that the frightful punishments inflicted by the Pindaris on anyone suspected of informing or giving help to their enemies was another reason for this refusal to co-operate with us. They would burn out eyes with a heated spear-blade, cut off ears, nose, and lips, and perform other horrible mutilations. We *sepoys* hated them cordially, and as we were servants of Government, they never spared us.

At this time[3] the Pindaris' fortunes seem to have been improving a little. We heard that the Mahratta chiefs had agreed to come to their assistance, but the Company's good fortune could not be resisted. The Mahratta army was beaten on the Sipra Nadi[4] near Ujjain, which was a long way from where we were. The news soon spread all over Bundelkhand, and the Pindaris broke up into small parties and were in flight throughout the countryside. They tried to escape into Maharajah Scindiah's[5] territories near Rampura but were intercepted in several places and cut to pieces. Added to which, numbers of their former supporters abandoned them. When the Pindaris saw the *Sirkar* everywhere victorious, and when they could no longer count on receiving information as had formerly been the case, their fear was like that of the deer when pursued by the cheetah. Karim Khan was defeated and eventually surrendered to one of our General *sahibs*; Chitu, the other chief, ran off into the deep jungle and is reported to have been killed by a snake.[6] The power of the Pindaris had now been completely broken, while the reputation of the Company *Bahadur* was correspondingly increased. The various columns of the army

[3] Presumably Sita Ram is referring here to events late in 1817, by which time three of the great Mahratta chiefs (Holkar, the Peshwa, and the Bhonsla Rajah of Nagpur) had taken the field against the Company. Scindiah of Gwalior would almost certainly have done the same had it not been for the presence on his territory of a large number of the Company's troops.

[4] Battle of Mehidpur, 21 December 1817.

[5] One of the leading Mahratta chiefs whose capital was (and still is) at Gwalior.

[6] Incorrect factually and chronologically. See introduction to Chapter 5, above.

were now broken up,[7] and my battalion was sent to Ajmer. However I was attached to a regiment returning to Agra as I had been given permission to return to my home for six months' sick leave.

Only twenty men in my regiment were killed during this campaign, but 180 died of cholera and fever, while nearly 100 were ruined in health and fit only to return to their villages. It was said that 700 followers[8] and servants died of the cholera, which was a disease which had not been encountered in those parts previously. The European officers and soldiers also died from it. Their Doctor *sahibs* had never seen it before and knew of no cure for it. It was more deadly than small-pox and a dreadful disease.

I arrived safely in Agra with the regiment to which I was attached and bought myself a pony for 11 rupees. I then set off for my village in the company of four or five *sepoys* who had also been given leave. I arrived at home early one morning before it was light and waited outside until daybreak. When my mother came out to draw water I called to her, but she did not recognize me. During the four years I had been away I had grown from youth to manhood, and I had also grown whiskers and a moustache. In fact I considered myself a rather handsome *sepoy*. My mother seemed so alarmed when I spoke to her that I also became frightened, but my father told me later that my uncle had written home to say I had been killed, and my mother therefore thought she had met my ghost. However my father now appeared from the house and I was pleased to learn that none of my family had died during my absence. Everything was exactly the same as when I had left home. I also had the great pleasure of experiencing some ease for the first time for many months. My health rapidly recovered. I also satisfied my ambition by seating myself on the same bench in front of our house where my uncle had sat and recounting stories of my own escapes to the crowd who came every evening to listen and gossip, as they had previously done when my uncle was with us. I soon became a man of some importance in my village. The old priest was still alive and greeted me most warmly; he prided himself on the efficacy of the charm he had given me when first I left home.

While I had been away my mother had arranged my

[7] The Grand Army of Bengal, its task accomplished, was dispersed in February 1818.

[8] Sita Ram presumably refers to the followers of his own battalion. The term 'follower' includes water-carriers, sanitary-men, officers' servants, cooks, grooms, grass cutters, and other menial workers *and* their families. On the basis of ten followers for every soldier, there would have been around 5,000 followers with Sita Ram's battalion. They would have suffered severely in any epidemic, but it is hard to believe that this was the first time the Company's armies had encountered cholera. However, Fortescue states that this was the case.

betrothal with the daughter of a local landowner. You will be aware, your Honour, that betrothals are arranged by our parents, and we are not allowed to see the faces of our wives until our wedding night. I did not much want to be married while I remained a soldier, but it was all part of my fate so what could I do about it? The priest fixed the auspicious day which was six months ahead. I often tried to get a glimpse of my be-trothed's face during this time, and asked her nurse[9] about her. All I was told was that she had a neck like a dove, her eyes were like doe's, her feet like a lotus leaf, and that she was consumed with love for me, and with this I had to be satisfied! I only saw her once while getting into a bullock-cart, but she was a long way off and I could not see her face. My mother and the priest told me that my wife's dowry would be quite enough for us to live on and there was therefore no longer any need for me to remain in the army. She nearly managed to persuade me to write to my uncle and obtain my discharge. However my father was not so keen for me to be married because the priest's marriage fees would cost him a lot of money. He also did not wish me to leave the service because his lawsuit about the mango orchard had not yet been settled. Now that I had returned home he wanted me to act as his agent in the courts, since my being in the *Sirkar's* service would give me an advantage over the other claimant who was now urging his suit.

I employed my time as formerly in looking after my father's farm, and my wound quickly healed; however it gave me great pain whenever it rained. One evening, when I was telling the story of how I was wounded, I happened to mention the incident of the little girl who was looking after the cows in the jungle, and who gave me water which saved my life. A Brahmin priest who was listening said that from my own description the girl must have been of a lower caste than even a sweeper, and that therefore I must be defiled from having drunk water drawn by her. I protested in vain that I drank the water from my own brass bowl, but he talked so loudly, and reviled me so much, that the news was all over the village in no time at all. Everyone now shunned me and refused to smoke with me.[10] I consulted Duleep Ram, our priest, who heard all my case and decided that I had broken my caste. He could no longer associate with me, and I was not even allowed to enter my father's house. I was plunged into despair. Through my father's influence a *panchayat*,[11] or court composed of five persons, was assembled to sit in judgement over me. After the priests had performed many ceremonies over me, and ordered me to fast for many days, I was declared clean and was given a new Brahminical

[9] The word used by Sita Ram is 'midwife' or 'wet-nurse'.

[10] Sita Ram presumably refers to the communal *hookah* which is passed from one smoker to the other among members of the same caste.

[11] The *panchayat*, or village court of five members, is as old as Indian history.

cord. I had to give feasts for the priests and also gifts, and all the money I had saved during five years' service was spent. But who can struggle against destiny?

The day for my marriage drew nearer. All the ceremonies for this were conducted without my being present; my mother, and the girl's mother, arranged all these with the priests. The ceremony was performed, and on the first night my bride's face was allowed to be seen by the members of my family. Her nurse's description of her turned out to be false. How *could* the moon be beautiful if it had suffered from small-pox? Moreover my wife's dowry was mostly property settled on herself. As my leave was soon finished I decided to rejoin my regiment, leaving my wife in the care of my mother.

I set off for Ajmer in Rajputana[12] where my regiment was supposed to be, or at least where it was under orders to go at the time I went on leave. There had been no letter from my uncle during my stay at home although I had sent him two. But in those days the posts were very uncertain, and letters were usually entrusted to people travelling to a place, wherever it might be, instead of sending them by the Government's posts. I arrived in a few days at Agra and went to the Adjutant-General *sahib* for information. He could not tell me much but thought my regiment had gone with a force to Nagpur. I was given two months' advance of pay and set off via Jaipur, meeting with no adventures until I arrived there. Jaipur is one of the cleanest cities I have ever seen. Its streets are broad and it is altogether a beautiful place. Peacocks walked about everywhere; all the animals were tame; the deer came close up to one; pigeons of all colours abounded; clear streams of water ran on either side of the streets; the shops were large; and the gardens all round were beautiful. 'There creepers bloomed on numerous trees, different kinds of flowers were in blossom, on which swarms of bees were gathering honey. Cuckoos were singing on the mango trees, and peacocks strutted about in shady places.'[13]

A priest told me that the town had been built by Maharajah Jai Singh, and that a French *sahib* had furnished the plans; however the people do not like to be reminded of the latter. I went to the king's garden and here I saw an animal that astonished me. It had a head like a nilghai[14] with a neck four yards long and hooves like a horse. Its skin was

[12] Rajputana is now known as Rajasthan, but one of the Indian Army's oldest regiments is still called the Rajputana Rifles. Rajasthan is the home of the Rajputs, one of the great warrior races of India.

[13] Sita Ram's translator put this passage into quotes but without specifying where the quotation originated. Attempts to identify the quotation have been unsuccessful.

[14] Nilghai: the Blue Bull, or Blue Cow, of northern India. It is a large slaty blue antelope with sloping shoulders and short horns. It is a great nuisance to the farmers and is gradually being exterminated.

covered with spots like a cheetah, but it did not eat flesh. It lived on the boughs of trees which it pulled down with its tongue which was a yard long. I asked the keeper about the animal and he told me it came from the great desert in Africa, 8,000 miles away, and that it was very gentle. I do not know its name or its species. All I do know is that it was a wonderful animal, and never has such a beast been described in any grandmother's tale.[15] This was an astonishing city, and truly a place of wonders. I soon saw yet another remarkable animal, a bird one hundred times as large as a turkey, and ten times as big as a sarus crane. It could run as swiftly as the wind, but although it had wings, it could not fly. Its keeper told me that its food was stones, and that it too came from Africa where the people use it instead of a horse.[16] This really was a city of enchantments. These marvellous animals were all presents to the Rajah from the Nawab of Surat, Nasiruddin, who had big ships trading with all parts of the world.

I remained in this place for several days and then proceeded to Ajmer. I could see the high hill of Taragarh beside Ajmer while still two days' journey away. I discovered that my regiment had left, and I therefore attached myself to some irregular cavalry[17] and went on with them towards Nagpur. After fifteen days I found my regiment[18] at Amboorah. My uncle was quite well although he had again been wounded in his right arm by a bullet. To my great delight I found my Captain *sahib* had returned, but he was much thinner and could no longer wrestle. However he was as brave as ever and was worshipped by his men. I have only met two other *sahibs* like 'Burrumpeel' *sahib*, and they were true Englishmen—not *sahibs* from the hilly island.[19]

I was now quite fit enough to take my place in the ranks and my old wound never bothered me except in damp weather. In a few days we were ordered to storm a village called Ahanpura, which was

[15] This was Sita Ram's first sight of a giraffe!

[16] The ostrich.

[17] Over and above the regular establishment of the Company's Bengal, Madras and Bombay Armies, there were numerous irregular corps which were often raised for a particular campaign and then disbanded. During the Pindari War, for example, some of the Pindari bands were taken on after defeat as irregulars. Many of these irregular corps were para-military, and can probably best be described as military police. Some of these irregulars have survived in the modern Indian Army, such as Skinner's Horse and Hodson's Horse of the Armoured Corps.

[18] It has been assumed that Sita Ram was posted to the 2/15th Bengal Native Infantry when the 'Flank' battalion, in which he had served during the Gurkha and Pindari Wars, was broken up. The 2/15th BNI had lost three companies during the Gurkha War and it is possible that Sita Ram's company was posted to it *en bloc* as reinforcements. He says that 'Burrumpeel' and his uncle, *Jemadar* Hanuman, were serving with him.

[19] Norgate's original translation has the following footnote: 'It is not very evident what Sita Ram means by the "hilly island"; all *Belait* (Europe) is imagined by the Hindus to be composed of different islands.' Perhaps he is comparing Englishmen with Scotsmen—to the disadvantage of the latter!

defended by Arab soldiers[20] in the pay of Apa Sahib.[21] These men were said to be the bravest in the world, and even a match for European troops. Nevertheless our Colonel did not hesitate to try and take the place with us Hindustanis. The Arabs fought desperately for their lives, and my regiment lost many *sepoys*; in my company alone eleven men were killed and wounded. As soon as one house was taken, the enemy retired to another. They did not run away, but died at their posts like men. They were expert marksmen and we always suffered severe casualties whenever we fought them. Even dislodging them from a few huts was a difficult business.

[20] Arab mercenaries were long recruited as bodyguards by Indian princes. The Nizam of Hyderabad, whose family has a long connection with the State of Qai'ti in South Arabia, maintained an Arab bodyguard until quite recent times. Presumably the loyalty of Arabs to the ruler's person was less likely to be tampered with in the plots and counterplots of an Indian court. These Arabs mostly came from Yemen and South Arabia, and the Yafa'i tribe from north-east of Aden provided a great many mercenaries.
[21] Apa Sahib is another name for Madaji Bhonsla, who acted as vice-regent for his imbecile cousin who was Bhonsla Rajah of Nagpur, and one of the leading Mahratta chieftains. He concluded a treaty with the British which he subsequently broke, allowing his troops to attack them at Sitabaldi on 26 November 1818. Nagpur was subsequently besieged and Apa Sahib fled to the hills and jungles. The campaign against him was long drawn-out but culminated with the capture of Asirgarh. Apa Sahib took refuge with Runjeet Singh, ruler of the Punjab, and later removed to Jodhpur where he died.

'. . . I therefore attached myself to some irregular cavalry'

'I saw her every day and my heart became inflamed with love'

6   The Lovely Thakurin

The last attempt by the Mahrattas to dispute the dominion of India with the British ended on 3 June 1818, when the Peshwa of Poona, the principal Mahratta chief, surrendered to Sir John Malcolm at Dhulkot in central India. The Peshwa was forbidden to return to the Deccan, but was exiled to Bithur, near Cawnpore, where he was provided with an annual stipend of £100,000 as some solace for the death of all his hopes. 'With him,' wrote Fortescue, 'the great Mahratta confederacy, which, but for the British would have mastered all India, passed finally away.' It had indeed been a remarkable saga, beginning as far back as Sivaji (1627–80), who raised the standard of revolt against the Mughuls and made his people the ruling power in the Deccan;[1] and it is sad that it should have ended amid a welter of palace intrigue and in alliance with a worthless collection of banditti like the Pindaris.

However, there still remained the Arab mercenaries, who refused to surrender, and the great fortress of Asirgarh which is situated midway between the Narbada and Tapti rivers. Asirgarh was a place of great natural strength, belonging to Maharajah Scindiah of Gwalior, and held for him by his kiladar, or fortress commander, Jaswant Rao. Although Scindiah had ostensibly ordered Jaswant Rao to surrender his charge to the British, he secretly directed him to hold the fort in support of Apa Sahib, who was still in arms against the British, and to Asirgarh there came all that remained of the Pindaris, as well as the few Mahrattas remaining in the field and their Arab mercenaries. The fortress towered 1,500 feet above the plain, and it was said that 'none but the hawk or lark ever saw inside Asirgarh'. When John Shipp arrived outside the walls with the Bengal column, he concluded that any idea of climbing up to such a place, or breaching its walls, seemed absurd.

And yet the fortress was captured by a combined force of Bombay, Madras, and Bengal troops under General Doveton and Sir John Malcolm, after a siege lasting from 18 March until 7 April 1818. Neither Apa Sahib, nor Chitu the Pindari, were among the prisoners, having made their escape before the final surrender. The British casualties were astonishingly light, amounting to one officer killed[2] and ten wounded, while 46 men were killed and 256 wounded; of these the Bengal column lost 36 killed and 108 wounded, the greater part of whom belonged to the 2/15th BNI who were killed or injured by the accidental explosion of an expense magazine.

Sita Ram was present at the siege and narrowly escaped death when the magazine blew up. His uncle, Jemadar Hanuman, was buried under the debris and never seen again, while 'Burrumpeel' sahib had a miraculous escape. Sita Ram was so badly injured that he was once again unfit for duty. He

---

[1] The Mahratta Light Infantry still use as their battle cry, 'Sivaji ki jai!' ('Long live Sivaji!'); there is a statue of him opposite the Gateway to India in Bombay.
[2] Lieutenant-Colonel Fraser of the Royal Scots was killed just after the capture of the lower fort.

*was carried in a litter to Aligarh in the UP and subsequently decided to volunteer
for a new unit which was being raised at Fategarh. He probably thought that
his uncle's death would remove any influence he had in his own regiment.
The Fategarh Levy which he joined eventually became the 63rd and 64th BNI in
the reorganization of 1824. Since he says that he did not report for duty at
Fategarh until July 1820, he must have spent a long period at Aligarh on sick
leave, or light duties.*

*Only a small cadre of British officers was provided to raise new
units, and Sita Ram has a lot to say about his new commanding officer who was
killed in a duel. Major 'Gardeen', as Sita Ram calls him, seems to have been a
difficult officer, hot-tempered and overconscious of his own importance, but
long service in India has always been notoriously hard on the liver. In any case
many of us can recall without much difficulty others of his type. Sir Patrick
Cadell has endeavoured to identify 'Gardeen', but without success.[3]*

*In this chapter Sita Ram also tells us of the great romance of his
life—his rescue of a beautiful Rajput girl of good family who was about to be
put to death by the Arab soldier who had forcibly made her his mistress. She was
the daughter of a minor Rajput chieftain (Thakur) from Bundelkhand, and
her honour had been indelibly disgraced by the indignities to which she had had
to submit, both as a woman, and also as a high caste Hindu lady at the hands of a
Mahommedan. After various vicissitudes Sita Ram married her, though by
a less formal marriage than that with his first wife, and by her he had several
children.*

Although we tried every means to dislodge the enemy
[from Ahanpura], we made little progress for a considerable time, but at
last the few remaining enemy escaped down a ravine, and these were
nearly all Mahrattas. While running along a lane in the village, I came
upon the enclosure of a house and entered it, expecting to find it deserted.
However I surprised an Arab in the very act of killing a girl who was
kneeling at his feet and imploring him to spare her life. The moment he
saw me he shouted out, 'Not yet!', and rushed at me like a tiger. He came
so frantically that he transfixed himself on my bayonet before I could
recover my surprise. I then fired my musket and blew a great hole in his
chest, but even after this he managed in his dying struggles to give me a
severe cut on my arm. These men live like jackals and they fight like
Ghazis.[4]

[3] *The Autobiography of an Indian Soldier*, edited by Sir Patrick Cadell,
Journal of the Society of Army Historical Research, March and June 1959.

[4] *Ghazi* is a word meaning a fighter for the faith, or one who fights
against infidels. They were particularly to be met among the Pathans on the Northwest

The girl threw herself at my feet and embraced my legs. She was in reality, with regard to beauty, what my wife's nurse had described my wife to be! I asked her who she was, and where she came from, and where her friends and relations were? She told me she was the daughter of a *Thakur*[5] in Bundelkhand, by name Mokum Singh. She had been carried off by the Pindaris who had sold her to this Arab, who had forced her to become his mistress. Her father had been killed, and many of her relations also, while defending their property. She also assured me that the survivors would never receive her back as she was disgraced beyond redemption, and she ended her sad story by telling me that I was her Lord and now her only protector.

The village had been set on fire and smoke was coming in dense clouds into the enclosure. I hastily bound up my arm with the turban of the dead Arab, and taking his sword as proof that I had slain him, I led the little fawn through the unburnt part of the village and rejoined my company. But I did not know what to do with the girl since I knew I should not be allowed to keep her with me. Our force retired some miles after the fight and camped behind Ahanpura. I told my uncle about my adventure and he advised me to abandon the girl and not encumber myself with a woman in these times of war. But how could I have left her in the village to be burnt to death? I went to my Captain and told him of the affair. He praised me very much and ordered the girl to be placed in the care of the man in charge of our followers.[6]

This young creature rode my pony but remained in the care of the head follower. I saw her every day and my heart became inflamed with love, for she was beautiful to look on and always called me her protector. I am an old man now but never before nor since have I seen any woman like her, not even in Delhi. For a week or more no notice was taken of me nor the girl, but at the end of this time the Adjutant sent for me and told me I could not keep her because women were not permitted to accompany the forces. At this my mind was filled with sadness and my heart became a target for the arrows of despair. I pleaded that if she remained with the followers, the girl could give no trouble, nor put the

---

Frontier, and in Afghanistan. Believing as they did that death in their cause was a certain invitation to eternal paradise, they were completely reckless of their lives.

[5] *Thakur:* a Rajput petty chief, or noble. Hence *Thakurin*, the feminine of *Thakur*. The Rajputs, a warrior race, pride themselves on their chivalry and are intensely jealous of their honour.

[6] The Hindi expression used by Sita Ram is *Bazar Chowdree*, meaning head man of the bazaar. The unwieldy collection of followers constituted what was sometime referred to as the regimental bazaar, and as there were probably itinerant shopkeepers among them, the expression is not inapt. There might also be dancing girls, jugglers, and musicians trailing along with the regiment.

Sirkar to any expense. The Adjutant then proposed to give me one hundred rupees for her, and ended by offering four hundred rupees[7] if I would give her up. But I could not bring myself to part with her although I now foresaw that I should soon lose her. My uncle strongly advised me to get rid of her as she would only bring disgrace on me. For the first time my uncle and I nearly had a quarrel. How true was the warning given me by the priest Duleep Ram: 'More men are entangled by the wiles of a woman than fish in the net of the most skilful fisherman. The arrows from their eyes wound more than the poisoned arrows of the Bhil.'[8]

If I had been in cantonments nothing would have been known, and no-one would have cared about my keeping this girl. Many of the *sepoys* constantly had women living with them, and the *sahibs* never forbade this because the women were all put down as relations. Had 'Burrumpeel' *sahib* asked me for her, it might have been different, but he never did this. He praised me for my kind action, took me to the Colonel, and told him about my killing the Arab. I presented the sword to the Colonel who was graciously pleased to accept it. At the same time he promised me promotion as soon as possible, and ordered me to be made a lance *naik* at once. This gave me no increase of pay, but I now had command of four men, and wore a stripe, and of course felt more important.[9]

My regiment marched from one hill fort to the next, sometimes with artillery and European troops attached to us, and at other times on our own. Once or twice we were repulsed, and in one engagement two officers were shot dead, and four wounded. Among the latter was the Adjutant *sahib* who received a severe cut from a sword in his right shoulder. These Arabs had been in Apa Sahib's service and were so highly esteemed for their bravery that they were paid twice as much as we *sepoys*. They were now fighting on their own account because they would not obey Apa Sahib's orders to give themselves up. Since no *sahib* could speak their language, and as they were always spoken to through a Mahommedan priest who pretended to know their speech, I think they did not properly understand the Government's surrender terms. These terms were that they should lay down their arms and leave India, but this order, whether they understood it or not, was never obeyed. They fought to the last, never asking for nor giving quarter. They destroyed nearly three entire companies of a newly-raised regiment, the 2nd battalion of the 10th under Major 'Esparks', having previously refused an offer to surrender

---

[7] A great deal of money for a humble *sepoy*—more than two years' pay.

[8] The Bhil are an aboriginal tribe of Central India who used to hunt game with poisoned arrows.

[9] Non-commissioned ranks were: *havildar* (sergeant), *naik* (corporal), and *lance-naik* (lance-corporal). In the cavalry a sergeant was a *duffadar*.

under a white flag.[10] Brigadier-General Adams *sahib* subsequently avenged this treachery and annihilated the party of Arabs and Gonds who were under their chief, Chyn Sab. Other engagements followed in which they were defeated, and then a truce was made, but this was soon broken.

      The *Sirkar* now had a large army with plenty of artillery. The fort of Hasser[11] was summoned to surrender but its governor, Jaswant Rao, would not listen to any terms and was determined to hold out to the last. He was a very brave man.[12] An English officer went down to the gateway to persuade Jaswant Rao to surrender; he pointed out that Maharajah Scindiah was a friend of the British, and master of the governor of the fortress, but no heed was paid to his words. Jaswant Rao was so confident in the strength of the fortress, and the bravery of his Arabs, that the officer was insulted and a shot was fired at him in defiance. This treatment of one of their officers enraged the British soldiers so much that they were keen to take the fortress by storm. It was very strong and had walls of great thickness. It stood on a hill, one thousand feet high, and all the approaches were exposed to a galling fire from the garrison. Many of the *sepoys* believed that it would stand a long siege, but my uncle told me that the Company had already taken it once [in 1803], and now that they had assembled such a strong army with so many heavy guns, it would easily be taken again.

      Until now my luck had been good, but even so I could not look on the fortifications without feeling some fear. My liver turned to water. The siege was opened by our heavy artillery, and the enemy made frequent sallies, but our shells (which were a new weapon for them) caused dreadful havoc among them. Great chunks of the fortifications came tumbling down, while the perpetual thunder of the guns was like the onset of the monsoon. A Colonel 'Frasan' *sahib*[13] forced his way into the town and took possession of some merchants' shops for two or three days, but he was killed while repulsing an enemy sortie. The morning after this happened the citadel was abandoned by the enemy and my regiment was ordered to occupy it. We were running forward to do this when the enemy

---

    [10] Sita Ram is inaccurate here. 2/10th BNI was not a newly raised regiment, but an old one. One company, *not* three companies, was surrounded by the enemy (Arabs) shortly after crossing the River Tapti near Multai. Captain Sparkes and his men fought gallantly but were wiped out, apart from nineteen survivors, of whom ten were wounded—20 July 1818.

    [11] Hasser was the old name for Asirgarh.

    [12] And also very fat, if John Shipp is to be believed.

    [13] 'Frasan' is obviously meant for Lieutenant-Colonel Fraser of the Royal Scots who led the party which had taken the lower town. According to Shipp, Fraser's men dispersed looking for loot, and the enemy, taking advantage of this, launched a counter-attack in which Fraser was killed.

suddenly blew up a mine under our feet.[14] I was blown up into the air and became unconscious. I knew nothing, saw nothing, nor heard anything for a long time. When I recovered consciousness I found two European artillerymen pulling me out of the rubble by my legs, and one of them forced some rum down my throat. They took me to a *sahib*, and I was sent back to hospital to die. My legs were not broken, but my left arm hung powerless by my side, and I had four severe cuts on my head from bricks or flying wood. I consider that I may count these as wounds, and this means that I have been seven times wounded in the service of the *Sirkar*.

I cannot say how many days I lay in that tent. The guns continued to thunder day after day, but one morning they ceased and on the day this happened I partially recovered my speech. I asked about my uncle and the fate of my company, and was horror-struck to be told by a wounded *sepoy* of my regiment that every man had been killed except for myself, Tillukdaree Gheer, Kadir Bux, and Deonarain. There were also four men away on guard duty who escaped, but forty-seven men were killed by this terrible explosion.

How right I was to have been afraid before the siege! My mind was oppressed with grief. My uncle's body was never found; the ruin was so widespread and there was no time to clear away the rubbish. How I longed to go and search for his body but I could move neither hand nor foot. The hospital tents were so full of wounded at this time that the officers even gave up their own tents for the wounded. My Captain was very kind to me, and Captain 'Burma' *sahib*[15] who was seriously wounded was in the same tent as me. 'Burrumpeel' *sahib* had had a miraculous escape. Although he was only a few yards from the mine when it exploded, he was thrown down, and nearly suffocated with earth, but otherwise was unhurt. Number 2 Company was destined to be destroyed. Number 1 Company had gone over the same mine a few moments before it blew up. The fort was taken and I was told all kinds of people were found inside it—Arabs, Baluchis, men from Kabul, and others. The *Sirkar* again failed to punish Jaswant Rao, but allowed him to go free. I asked my Captain why Jaswant was not executed, and he replied that he had only obeyed the orders of his master, Maharajah Scindiah, who had pretended to be a friend of the Company *Bahadur*, but who was in reality its enemy. He would be the one to be punished. The justice of this Government is indeed remarkable, and its conduct inexplicable. What is the use of fighting if you do not destroy your enemy? These were strange customs for the

---

[14] It was not a mine but a magazine, constructed well forward and close to the walls, for explosives and mortar shells.

[15] This was probably Captain F. L. Burman of the 7th Madras Native Infantry who was wounded at Asirgarh.

people we were fighting. They thought the *Sirkar* was crazy for showing mercy, and they sought in every way to take advantage of their kindness and often succeeded. But Lord Malcolm *sahib*[16] was such a mighty chief that they seldom deceived him. There were few Lord *sahibs* like him. It only goes to prove what I have already said—the *sahibs* and the European soldiers like fighting for the sake of fighting. And as for the latter, providing they have enough of their beloved grog they are happy. War is an amusement, or kind of game, so far as they are concerned.

This war being now finished, the army broke up and the different regiments marched to their stations. My battalion was ordered to Aligarh, and I was carried all the way in a hospital litter. I could have got sick leave again at my home but for certain reasons I did not want to go just then. I was allowed to live in a hut by myself and the young Thakurin lived with me and looked after me. I was happier than I had ever been in my own home, and within a few months I had recovered sufficiently to be able to walk.

Several new battalions were being raised at this time for the Government, and my Colonel *sahib* told me that if I felt inclined to join one of these battalions, I could gain promotion to *naik*. Since my good and kind uncle was dead, and nearly all my comrades in my company as well, I decided to leave my old corps. But I felt the most painful thing in my undertaking was leaving my Captain *sahib*. There was only one 'Burrum-peel' *sahib* who ever left England, and he was in my old regiment.

I joined the headquarters of the new battalion at Fategarh in July 1820, and found it consisted of only two companies made up from men of different regiments as a foundation for the new regiment the *Sirkar* intended to form. There were only two British officers, Major 'Gardeen' *sahib*, and the Adjutant. The Major was very tall and dark. He was in the habit of coming on parade in shooting dress[17] and throwing his heavy stick at the recruits' heads, and sometimes even at the drill instructors' if they did anything to annoy him. As a result he was much disliked, but also feared. He told the Indian officers that he had been removed from his own regiment against his wishes and sent to command them and he hated them all. In fact, through fear of him we only recruited forty men in four months. After this we were given four more *sahibs* from other regiments and three new cadets. More men also arrived and the drill commenced.

The Major *sahib* was not liked by the English officers;

[16] Malcolm combined the duties of soldier and political officer. From all accounts he was a most attractive personality with a remarkable insight into Indian character.

[17] Presumably the clothes he wore when he was shooting game.

they never spoke to him before or after parade, nor did they seem to associate with him in any way. The only person he appeared to be friends with was an old butler, and no-one knew why this man had so much influence over the *sahib*. However I do know that any *sepoy* wanting leave, or any other favour, always tried to secure the good graces of the butler to put in a good word to his master. One day when I was on guard at his house the Major was about to start smoking his *hookah* in the evening; the tobacco would not draw, and he flew into a violent passion, throwing the lighted bowl at the *hookahbadar*'s head.[18] The red-hot charcoal rolled over the room and set fire to the floor matting, which in turn set fire to a tent in the next room. The servants and the guard rushed in and managed to extinguish the flames, but the tent was nearly destroyed. Throughout this scene the *sahib* never moved from his chair, but then the butler came and spoke to him and his rage subsided in an instant. However, giving way to his irritation had cost him dear, for the tent was almost new and must have been worth three hundred rupees. We endeavoured to discover the secret of the butler's influence over this *sahib* but we never succeeded. Some said he was a near relation.

There was no doubt that the Major was slightly mad. His habits were quite different from other *sahibs*. He used to walk up and down his veranda for hours at a time, with his hands behind his back, muttering to himself and kicking the wall with his foot every time he turned round. He spoke our language perfectly but his chief delight lay in teasing our recruits. He would make them tell him whether they were married or not, and also the names of their wives, which is a great shame for a Hindu to mention. I could also see that his attitude towards the other officers of the regiment was very odd. The Adjutant *sahib* was never allowed to sit in his presence, while his servant never offered a chair to any of the *sahibs* who came to see him unless the Major told him to do so.

An officer now joined the regiment who was quite as old in appearance as the Major and I happened to be on guard at the Major's house when this officer came to pay a call. I was curious to see whether the Major would offer him a chair, but he remained standing for a short time, and then took one himself and sat down. A storm of abuse then followed and I saw the Captain strike the Major and knock him down. He then left speaking very loudly. The following morning, while returning from the fields,[19] I saw four officers behind the rifle butts. They were some way

---

[18] The bowl of the *hookah* would contain a mixture of tobacco and charcoal. The smoke passed through water before it was drawn into the mouth, and it was the *hookahbadar*'s responsibility to make sure that the *hookah* was lit properly and drawing evenly.

[19] In the absence of latrines, the fields were resorted to by the *sepoys* in the early mornings.

from the lines and near some gullies. Since the officers were often in the habit of practising with their pistols, I did not take much notice at first. But as I drew nearer I saw that the Major and the Captain were both present and, as I knew it was the custom among the British officers to fire pistols at each other in the event of a quarrel, I stopped to see what was happening. The Major was placed a short distance in front of the Captain by another officer, and there was another officer attending upon the Captain. They both fired and the Major fell forward on his face. I now ran up and found that the Major was dead. He had been shot through the head. I went to the hospital for a litter and the news was round the lines in a moment. The Major was carried to his own house and was buried in the evening. The only person who seemed to be affected was the butler. No *sahib*'s face displayed any grief.[20]

How curious are the customs of these foreigners! Here, in this case, no revenge was taken at the time when they were heated with anger, nor was the fight with swords. No words were spoken, nor was there any abuse. The *sahibs* were as cool and collected as when on parade. I did not know at the time that the officer attending on the Major was a great friend of the Captain, and both the attendant officers spoke to each other, and were friends, as they shared the same house. The English have very strict rules about honour and if insulted they must fight, since otherwise they are never spoken to by their brother officers again. In those days the *sahibs* often fought one another, and after the fight they frequently became greater friends than ever. I have not heard of *sahibs* fighting each other in recent years; if they do, it is done secretly, as if nowadays they are ashamed to be seen. But I believe the real reason is that they fear the new rules about duelling. The *sahib* who now takes part in a duel is tried by Court Martial and dismissed the service without any excuse being taken. I have heard that the King of England was forced to put an end to this habit because he lost so many good officers from it, and the family of the dead *sahib* had to be supported by the state. I cannot imagine how they can fight after their tempers have cooled, but this, like everything else they do, is managed by their remarkable arrangement of their affairs. The European soldiers do not fight among themselves with pistols; they use their fists instead, which is just as dangerous for I have known several men to be killed. After their fights, however, they soon become friends again, but even among the soldiers they lose face if they refuse to fight.

Another officer was sent to command the regiment. He was Colonel 'Hamilteen' *sahib*. He was quite different from the Major and

[20] There must have been many deaths from duels, but only 22 are recorded in the Bengal Army. In a land where death came swiftly, they would have been easy to hush up.

was popular with both officers and the soldiers. The regiment was now a thousand strong and composed of fine, tall young men. For two or three years nothing much happened except that we marched to Meerut. I had spent a lot of money in order that the Thakurin could regain her caste, and I was married to her by the ceremony called *gardab*.[21] While we were at Meerut 'a joy of the world' was born to me—a son!

[21] *Gardab*: a second marriage, but not as binding as a first marriage.

'. . . I saw four officers behind the rifle butts'

'Darjan's people fought desperately'

7   *The Bulwark of Hindustan*

The great fortress-city of Bharatpore,[1] near Agra, was sometimes described as the 'Bulwark of Hindustan', and in 1805 General Lake's victorious progress was halted by its walls. He made four separate attempts to storm Bharatpore and on each occasion was repulsed with heavy loss. There was an ancient prophecy that Baharatpore would only fall when a crocodile came from across the seas and drank all the ditches dry, and since there was a wide belt of desert and jungle between Baharatpore and the nearest crocodile, the likelihood of this occurring seemed highly remote. But in 1824 Lord Combermere succeeded General Paget as Commander-in-Chief of the Bengal Army, and his name, as pronounced by the Indians, bore a marked resemblance to the vernacular word for crocodile.

Bharatpore was the capital of the Jats, Hindu yeomen who make excellent soldiers, and its ruler, Rajah Baldeo Singh, had come to terms with the powerful Company and managed to retain his independence. However, trouble began when he tried to settle the succession to his throne. He put forward his six-year-old son, Balwant Singh, and tried to ensure the child's inheritance by enlisting the support of General Ochterlony, who was the Company's Resident in Delhi. Ochterlony promised his support, and when the Rajah died early in 1825, the child was installed on the throne. However, this was followed by a palace revolution, as a result of which Darjan Sal, nephew of the dead Rajah, seized the citadel, murdered the guardian uncle, and proclaimed himself viceregent, filling all the offices of state with his own creatures.

Ochterlony responded with his usual vigour. He denounced Darjan Sal as a usurper, promised support to all who rose against him, and assembled an army to march against Bharatpore. The Governor-General, Lord Amherst, took exception to Ochterlony's action and said so in an extremely offensive dispatch. The troops were dispersed, and Ochterlony resigned. He was succeeded as Resident by Charles Metcalfe, who had already served in Delhi. He soon recognized the danger of the situation, for by then Darjan Sal had ousted the infant Rajah and placed himself on the throne. Metcalfe advised Amherst that the claim of the infant Rajah must be supported—'not by any positive engagement to the Bhurtpore state, nor by any claim on her part, but by our duty as supreme guardians of general tranquillity, law and right'—and Amherst changed his instructions. A force was assembled under Lord Combermere and marched to Bharatpore in December 1825. Sita Ram's regiment[2] formed part of the First Division commanded by Major-General Reynell.

Bharatpore was immensely strong. The city, containing nearly 100,000 people, was situated in the middle of a level plain and was surrounded by

---

[1] The old rendering was Bhurtpore, and as such it appears on the Colours of the regiments which fought there. The modern rendering of the Hindi into English is Bharatpore.

[2] It has been assumed that Sita Ram was serving with the 63rd BNI.

a high wall of mud brick, strengthened throughout its length by rows of tree trunks buried upright. Beyond the walls was a deep and wide ditch with perpendicular banks. Each of the nine gates was protected by an extensive earthwork, and towering above the walls was the citadel, reputedly the strongest place in India. Lake had lost nearly 3,000 men killed and wounded in his attempts to storm Bharatpore, but he lacked the siege artillery which Combermere was able to assemble. However, even siege guns had their limitations since the mud brick walls merely crumbled when hit. 'What was needed,' wrote Fortescue, 'was shell, and shell was as yet projected not by horizontal but high-angle fire. Shell could only be dropped upon a surface, not driven into the heart of an obstacle to burst within it.'

In the event, Combermere succeeded where Lake had failed. Bharatpore fell on 18 January 1825, and Darjan Sal was taken prisoner. The big gun referred to by Sita Ram was over fifteen feet in length and six feet in circumference at the muzzle. The campaign has several interesting features. It was the first time British cavalry used the lance in Battle.[3] It was the first of many battlefields on which the Gurkhas fought for the British.[4] It was also one of the few occasions in India when British soldiers deserted and actually fought for the enemy. Three artillerymen deserted and served the enemy's guns. Two were men of bad character, but one of them, Sergeant Herbert, had fought at Waterloo and was highly regarded. All were captured and Herbert was hanged on the north-west bastion; the other two, much to the indignation of the army, escaped with transportation to Botany Bay.

A long period of peace followed the capture of Bharatpore, and Sita Ram rose to the rank of Havildar. He became pay-havildar in his company, a much-coveted post. Most of the sepoys kept their pay with the pay-havildar until they went home on annual leave, and custom permitted the pay-havildar to lend money to British officers, who, according to Sita Ram, were often in debt. The Captain of his Company unfortunately lost all his property when a boat containing it sank in a river, and Sita Ram lent him 500 rupees. There was a sudden call for the money banked with Sita Ram by the sepoys, and the combined resources of the Captain and himself fell short of the amount required. Sita Ram was therefore court-martialled for breach of Regulations and lost the appointment of pay-havildar, although he retained his rank as there was no imputation on his honesty.

He rambles a good deal in this chapter, discussing, among other things, the curious rules of the army, and the need for British officers to remain longer with their men than was usually the case. It was inevitable that the

[3] The 16th, Queen's Lancers, who had been equipped with the lance in 1818, charged with their lances against the Jat horsemen on several occasions.

[4] 1st Nasseri battalion and the Sirmoor battalion of Gurkhas were raised in 1815 during the Gurkha War. The former is now the 1st Goorkha Rifles, Indian Army, and the latter the 2nd King Edward VII's Own Gurkha Rifles, British Army.

more clever and ambitious officers should try to escape from the monotony of regimental life in some up-country garrison and find wider scope for their energies in semi-civilian employment, but it meant a constant chopping and changing within units. Sita Ram was not so much concerned that his officers should be efficient, as we might define the word, but that they should remain long enough at regimental duty for their sepoys to get to know their foibles and idiosyncrasies.

Although there was always a 'bush-fire' operation of one sort or another taking place in India, or in places dependent on India like Aden, none of these was of any real consequence. Sita Ram was able to soldier along quietly and watch his children grow up. But these were years of change for the Company's army, and Sita Ram by no means approved of all the changes. Lord William Bentinck, the Governor-General for much of this period, was an ardent reformer and it was during his time in office that such evils as the burning of widows (suttee) and thuggee were eradicated. He also turned his attention to the army, and was subsequently accused, by Sita Ram among others, of having damaged discipline by reforms.

A General Order of March 1827 had abolished corporal punishment for Indian troops, apart from the crimes of stealing, marauding, and gross insubordination. Eight years later flogging was abolished altogether, and dismissal from the service substituted. There was an immediate outcry after the introduction of both these reforms, and more particularly after the latter. Unfortunately there is ample evidence to show that discipline did decline very rapidly from 1827 onwards—'The Army had ceased to fear'. There were of course other reasons for this decline, and not least the removal from units of their best officers for employment in other fields, but the abolition of corporal punishment undoubtedly played some part. Moreover, the fact that it had not been abolished in the British Army, and that European soldiers could still be flogged, and were flogged, on garrison parades for offences which the sepoy could commit without fear of flogging, must have had a detrimental effect on discipline, and on relations between the British and Indian soldiers. Flogging was reintroduced in 1845 after some serious mutinies among regiments ordered to Sind, which was an unpopular garrison.

About this time it was generally reported that the *Sirkar* was going to provide assistance for Rajah Balwant Singh of Bharatpore who had been driven from his throne by his brother Darjan Sal.[5] The Rajah had begged and prayed the *Sirkar* to support his right to the throne,

[5] Balwant Singh was ousted from the throne by Darjan Sal, a nephew of the late Rajah; he was not a brother of Balwant Singh.

but he was only a boy and there was a strong party against him at Bharatpore. General 'Loneyackty'[6] was then Governor of Delhi and he gave orders for an army to be assembled. My regiment received instructions to march to Agra, but it only went four or five marches and was then recalled to Meerut.[7] Great was the disappointment of the officers for they longed for their new regiment to see service and make a name for itself. After a month[8] orders were again received and we marched to Agra where a large army was encamped. We remained here for some time.

Some people thought that Darjan Sal, hearing that an army was advancing against him, would give up the fortress without a fight. On one day he would send to say that he would do this, and then on another day that he intended to fight. All this was done in order to gain time for the collection of more men and arms. The English had besieged Bharatpore before in 'Lad Lick's' time and had lost half an army there; the place had been delivered up but had not surrendered.[9] This was well known to everyone, and was also well remembered. The place was much stronger now than formerly, and was reported to have many large guns which could throw a cannonball six miles. The Bharatpore people put great trust in this artillery and considered the place impregnable.

The English Commander-in-Chief,[10] getting tired of these useless negotiations, marched the army from Agra and laid siege with many large guns. The great annoyance now came from the enemy's horsemen who always hovered round our camp and cut up large numbers of our followers and stragglers. Whenever they were chased by our cavalry they always galloped under the guns of the fort, or into some gateway known only to them. The *Sirkar*'s guns were of no use in making a breach; the walls were so thick that a company could have been drawn up in column upon them and been wheeled into line. The enemy made many attacks on our camp at night, and all the neighbouring states were waiting to see the fortune of the *Sirkar*. If a reverse had taken place, they would have come down on our camp from the rear where the jungle was thick and difficult to guard.

The Sappers and Miners were set to work to mine under

[6] Major-General Sir David Ochterlony. See note 23, Chapter 3.

[7] This would have been the first, abortive, attempt by Ochterlony to march against Bharatpore, which was countermanded by the Governor-General (Lord Amherst).

[8] Sita Ram's chronology is once again at fault. Nearly a year passed between the cancellation of the original plan and the decision to advance against Bharatpore.

[9] Lord Lake's failure to take Bharatpore in 1805 was due mainly to the lack of sufficient siege artillery. He made four attempts to carry the place by assault, and then made a treaty with the Maharajah which was faithfully observed by both sides.

[10] Sir Stapleton Cotton (1773–1865), Wellington's old cavalry commander of the Peninsula, had been raised to the peerage as Viscount Combermere.

the walls. I was on guard one night at the entrance to one of these galleries, and about midnight a sentry reported that water was spreading over the surrounding fields. The enemy had let the water out of the big moat, and if I had not given warning in time, all the Miners would have been drowned, as mice are killed in the rains.[11] However the Sappers soon constructed walls of earth and diverted the water from the mine. This was on Christmas Day. Some weeks after this the gallery was continued under one of the bastions and we heard that the mine would be exploded. All our troops turned out to see the effect and the enemy, thinking an attack was imminent, manned the walls, and were busy bringing into action an enormous cannon which was positioned on the bastion under which the mine was laid. For a time there was a deep silence throughout our camp but the mine did not explode. The Sapper officers were very anxious, thinking that the enemy had countermined. Several of them rushed to see whether the fuse had burnt out, when off went the mine and the bastion, together with the big cannon, men and all, were hurled into the moat. A hole was left in the fortress wall big enough to march a company through it.[12] The enemy fire ceased for a time for they were quite thunderstruck by the explosion. Our artillery kept up a brisk fire on the breach throughout the night, and next morning a storming party was formed. My company, and part of another, were included in the attacking column. Darjan's people fought desperately, but who can stand up against the charge of European soldiers?[13]

By ten o'clock that morning[14] the far-famed fortress of Bharatpore was in the hands of the *Sirkar*. Darjan himself was captured while attempting to escape. There was plenty of loot and many *sahibs* acquired very valuable property.[15] I found a handsome necklace on a woman who had been killed, and decided this would be my share. I thought I would put it round the neck of my son but I was seen by two European soldiers who took it away from me by force. They cut it in two, each taking half, but I later came across one of these men who was dead-drunk and I easily regained one half of the necklace without any need for

[11] Part of the defences were a series of *jheels*, or marshy ponds, from which sluices controlled the level of water in the moat. The sluices were captured early in the siege.

[12] The explosion was tremendous. Brigadiers McCombe and Paton, who were to lead the storm, were struck down, and Combermere, who was beside them, dashed forward to lead the stormers but was forcibly restrained by his aide-de-camp.

[13] The *sepoys* performed just as gallantly, according to Major John Luard of the 16th Lancers, who wrote: 'All who witnessed the conduct of the *sepoys* on this day bear testimony to their gallantry, and the King's officers have declared that their forwardness was not outdone by the British soldier.'

[14] Actually 3 p.m. on 18 January 1825.

[15] The prize-money amounted to £480,000 of which Combermere's share was £60,000, later to be lost by him to a dishonest banker. The rank and file received £4 apiece.

force. Great numbers of the enemy, or rather people of the city, had been killed by shells and numbers had been destroyed by the mine. I went to look at the place of the explosion, and it was incredible. The large cannon had fallen into the ditch, crushing men beneath it like Juggernaut, but all these men had died at their guns and what better death could they have chosen?

This gun was called *Fateh-jang-sir-phorhua*, or the 'victorious in war—the head-smasher'. It was three musket lengths' long and the cannonball was the size of a large earthen pot. Engraved on the gun was the charge which amounted to 150 pounds of gunpowder. I have heard the *sahibs* talk of the big new guns they have in England but I can hardly believe that they are any bigger than four or five of the guns I saw at Bharatpore. In spite of all that had been said about this fortress, it did not cost us much to capture it.[16] Not more than 50 *sepoys* were killed, and in the storming party furnished by my regiment we lost only 5 men killed and 15 wounded. The European troops lost about the same, but many *sahibs* were wounded because they persisted in going close up to the walls to fire their shot-guns and their rifles. This was strictly forbidden but the orders were disregarded. After this siege my regiment was sent to garrison several small forts in the neighbourhood, and my company was ordered to Biana Garhi. These places were soon dismantled, and the regiment then returned to Meerut after an absence of about one year.

There now came a new *Lad Sahib* to India who was much disliked by all the officers.[17] He wished to reduce their pay and the *sahibs* nearly mutinied. They held many meetings in their own houses and were greatly disturbed. Many of them said they would serve the Government no longer. This *Lad Sahib* was sent by the Company *Bahadur* to save money, for, as a result of the great expense of the wars, they said they were very poor. But who can credit this? When did the *Sirkar* ever lack for money? I heard that the officers of one regiment asked the officers of another whether their men would stand by them if they marched to Calcutta to compel the *Lad Sahib* to give them their rights. I was also told that the European soldiers said they would not act against the officers of the Bengal Army so long as their object was the *Batta*[18] alone. Every *sahib* at

---

[16] No complete return of losses appears to have been submitted, but a rough estimate is 180 killed, 780 wounded and 20 missing.

[17] This was General Lord William Bentinck (1774–1839) who was Governor-General from 1825 to 1835. He was the last Governor-General to be Commander-in-Chief as well. Sita Ram is quite correct—he was sent out to India to effect economies. *Lad Sahib* was the vernacular term for the Governor-General, and later for the Viceroy.

[18] *Batta:* field allowance. There was much discontent but Sita Ram is probably only repeating bazaar gossip.

this time was angry and spoke much aginast the *Sirkar*, but most of the blame was laid on the new *Lad Sahib*. They said he was carrying out this injustice without orders, and only because he wished to curry favour with the Company.

The *Sirkar* compelled the young Rajah Balwant Singh to pay all the expenses of the war [at Bharatpore] now they had restored him to the throne, and this amounted to more than one crore of rupees.[19] This was regarded as a great insult by many of the rajahs and nawabs who had hitherto looked upon the *Sirkar* as their friend and not as a paid ally. Some of them now boasted that they could hire the services of the English whenever they wanted them. I have heard that one rajah sent an agent to the *Sirkar* to enquire how much they would require to wallop another rajah who had insulted him, but this was bazaar gossip and may not be true. All kinds of news, both true and false, are discussed in the bazaars of large military stations, and anything injurious to the fortune of the Government is listened to with the keenest interest. This induces idle people with nothing better to do to invent news, and the greater the lie, the more it is believed—that is, if it is any way detrimental to the *Sirkar*. I remember during the Russian war, which was the only time when there was no war in India, that news was always fabricated to show that the *Sirkar* was usually defeated, and that the Russians had destroyed all the English soldiers and sunk all their warships. This idea was fostered by interested parties with the result that when the Mutiny broke out, most Indians believed that the *Sirkar* had no other troops than those which were already in India. Nothing could exceed the surprise of the rebels when they saw regiment after regiment pouring into the country. They then lost heart, realizing they had been deceived, and soon discovered it was useless to oppose the mighty power of the English.

After remaining two years at Meerut my regiment was sent to Shahjahanpore, and from thence to Karnal, and later to Ludhiana.[20] Nothing of note happened during these years except that there were some alterations in the *sepoys'* uniform, and rifle companies were formed in many regiments.[21] Small wars took place every year in some part of

[19] One crore of rupees: £1,000,000.

[20] Sita Ram's account of the movements of his battalion does not coincide with the actual movements of the 63rd BNI, if he did in fact remain with that unit after the Bharatpore campaign. Karnal was a big military garrison not far from Delhi and he may have been there on detachment; it was very unhealthy and was abandoned in the 1840s. Ludhiana was the main frontier garrison in the Punjab.

[21] There were constant changes in dress, but Sita Ram may be referring to change from drawers (shorts) to trousers. Rifle companies were formed after the gradual introduction of the muzzle-loading 'Brunswick' rifles in 1840, and about the same time forage caps were issued for general duties. Armies generally devote more attention to dress in peacetime than they do while campaigning.

Hindustan but my regiment did not take any share in them. I had been promoted to *havildar*, and also held the appointment of pay-*havildar* which in those days was a much sought-after appointment. Most of the *sepoys* in the company kept their money with me, and as this was seldom required by them except when they went on leave, I used to lend some of it at good interest. The money was shown at the end of every month to any *sepoy* who wanted to satisfy himself that it was safe, and this went on every month until I had accumulated the sum of 500 rupees. Pay-*havildars* also used to lend money to the *sahibs*; since all the *sahibs'* pay passed through our hands, there was little risk of losing the money unless a *sahib* died, in which case we did not dare to make a claim against his estate. The practice was forbidden but I seldom heard of anyone being punished for doing it. The officers' pay was large but it seldom sufficed for their wants. There were only two officers in my regiment who were not in debt, and many of them owed large amounts.

They spent a great part of their pay in giving entertainments; some gambled, while others lost large sums on the race-course. They are passionately fond of this sport. All the married *sahibs* were permanently in debt for their expenses are great. But some became poor through misfortune. The Captain of my company lost all his property when his boat sank in a river.[22] He had no money with which to replace his property and I lent him 500 rupees. Unfortunately the time of furlough was at hand and the *sepoys* required their pay. Having lent some of theirs with my own, I was unable to make good the whole amount I should have had in my hands. I was reported to the Colonel *sahib*, and although I sold everything I possessed, and the Captain tried all he could to raise the money, I was still 137 rupees short. I was tried by court martial, found guilty of disobedience of orders, and sentenced to be deprived of my appointment as pay-*havildar*. Had it not been for my previous good conduct, I should have been reduced to the ranks again.

This was the first court I had ever appeared before. How entirely incomprehensible are the laws of the English for us Hindus! I was found guilty by a number of Indian officers of my own regiment, not one of whom thought I had done anything wrong, and every one of whom would have acted as I had done if they had been placed in my position. And yet, because they thought the Colonel desired me to be punished, they found me guilty. The European officers were equally well aware of the facts of the case, but the custom of the service required my punishment. The Articles of War are often read out to regiments, but the language is seldom understood, being nearly all Persian and Arabic. Some of it is of course intelligible, but the greater part, as with the orders of the Governor-

[22] A large amount of travel up-country was carried out by riverboat.

General, etc., is far beyond the comprehension of any but those who have had a good education. As a general rule only two or three *sepoys* in a company understood what he must or must not do after hearing these orders read. In the first place the Interpreter *sahib*[23] nearly always reads too quickly, and secondly, he frequently mispronounces the words. Your Honour, a *sepoy* does not require a lot of rules and regulations to be read out to him. They only fill his head with doubts and fears. He should look upon his Commander as his father and mother, his protector, his god, and as such be taught to obey him.

We do not understand divided power; absolute power is what we worship. Power is much divided among the English. The Commanding Officer certainly has some power; also the Adjutant, and sometimes more than the Commander. The Commander-in-Chief has a great deal, the Governor-General still more, but they each have to ask some even higher authority before they can do anything. The Commanding Officer has to ask half a dozen officers before he can punish a *sepoy* and the permission takes months before it is received.[24] By the time the punishment is inflicted, half the men will have forgotten all about the case and the effect of the punishment entirely lost. I remember in one regiment that a *havildar* was tried by a court martial and dismissed the service for insolence to a superior officer—a crime for which he ought to have been flogged.[25] When his sentence was read out to him on parade, he turned and told his Commanding Officer that he would go straightaway to the Commander-in-Chief *sahib* and lodge an appeal. Another *havildar* was promoted in his place, but he went up to Simla, threw himself in front of the Governor-General's lady, and cried out for justice and mercy. Within three months he was restored to the service and sent back to his old regiment, thereby laughing in the face of the General, Brigadier and his Commanding Officer. No *sepoy* worried about a court martial at that time, but this was in the days when any complaint received attention from the Commander-in-Chief. The Colonel *sahib* was furious, but he had no power, and what could he do?

The Commander ought to have the power of life and

[23] The appointment of Interpreter was usually filled by a junior British officer who had passed the prescribed examination in languages. Persian was essential since it was the court language in the East, as French was in the West. Most official documents were written in Persian which would be incomprehensible to a Hindi-speaking *sepoy*. Language continues to be one of India's principal problems—more than a century after Sita Ram's death.

[24] Sita Ram is here inveighing against the changes in the disciplinary code introduced by Lord Bentinck, and in particular against the length of time required before the sentence of a court martial could be confirmed.

[25] Flogging was first abolished in the Bengal Army in 1835—many years before it was abolished in the British Army.

death. When the sword is 600 miles away,[26] who fears it? When *sepoys* find that their Commander is not really their Commander, they will always look up to some higher power. This was one reason for the Mutiny.

I have already said that the people of India worship power. They also love splendour and the display of wealth. A great impression is made on the masses by this—much greater than the English seem to believe. Our idea of the power and might of our kings and princes was always associated with magnificent equipments shining with gold and silver. Have we not thought this since we were children? Is it not the theme of every tale that is told? What then can we think of a Governor-General, or Lieutenant-Governor, when we see him as a *sahib* driving in a buggy without any ornaments or retinue? People in Government employment know that he has power, but the ordinary people consider him all sham, and he does not match up to their idea of a Rajah, Nawab, or even a minister. They then make comparisons which the *Sirkar* would not like to know. I have often asked the *sahibs* why they do not take a lesson from some of their *memsahibs* and wear more jewellery, for I have seen some English ladies looking as princesses ought to look when they go to their balls and dances. They have replied that it was considered shameful for a *sahib* to wear jewels or ornaments unless these happen to be awards of honour, but what I have seen of the latter have seemed to me to be very paltry. One *sahib* told me that his *memsahib* spent so much money on her jewels that it was impossible for him to wear any even should he feel inclined to do so.

We sometimes pay homage to peculiarities of character and superiority of intelligence but not so much as to outward pomp and magnificence. General 'Nickalseyn' *sahib*[27] was believed by some to be an incarnation of the Deity, and there are those who still mourn his removal from the world. General 'Jacum'[28] was looked upon as next to the Prophet Mahommed by many of the hill tribes, but I am told that he is also dead. The *Sirkar* should remember that the value of a regiment

[26] Presumably the reference is to Calcutta and Simla, the winter and summer capitals of the Government of India.

[27] Brigadier-General John Nicholson (1821–57). He began his service with 27th BNI and was taken prisoner during the First Afghan War. Later he gained a great reputation as a soldier-administrator on the north-western marches of the newly conquered Punjab. He so impressed his personality on the wild tribesmen he ruled that some of them saw in him the incarnation of the divine and formed a sect to worship him. He died of wounds received at the storming of Delhi on 14 September 1857.

[28] Brigadier-General John Jacob (1812–58). Another great soldier-administrator who was largely responsible for the pacification of Sind after its annexation in 1843. His name lives on in Jacobabad, the town he founded, and in the Scinde Horse, now an armoured regiment in the Indian Army, but which began its existence as Jacob's irregular cavalry.

of *sepoys* greatly depends on the Commanding Officer. If the men like him, if he understands them and can enter their feelings and has their confidence—which is not to be done in one day, or even in one year—and above all if he has power and is just, they will do anything, will go anywhere, and his word is law. But when someone completely strange to them and their feelings is sent to command them there is always discontent. Among us there is a great dislike for new ways. One *sahib* upsets what the other has done, and we do not know what to do because what we have been taught one day is wrong the next. I have known four Commanding Officers come to a regiment within a year, and three Adjutants, and two Quartermasters; and this was not as a result of officers having been killed in war. It takes us a long time to learn the ways of a *sahib* and once the men have got used to him it is wrong to have him removed.[29] Before the Mutiny any clever officer was always taken away from his regiment for some appointment, and he never came back for years. When he did come back he knew very little about the men. The Indian is not alone in his likes and dislikes of Commanding Officers; I can remember a European regiment which refused to advance against a Sikh battery of guns because

'*All the married* sahibs *were permanently in debt*'

77

they disliked their Colonel. They preferred to be turned into dust by cannon-fire rather than move. I heard that this officer was wounded—some say by his own men—and was succeeded by a popular officer. The men then instantly took the battery and drove the Sikhs like dust before the wind!

[29] This will be a familiar complaint for anyone who has ever served with Indian or Arab troops, and, for all I know, with Africans as well. I remember Glubb Pasha telling me exactly the same in 1955 when I completed my tour with the Arab Legion. Whenever a new British officer joined the Federal Army in Aden, I used to tell him that it was not so much a question of his getting to know his Arab soldiers, as of giving them plenty of time, and every opportunity, to get to know him—a much slower process. It should be remembered that Sita Ram is referring to the 1830s and 1840s when the East India Company's dominions had enormously increased, and Army officers were in great demand for civil employment, ranging from the political department to the organization of famine relief. There were never enough European civilians to fill the required appointments and the Army had to make up the deficiencies.

'. . . one valley called Dadhar which was the mouth of hell'

8   *The March*
into Afghanistan:
1838-1839

Sita Ram begins this chapter with a criticism of the new Bengal Army that had arisen phoenix-like from the ashes of the old army which had mutinied in 1857. It is hard to say whether his criticisms are justified, or whether there is any truth in his allegations of disloyalty among the Punjabi sepoys. As a soldier of the old school of pipeclay and close-order drill, Sita Ram probably resented the freer and easier ways of the new army. The fact that it contained a much larger number of Moslems than the former army also aroused his religious prejudices. But it must be remembered that he was old, tired and disillusioned by the time he wrote his memoirs. There undoubtedly was a good deal of discontent in the years immediately after the Mutiny, as well as a break in relations between Indians and British, but there can be no doubt that the Bengal Army post-Mutiny was a much better disciplined and officered force than its predecessor.

For the most part, however, Sita Ram deals in this chapter with his experiences at the outset of the First Afghan War. The causes for that war have already been discussed in the Introduction, and it suffices to say here that it was the greatest disaster British arms were to suffer in Asia until the surrender of Singapore almost exactly one hundred years later. Fortescue has written that the campaign brought 'nothing but disgrace', and that harsh verdict is probably true. It severely damaged the prestige of the Company in India and had far-reaching effects on the discipline and morale of the Bengal Native Army.

Sita Ram took part in the campaign as a havildar *in a force recruited in India by Shah Shujah-ul-Mulk. It was known as Shah Shujah's Levy and was intended to ensure Shah Shujah's security on the throne of Afghanistan after the British had withdrawn from that country. In fact the Shah succeeded in alienating his own troops, British officers and sepoys alike, as successfully as he had alienated his own countrymen.*

It will be recalled that the aim of the British was to restore Shah Shujah on the throne from which he had been ousted by Dost Mahommed Khan. They believed he would prove to be a more trustworthy and dependable ally than Dost Mahommed, but seldom has any government been proved more wrong. After four years' campaigning, and at great cost in blood and treasure, the British were to learn how grievously they had miscalculated the respective worths of Shah Shujah and Dost Mahommed. In this chapter we are told of Sita Ram's experiences during the first phase of the campaign—the assembly of the expeditionary force and its march across the Sind desert and through the Baluchistan mountains to Kandahar. It was virtually bloodless so far as battles were concerned, but thousands died of hunger, thirst, and disease. Most of these were followers, of whom 38,000 accompanied the Bengal Division alone, but both the British and Indian troops also suffered severely from privations.

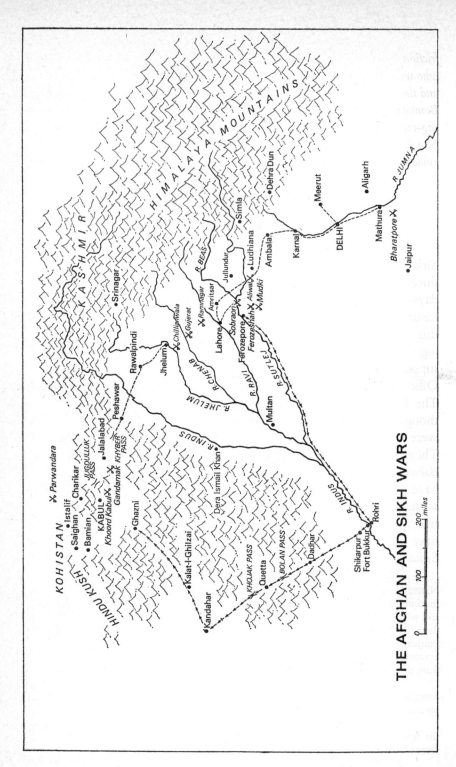

THE AFGHAN AND SIKH WARS

From the outset the campaign was mismanaged. There was friction between the generals; between the generals and the political officers who were supposed to be advising them; between officers of the Royal Army and the officers of the Bombay and Bengal Armies; between the officers of the Bombay Army and those from Bengal; while all were united in despising the rag-tag and bobtail who had joined up in Shah Shujah's Levy. No wonder that Sita Ram expresses his astonishment at the ineptitude of his generals, and the evident mismanagement of the campaign.

And now, my Lord, I shall say something about the *Sirkar's* new army, and by this I mean the army which has been raised since the Mutiny.[1] As far as I know, everyone dislikes the service nowadays—Hindus, Mahommedans, Sikhs, Pathans, and Dogras. They get no leisure; they never know their work; they have to learn one kind of drill this year, and another the next, and they are punished for not remembering the new drill. They now have examinations and promotion goes by supposed merit, which means in effect at the pleasure of the Commanding Officer, which is a very precarious thing to depend upon for promotion.[2] The Punjabis and Sikhs only entered the *Sirkar's* service because they thought there would be opportunities for plunder, and not because they were pleased at joining the service, or looked on it for bread and pension. They do not respect the Government as we used to respect the Company *Bahadur.* If Delhi had not fallen at the time it did, the British would not have persuaded so many Pathans and other northern men to enter their service. It is well known that these men hung back, waiting to see which side was likely to win. Their great hope was that the Punjab would also have been disturbed,[3] in which case they would have gone against the *Sirkar* with the same alacrity as they displayed when entering its service.

[1] There were upwards of ninety regular infantry battalions in the Bengal Native Army at the beginning of 1857—the year of the Great Mutiny. Two-thirds of these mutinied and were disbanded; of the remainder, several hovered on the verge of mutiny and were later removed from the Army List. The newly raised regiments which replaced them were composed mainly of men from northern India—Pathans, Sikhs, Dogras, and Punjabi Mussalmans. Sita Ram, a Brahmin from the heart of Hindustan, regarded these newcomers as rude and uncouth, even when they were co-religionists such as the Dogras from the Kangra and Kulu valleys.

[2] These views conflict with those expressed previously, but Sita Ram doubtless considered that the old days and old ways were in every way superior to the present. This has been the old soldier's privilege since long before *Tristram Shandy*!

[3] The Punjab would certainly have burst into flames had it not been for the strong hand of John Lawrence, the Commissioner, and his team of assistants, who worked on the principle, 'Act first, and ask afterwards'.

Their sole object was love of loot. More than half the men of these regiments now want their discharge, and the other half only remain because they think there may be a chance of plunder for them in China or elsewhere. But thanks to the amazing good fortune of the *Sirkar*, all prospect of war has been extinguished, like hot ashes after sprinkling from a waterskin, and as peace is likely to last for many years to come, most of these men will wish to leave the service. If they are prevented from doing this they will only be unwilling servants.

Numbers of young men can always be found to enlist but once the novelty has worn off they will soon want to leave a service which is daily becoming more distasteful to them. Their officers will have had all the trouble of drilling them for nothing. In the Punjab the Sikhs will take service because they are near their homes, but they do not care for any other country.[4] There is also an uneasy feeling about pay. The cavalry trooper has had his pay increased, but the foot soldier's remains the same. Since throughout Hindustan everything nowadays has become so much more expensive, and since the Government allows the moneylenders to do as they please, the pay of seven rupees a month will not support either Sikhs, Punjabis, or Mahommedans. So far as the latter are concerned, they always think they will reconquer Hindustan from the foreigners and they look forward to that day, flattering themselves that it is not far off. They have not seen what I have, or they would not entertain such foolish notions, but they love to boast of what they have done and what they one day will do again. They might have some idea of the absurdity of these ideas when they remember that they could not hold Delhi even with the Company's army in their service, and its artillery in their possession, against four or five European regiments and a few hastily raised regiments of dirty Punjabis. After the Mutiny I was posted to a Punjabi corps, and I know what I have said to have been the general feeling. I also know that if the people of the Punjab should rebel and fight the *Sirkar*, there would be 100,000 Hindustanis ready and willing to take service against them, if only to pay off old scores.[5]

The Government's practice of keeping several regiments of Native troops together at the same station is unwise. It is then that the young men become full of their own importance and swagger about the bazaars puffed up with vain conceits and talking about things they had better not. They forget the giver of their salt. There are plenty of rascals in

[4] It is strange that Sita Ram should take this view of the Sikhs who are some of the greatest travellers in India, and certainly among the most enterprising of India's many races and sects.

[5] Sita Ram was posted to the 12th Punjab Infantry after his own regiment had mutinied. This would have been composed of men from northern India, with probably a preponderance of Mahommedans and Sikhs.

every city, and in most *Suddar* bazaars,[6] who encourage the *sepoys* in every kind of villainy. This idle behaviour has much increased since the Mutiny. Before that time I never heard much about it, but now that calamity has afflicted Hindustan, it has become common practice. These bazaar ruffians have nothing to lose, and they reckon that in times of confusion and disorder they will benefit, as many of them did during the rebellion. Meerut, Cawnpore, and some other cities are full of these men who escaped punishment for their evil deeds and boast of the fact. Some bad men will be found in every regiment and their influence should be well guarded against—especially among the young soldiers.

For several years nothing happened in my regiment. My son became a fine young man and was enlisted into my corps. In the year 1837 it was common gossip throughout India that the *Sirkar* was going to assist Shah Shujah-ul-Mulk, the Amir of Kabul,[7] to regain his throne. Every day the rumours grew stronger and there was great excitement throughout Hindustan. Some said the *Sirkar* would meet the Russians in Afghanistan and that they had promised to help the Amir Dost Mahommed Khan, who was the favourite ruler among the Afghans. Therefore the whole country, supported by a large army of both Russians and Persians, would be against the English. Many people said that the *Sirkar's* army would be beaten, while others considered that the English would succeed in taking Kabul because there was a strong party which favoured the deposed king, Shujah-ul-Mulk. The *sepoys* dreaded crossing the Indus because it was beyond Hindustan; this is forbidden by our religion and the very act means loss of caste.[8] Consequently many *sepoys* obtained their discharge, and many deserted. The Mahommedans said that a large army was coming to invade India and tried by every means to excite the feelings of

---

[6] In most instances the military lines, or cantonment, were situated some distance from the city or town. This was partly for defensive purposes, partly to overawe the local population, and partly for hygienic reasons since disease was endemic in almost every Indian city. Bazaars, or markets, to serve the soldiers and their families sprang up in every cantonment, and were known as *Sudder* bazaars.

[7] 'The inhabitants of India, although they talk of an Afghan, seldom call the country Afghanistan; with them it is Kabul. Kandahar, Jellalabad, Ghazni—all are Kabul.' [Footnote in Norgate's original translation.]

[8] The reluctance of high caste Hindu *sepoys* to serve overseas, or beyond what they considered to be the confines of Hindustan such as the river Indus, was a perpetual problem in the Bengal Native Army. The 47th BNI mutinied in 1835 rather than take part in operations in Arakan and there are many similar instances. Neither the Madras nor the Bombay Armies seem to have suffered from this problem, or at least to a much less extent, and some authorities have attributed this to the fact that they recruited *sepoys* of lower caste. Nevertheless the Bombay Army recruited some of its soldiers from the same areas in Oudh as the Bengal Army but had much less trouble with them. Discipline was certainly stricter in the Bombay Army and there was much less disposition to coddle the men.

the people. They gave out that this invading army was supported by a large force of Russians; when it made its appearance on the plains on this side of the passes, it would be a signal for the entire Mahommedan population to rise against the *Sirkar* and drive the foreigners out of India.

These reports daily gathered strength until fear filled the mind of the whole Native Army. The Russians were said to have an army of hundreds of thousands and untold wealth. Their soldiers were represented to be of enormous stature and as brave as lions. The end of the *Sirkar's* rule was predicted, for how could they withstand their enemies with only twelve or thirteen regiments of Europeans, which were all that were then in India?[9] There were some people, however, who still believed that the Company's astonishing good luck would enable it to overcome everything, but even they were appalled when they learned of the mighty armies that were being assembled to invade India. Nevertheless troops began to be moved up-country, and a force was assembled at Ferozepore, where my corps was stationed in October, 1838.[10] Ten thousand soldiers were collected, and also an army in the pay of Shah Shujah, but which was officered by English officers.[11] It was composed of men from all over India who felt inclined to try the fortunes of war.

I was offered a *havildar's* appointment in this Legion, with higher pay, and I joined one of the regiments, having lost any chance of promotion in my own because I had been tried by court martial. It was said at the time that this army would be paid by the Company *Bahadur*,

[9] Sita Ram's figures are wrong. There were 4 British cavalry and 20 infantry regiments serving in India at this time, and there were in addition 4 or 5 of the Company's European regiments. Of these only 2 cavalry and 8 infantry regiments were serving in the Bengal Presidency—a total of not much more than 10,000 British troops. The Bengal Army at this time totalled 86,500, which figure includes 6,150 Europeans.

[10] The original plan called for a force of two divisions from the Bengal Army which was given the grandiloquent title of the 'Army of the Indus', and placed under the command of Lieutenant-General Sir Henry Fane, Commander-in-Chief of the Bengal Army. It was to march down the Indus as far as Sukkur where it was to join forces with one division of the Bombay Army, marching from Karachi under Lieutenant-General Sir John Keane, Commander-in-Chief of the Bombay Army. The combined force, under Fane, was then to cross the Indus and enter Afghanistan via the Bolan Pass and Baluchistan. However, when news was received of the withdrawal of the Persian Army which had been besieging Herat (September 1838), the Bengal Army's contribution was reduced to one division and Fane withdrew from the command which was then given to Keane.

[11] Shah Shujah was encouraged by the Company to recruit an army in India which was subsidized by the British. It consisted of some artillery, two regiments of cavalry, and six of infantry. It was to be officered by British and Indian officers lent from the Company's army. It attracted more than its fair share of ne'er-do-wells and suffered both from lack of discipline and intermittent pay; much of the cash provided by the Company for the purpose stuck to the palms of Shah Shujah and his minions. At one stage it was commanded by General Abraham Roberts, father of Field-Marshal Earl Roberts. After the First Afghan War the 3rd Battalion, which had fought well at Kalat-i-Ghilzai, was taken into the Line as the 12th Bengal Infantry.

but all I know is that when the Shah regained his throne, he could not pay his own bodyguard. This army consisted of artillery, cavalry, and infantry, and was called Shah Shujah's Levy. Only one weak regiment of Europeans from the Company's army accompanied us to Kabul, as well as the *Burdwan, Castor,* and *Grand* infantry regiments, and two others.[12] The nearest road to Kabul would have been through the Punjab, which at this time was ruled by Maharajah Runjeet Singh who was a great ally of the *Sirkar.* I believe he offered to let the army march through his territories, but he told Lord Fane *sahib* that his force was too small and a collision might therefore take place with some of his own troops, whom he could hardly control, up in the northern part of the Punjab. The order was therefore given for the force to march down into Sind and enter the country of the Afghans by the Bolan Pass.[13]

We marched by the side of large rivers[14] with thick low jungle along their banks. It was a vile country and the people were very wild. After a march lasting two months, during which half the army was attacked with low fever, we arrived at Rohri on the river Indus. A bridge of boats was constructed after a good deal of toil and trouble, and the army crossed over to the dreaded other bank of the Indus, which was now trodden for the first time by the Hindustani *sepoy*. The country was much the same on the other side as this, and the people were also the same; they were a nasty and dirty lot. I was crossing with my company when the bridge broke and three boats were carried away and swept down past Fort Bukkur with frightful force. The boatmen were unable to stop the boats until they had gone six miles. Four *sepoys* were drowned and the company had to remain out all night in the thick wet jungle. No-one knew the way, but in the morning we discovered the headquarters.

The Commander-in-Chief suffered so much from fever that he went away to Europe.[15] The Bombay army joined the Bengal

[12] Sita Ram is not very accurate here, but he was writing thirty years on, and entirely from memory. I would not find it easy to give an accurate rendering of the composition of the 1st (Burma) Division with which I went to war in 1942! The Bengal Division, commanded by Major-General Willoughby Cotton, contained three European regiments—HM 16th Lancers and 13th Foot, and the Company's Bengal European regiment. There were also 3 Native cavalry regiments, and 7 infantry, of which Sita Ram gives three by their popular names. However, 2 BNI (*Burdwan-ki-Paltan*), 5 BNI (*Grand-ki-Paltan*) and 53 BNI (*Castor-ki-Paltan*), did not form part of the 'Army of the Indus'. They did take part in the First Afghan War but at a later stage in the campaign.

[13] There were several reasons for the decision to enter Afghanistan by the long way round, instead of by the direct route through the Khyber Pass, and a fear lest the lines of communication across the Punjab would be at risk to the Sikhs was one of the reasons.

[14] The Rivers Sutlej, Ravi and Chenab.

[15] Lieutenant-General the Honourable Sir Henry Fane was Commander-in-Chief of the Bengal Army from 1835 to 1839. He was due to relinquish command, and when

army and we marched on to Shikarpur. The people of the country were all Mahommedans whose language we did not understand and everything belonging to them was unclean. They offered no opposition to our force and no robberies or murders occurred at first; it was only after leaving Shikarpur that our real troubles began. The whole country was a vast sandy desert. The water in the few wells was bitter and everything, even firewood and water, had to be transported on camels. The Baluchis now began to harass us by night attacks and drove off long strings of our camels. Their method of carrying off these camels was very curious. A Baluch horseman would watch a line of them going out to feed, or detached with the baggage. He would then thrust a spear with a rag covered in camel's blood in the face of a bull camel, and would excite the animal with it until it rushed after the robber, followed by the whole string. The Baluch would thus lead off twenty camels at a time for many miles into the hills. This frequent loss of camels was a great problem for the army. Although many others were procured, many of them were unbroken, and almost invariably threw off their loads and ran off into the desert.

Our march was in the middle of the cold weather and yet the heat was such that numbers of European soldiers and *sepoys* died from the effects; on one day thirty-five men fell victim to it. At this stage the *sepoy* army had almost determined to return to India and there were signs of mutiny in all three armies.[16] However, partly on account of the lavish promises of Shah Shujah, and partly for fear of the Baluchis who grew in numbers every day, the armies marched on, and the *sahibs* did all in their power to encourage their men. Our sufferings were frightful and the livers of all the Hindustanis were turned to water. We went through one valley called Dadhar[17] which was the mouth of hell. It was low-lying and surrounded by hills so that no air ever came there. It was worse than my tomb in Bundelkhand. Then we came to the Bolan Pass,[18] and here many people were killed by the tribesmen. They murdered everyone whenever they had the opportunity, and rolled large boulders down the mountain sides.

---

it was decided that he would not command the force entering Afghanistan, he decided to sail down the Indus to Karachi, accompanying the Bengal contingent as far as Bukkur in Sind.

[16] The Bengal and Bombay contingents, and Shah Shujah's Levy.

[17] There is a local saying which runs—'Oh Allah! Wherefore make hell when thou hast made Dadhar?' It lies at the foot of the hills, between the desert and Baluchistan, and is hot for most of the year.

[18] The Bolan Pass rises from sea level to almost 6,000 feet. Torrential rains added to the misery of the army and it took nearly eight days to traverse the pass. Every yard of the way was marked by an abandoned camel, a foundered horse, or a camp follower dying from exhaustion. 'Tents, camel trunks, wine chests, cooking pots, bundles of blankets, and overturned bullock carts marked the progress of the Army of the Indus through the Bolan Pass, as the shore is littered with sea wrack after a storm.'

The watercourses were all blocked, and the wells were filled with *pilu* wood[19] that made the water stink, so as to make one sick even when approaching the well.

We next arrived at Quetta. Here it was very cold and the sudden change in temperature caused many of us to fall sick with fever. Eventually Kandahar came in sight. All the opposition came from the Baluchis and the hill tribes—we were not opposed by the people of Kandahar. It was said that the Afghans had never expected the *Sirkar*'s army to enter their country by such a circuitous route. They believed it would come over the Khyber Pass, near Peshawar, or through some of the other northern passes. Consequently they had defended those places and all their forces were collected there. I dare say the Commander-in-Chief knew this and put out information through his secret agents that the English army intended to come by the Khyber Pass, but I know that all the *sahibs* with our army were much astonished that there was no enemy, and that we were not resisted on the Kabul side of the passes. The hill men do not like venturing far into the plains and seldom leave their homes for more than a few miles to raid a village or attack a caravan. They are very formidable behind their rocks from where they can fire their long *jezails*[20] that throw a ball three times the size of a musket-ball with accuracy at 400 yards, but they could never withstand a volley of our musketry at close quarters. They fight as individuals, and not in formed bodies like the Company's troops.

Everyone passing through these hills is robbed and attacked, no matter if he be friend or foe. They are often bribed to allow caravans to traverse their country, and these are accustomed to visit India with dried fruits, skins, and other products of their country. They return with the produce of Hindustan. These caravans pay large sums of money to ensure safe conduct, but there is always one tribe or other that declares it has never received any money and loots the caravan. These hill tribes are supposedly subject to the ruler of Kabul, and Shah Shujah sent frequently to inform them that the English were his friends. However, this made no difference—they fired at, and attacked, the Shah's soldiers just as much as the *Sirkar*'s. Truly they were a lawless set of bloodthirsty savages. In a short time our army arrived at Kandahar, and it was hot when we arrived there, although not as hot as in Hindustan. The *Sirdars* came out at first with a small force, but suddenly, when they saw the red coats of the

---

[19] A desert scrub. The smoke from this wood is so offensive as to cause nausea and spoils any food cooked by it.

[20] *Jezail:* a long barrelled musket, often fired from a rest, which was considerably more effective at long range than 'Brown Bess'. The Afghan tribesmen used it with great effect.

Sirkar's army, fear seemed to fill their hearts, and they ran away.[21] If they had defended the Bolan Pass, which took seven or eight days to pass through, half our army might have been destroyed.

It was during this march of unheard of hardship that I saw, for the first time in my service, dissensions arise among the officers. The Bombay Commander-in-Chief and the Bengal general quarrelled.[22] The former thought his army the best. All the Bombay officers looked with contempt on the Bengal Army, and we[23] were much abused by the regular *sepoys* who called us 'irregulars'. 'Lad Kain' *sahib* was of higher rank than our general and he gave orders for some of the force to be left behind in Sind. The good management, for which the *Sirkar* is so celebrated, seems to have left the heads of both the commanders. As we approached Kandahar the truth began to dawn on us that despite all the assurances Shah Shujah had given us in Hindustan, that the Afghans were longing for his return, in reality they did not want him as their ruler.

Once again fear and remorse entered into the hearts of the *sepoys*. They imagined they had been deceived by Shah Shujah's promises and even thought that the *Sirkar* itself had been misled. However, as a result of the wonderful example set by the British officers, the army marched on with nothing worse than lamentations and grumblings, and our hearts were cheered by the thought we should in the end be rewarded by the Government if we survived, and this despite Shah Shujah's failure to live up to his promises. When we saw the fertile country around Kandahar, where gardens with flowers and many kinds of fruit abounded, we began to feel happier. I cooked my food beneath the shade of fine trees with pure water running beside me. None of us had ever enjoyed a good meal since leaving Shikarpur. All we had had to eat was parched grain or barley, or a small quantity of musty flour. The country we came through must surely have been on the confines of hell! It was a land of stones with nothing green except the camel-thorn, and no birds apart from the vultures that feasted on the carcasses of our baggage animals, and on the bodies of our comrades we were unable to bury.

[21] Hadji Khan, who was charged with defending Kandahar for Dost Mahommed, betrayed his trust and delivered up the second city of Afghanistan without firing a shot. He was renowned for his faithlessness, and betrayed Shah Shujah later.

[22] Lieutenant-General Sir John Keane, Commander-in-Chief of the expeditionary force, was not a popular officer. He was described as 'an apt, clever officer, but hardly deserving the name of general'. He belonged to the British Army and had next to no experience of Indian warfare. Major-General Willoughby Cotton, commanding the Bengal Division, was a much more polished individual, popular and fairly tactful. He also belonged to the British Army but had considerable experience in India. He quarrelled with Keane, but so did most people.

[23] Sita Ram does not make it clear whether he is referring to the Bengal troops, or Shah Shujah's force—probably the latter.

There were no animals in that vile country until our army came there, for what was there for them to live on? Troops of jackals followed in our track right across the desert and grew sleek and fat by their attendance. There was no wood with which to perform the funeral rites when a Hindu died, and he was far from holy Benares and the pure Ganges. His fate was unhappy for he was conveyed about in divers places in the bellies of hungry jackals! Now I understood why it was forbidden to cross the Indus. The fate of those who do so is truly bad, and our misfortunes were increased by the knowledge that we had done that which is forbidden by our religion.

The armies entered Kandahar,[24] Shah Shujah-ul-Mulk was restored to his throne, and there were rejoicings among the people. The Shah's army entered first, before the *Sirkar*'s, and there were great celebrations. At first the people seemed to be pleased at his return, but it was said that they despised him in their hearts, and only the fear of the *Sirkar*'s army kept them civil. I think that the common people did not much mind who ruled them, but the *sirdars*[25] and head people were offended that Shah Shujah had returned with a foreign army. They said he had shown the English the way into their country, and that shortly they would take possession of it. They would use it as they had done all Hindustan and introduce their detested rules and laws. It was this that enraged them. They said that if the Shah had come with his own army alone, all would have been well.

After the king had been a short time in Kandahar, I knew the people did not care the least about him, and their anger grew when they saw that the English army was not returning to Hindustan. Instead they turned the place into a regular cantonment. We found many Hindu merchants[26] in Kandahar who had forgotten even when their ancestors had arrived there. We were all surprised by this, but a merchant will go wherever he can cheat. We found them afterwards in Ghazni and Kabul, and I have heard that some of them have even penetrated into the land of the Russians. We remained some time in Kandahar doing nothing, but the time for harvest was approaching and we had to wait until the corn was ripe before we could march on. So miserable was this Kandahar that sufficient corn could not be found. Either the storekeepers buried all their stores, or they really did not possess the amount required. It took a long time to collect sufficient for our onward march.

[24] Kandahar was reached on 26 April 1839, and Shah Shujah was formally installed on the throne on 8 May. There had been few casualties in battle, but thousands had died from privations or disease.

[25] The Chiefs or nobles in Afghanistan style themselves *sirdar*. It is also a title much used by the Sikhs.

[26] The word used by Sita Ram is *bannia*, meaning a corn or seed merchant. They were also moneylenders and bankers. As a Brahmin he despised them, but their enterprise was remarkable.

Kandahar was in reality a very poor city and not to be compared with many smaller places in Hindustan. The people did not dare to build any large houses on account of the earthquakes, which are stronger and more frequent here than in Hindustan. The only large building is the tomb of Ahmed Shah.[27] The *sahibs* had expected stiff fighting and were disappointed. The *sepoys* could see no signs of Shah Shujah giving them the presents he had promised. In fact he only reigned in Kandahar and its vicinity. He was not King of Afghanistan at all. I never knew why the *Sirkar*'s and the Shah's armies halted there so long. By doing so they gave Dost Mahommed time to prepare things better for defence and call up support from the tribes. The presence of the Europeans aroused the feelings of the people who regarded them as unwelcome intruders. Although they were told that the English had not come to conquer or take their country away from them, they remembered the history of Hindustan. They could not believe that they had come only to put Shah Shujah-ul-Mulk Sudozai on his rightful throne.

[27] Ahmed Shah (1722–72). He founded the Durani dynasty in Afghanistan and invaded India on several occasions.

'. . . *and rolled large boulders down the mountain sides*'

'. . . *made the place look like the* Diwali Pujah'

9   *Ghazni and Kabul*

Keane halted for two months at Kandahar in order to rest his troops and collect supplies, and then moved on towards Kabul. He left a garrison in Kandahar under Major-General William Nott, a cantankerous and irritable officer of the Bengal Army who was one of the few senior officers to come out of the campaign with any credit. The fortified town of Ghazni lay between Kandahar and Kabul. It was reputedly a place of some strength, but Keane, for some unaccountable reason left behind his siege artillery at Kandahar. These guns had been dragged with immense difficulty all the way from Ferozepore and were discarded at the time they were most needed. Keane was severely criticized for his action, and particularly by Henry Havelock,[1] serving with the 13th Foot, but he may have been influenced by the difficulty of finding sufficient fodder for the train of elephants and bullocks required to drag the guns.

Whatever his reasons for leaving the guns behind, Keane must have regretted his decision when he first set eyes on Ghazni. It was one of the strongest fortresses in Afghanistan and his light horse artillery guns were useless for making a breach in the walls. However, a traitor was found, as so often in Afghanistan at that time, and he reported that the Kabul Gate was only weakly defended. The place was taken by coup-de-main, by a 'forlorn hope' from the European regiments, after the gate was blown in just before dawn. There was severe street fighting before Ghazni capitulated, and Sita Ram's regiment was involved in this. Once again he marvels at the clemency of the British when the fighting is over, and is amazed by the admiration they showed for the outspoken defiance of the Afghan chiefs. Sita Ram does not, however, make it clear whether he respected the British for this aspect of their character, or merely thought them mad—probably a bit of both.

From Ghazni the army marched to Kabul. Dost Mahommed's forces melted away in front of them, and Dost Mahommed himself escaped with his favourite son, Akbar Khan, to Kohistan beyond the Hindu Kush. There he survived to fight another day, but not before undergoing some unpleasant adventures in Bokhara where he sought refuge with the bloodthirsty amir who imprisoned him for a time. Shah Shujah-ul-Mulk was restored to the throne by the British, and forthwith proceeded to alienate his few supporters by his arrogance, meanness, and choice of ministers. He was also hated by his subjects for his reliance on British bayonets to keep him on the throne. Sita Ram is critical of Shah Shujah, and also of Sir William Macnaghten, the British Envoy, who consistently maintained that the Shah's rule was popular.

[1] Henry Havelock (1795–1857) was described by Lord Hardinge, Governor-General of India, as 'Every inch a soldier, every inch a Christian'. He took part in the Afghan War with his regiment, HM 13th Foot, and won a high reputation. He was to add to this during the Indian Mutiny by his efforts to relieve Lucknow.

The expeditionary force was reduced in strength after the entry into Kabul. The Bombay contingent returned to India by way of Kandahar and Quetta in Baluchistan. The Bengal contingent was reduced by several regiments. and Major-General Sir Willoughby Cotton succeeded Lieutenant-General Sir John Keane as commander of the force. The intention was to hand over more and more responsibility for internal security to Shah Shujah's Levy, but the efficiency of this force, never high, declined rapidly. However, conditions improved temporarily in those areas where the Company's troops were garrisoned, and a cantonment was constructed in Kabul itself. Although most officers, including Cotton, wished the troops to be garrisoned in the Bala Hissar, the fortress-palace of the kings of Afghanistan, Shah Shujah insisted that this would be a derogation of his sovereignty, and was supported by Macnaghten. In consequence the cantonment was constructed outside Kabul in an area that was difficult to defend, being surrounded by orchards and gardens and overlooked from the nearby hills, and was laid out on a pattern more suited to the peaceful conditions of Madras than a city as turbulent as Kabul.

There the British officers did their best to reproduce the cantonment life to which they had been accustomed in India, with horse racing, dinner parties, cricket, and shooting and fishing. Early in 1840 some of them were joined by their wives who had made the long and dangerous journey from Delhi and beyond in camel litters and on horseback. Among them were Lady Macnaghten, the British Envoy's wife, and Lady Florentia Sale, wife of the Colonel of the 13th Foot who had recently been appointed to command a brigade. Lady Sale took her daughter with her, as well as some packets of sweet peas and assorted 'hardy perennials'. She made a deep impression on Sita Ram, who was later to see her displaying great courage during the retreat from Kabul, and he would probably have preferred being commanded by her than by her husband, who was described on one occasion as 'stupid, blundering old Sale'. But he did not lack for courage.

Sita Ram also describes the amorous relations of certain British officers with high-born Afghan ladies. That this did happen cannot be denied and it undoubtedly aroused much ill-feeling among the Afghans. Dislike of having their women interfered with by foreign soldiery is a trait by no means confined to the Afghans, but in a Moslem country, and among a people as proud and hot-tempered as the Afghans, it became even more unendurable. It is astonishing that Macnaghten, whose own conduct was unimpeachable, should have permitted such behaviour; but his senior political officer in Kabul, Lieutenant-Colonel Sir Alexander Burnes, is reputed to have been one of the worst offenders. It is possible that Macnaghten, who worked so hard at his papers that he never had time for anything else, was unaware of the state of affairs, and perhaps neither Shah Shujah nor anyone else bothered to *enlighten him, but if so, it was a fatal mistake. The British were sufficiently disliked as foreign invaders and usurpers and, as if this was not enough for the wretched Afghans to endure, they now appeared to be cuckolds as well. There can have been no better grounds for the tragedy which was shortly to follow.*

After some months' stay, the army moved on towards Ghazni. Ghazni had refused to acknowledge Shah Shujah and lay about 280 miles from Kandahar. The road was very bad in places and yet quite easy compared with our previous marches. To everyone's astonishment Lord 'Kane' *sahib* only took light guns with him, and left behind all the heavy artillery, which we had such labour and difficulty in dragging through the passes, at Kandahar, where a garrison of two or three thousand men from our force was also left. When we came in sight of the fortress of Ghazni it was seen to be place of great strength and unlikely to be taken without the assistance of heavy guns. The enemy came out in great force as we approached the town and sharp firing took place, but they were soon driven back again. This was the first time we had any fighting since we entered Afghanistan. The governor of Ghazni was Hyder Ali Khan[2] and all the inhabitants supported Dost Mahommed, and were opposed to Shah Shujah. They felt secure in the strength of the place. The walls were too high to scale and the horse artillery guns were of little or no use against them.

The armies of the *Sirkar* and the Shah were about to leave the place untaken when one night a deserter came to our camp. He said he wished to be taken direct to our General, and it was believed that he pointed out a gate by which we could enter the fortress.[3] This man was one of the many sons of the amir, with whom he had quarrelled, and he now sought to revenge himself on his father by betraying the secret of the door. In a few days a storming party was told off. Orders were given to keep up a hot fire on that side of the fortress away from the gate in order to deceive and distract the attention of the *Ghazis*,[4] while a party went up to the gate to blow it open with several bags of gunpowder.

[2] The governor was one of the many sons of Dost Mahommed.

[3] Ghazni was betrayed by a nephew of Dost Mahommed. He told Keane that the Kabul gate was less strongly defended than the other gates, and since the lack of a battering train precluded any attempt to lay siege to the fortress, it could only be captured by a *coup-de-main* after blowing in one of the gates.

[4] Sita Ram appears to refer to all Afghans as *Ghazis* although by no means all Afghans fought as savagely as these fanatics.

The wind blew hard on this night and the clouds of dust which were flying about made everything darker than usual. When the guns opened fire, we saw the *Ghazis* running with torches, which suddenly made the place look like the *Diwali Pujah*.[5] After waiting some time we saw a flash high in the air, but we heard no noise on account of the firing of our guns. The bugles sounded the advance and the storming party rushed forward. They consisted of the 13th Europeans, the 16th Grenadiers, and two companies of my regiment.[6] No-one knew whether the gate had been blown in or not. The Shah's soldiers hung back a little until, hearing the continued firing of musketry and the bugles still sounding, and with morning also beginning to break, they went forward. The *Ghazis* fought like demons but to no avail. Our musketry swept them away. There was much confusion at this time. Some said that the gate had not been blown in; others said that the stormers had gone through. Our Brigadier halted the columns which were in reserve and sent forward an officer. However, it was now getting light and we could see the red coats inside the fortress. The *Ghazis* crowded to the gateway and defended it sword in hand. Some companies of Europeans were driven back and two companies of *sepoys* charged and carried the gateway. The Europeans were so pleased by this that they shook hands with every man of that regiment. I heard that the Brigadier *sahib* was severely wounded by a *Ghazi* who attacked him. The place was taken and was soon swimming with blood.[7]

The leading citizens and the women all came out and begged protection from the English General *sahib*. The Governor could

[5] *Diwali Pujah*: Hindu festival marking New Year (October to November). Lamps are ceremonially lit, housefronts illuminated, and presents are exchanged.

[6] Ghazni was stormed in the early hours of 23 July 1839. The storming parties were all European—found from HM 2nd, 13th, & 17th Foot, and the Bengal European Regiment. No *sepoy* regiments were employed in what might easily have turned out to be a forlorn hope, but several were involved in the street fighting that followed, and these presumably included Sita Ram's battalion from Shah Shujah's contingent. Robert Sale commanded the troops who were to follow the stormers. When he arrived outside the Kabul Gate in the half-light of early dawn, an excited engineer officer told him the breach was choked with debris and the dead. Sale was about to order the 'withdraw' to be sounded, but he then received contrary information. While he was hesitating, an unknown bugler sounded the advance, and the 13th Foot surged forward and stormed into Ghazni. Sale was wounded, as Sita Ram says. The 16th BNI particularly distinguished themselves and were later made a Grenadier regiment.

[7] Major-General Sir Robert Sale (1781–1845). He commanded the 13th Foot, by whom he was greatly respected on account of his gallantry in battle. Later in the campaign he commanded a brigade and successfully defended Jellalabad. He was killed during the Sikh Wars at Mudki in 1845. His wife, Florentia, joined him in Kabul, and was taken prisoner by the Afghans during the retreat. Her account of her experiences in *Lady Sale's Diary* (John Murray) is one of the best accounts we have of the disaster in Kabul.

nowhere be found and no-one knew whether he had been killed or not. After looking for him all over the place an officer found him hiding in a house. He was just about to fire at him when the man called out that he was Hyder Ali. He was taken to the General who treated him very kindly. This man spoke out very boldly to the Commander-in-Chief. He said he was fighting for his country and his amir. The Afghans had never annoyed the British; why, therefore, had they come into his country to set up a king whom they all hated? They had brought death and desolation into many Afghan families. He ended by saying—'kill me if you like, but if you let me go, I shall ever be found as your enemy, and do all in my power to excite the people against you, and drive you all out of Kabul!'

The General *sahib* was not angry. He told Hyder Ali that he was a brave man and that he respected his feelings. But he, the General, was acting under the orders of his Government, whose servant he was. Once again I saw here the curious customs in war of the English. Had this man said half as much before a rajah or nawab, he would have been cut to pieces on the spot. And yet, in this instance, and in open *durbar*, the very *sahibs* who had fought against him cried out *Barekilla! Barekilla!* (Bravo! Bravo!). This was wonderful! Why do they fight? Not to kill their enemies but to have the pleasure of capturing them and then letting them go! Truly, their ways are unaccountable. It was also very odd that this man so brave in speech was found in hiding after the battle![8]

Ghazni was a large town, surrounded by a high wall, and with a lofty citadel. The Afghans thought the place secure against any invaders, and it certainly would have been against any of their tribes. But what place can withstand the amazing good fortune of the *Sirkar*? A son of the amir, Akbar Khan, was reported to be marching on Ghazni to attack the English army, but when he heard that the place had fallen, he hastily retreated. More *sahibs* were killed and wounded in the capture of this place than I can recall at any other siege, but our loss in men was small—not more than 180.[9] The cavalry of our Levy distinguished itself very much and the Shah's army made a name for itself.[10] This siege took place in the middle of the hot season of 1839.

[8] Some of the admiration for Hyder Ali's open defiance was due to the contempt felt by most British officers for Shah Shujah. He was a man of fine presence but of the most arrogant character and pusillanimous temperament.

[9] The casualties were surprisingly light. 17 men were killed, 20 officers and 153 men wounded, and 2 missing. Ghazni earned Keane the GCB, and later a peerage as Baron Keane of Ghazni and Cappoquin. He was also given a pension of £2,000 a year.

[10] This reputation did not last long. General Nott reported six months later on the 2nd Cavalry Regiment of the Shah's army: 'I think it my duty to acquaint you that the regiment is quite inefficient. The majority of men are of that description which assures me they can never be brought to a serviceable state. . . . Out of 705 horses I conceive there are not at present more than 50 fit for any kind of duty. . . &c.'

Some *sahibs'* ladies came up to this country with the other army, but how they got up here I do not know.[11] They are wonderful for courage. The General *sahib* had his lady, who was a real warrior *mem-sahib*.[12] I never knew how these ladies came, because the *sepoys* told me that there was much fighting in progress by whichever route they had taken. But after having seen a lady lead a column through a pass, I can wonder at nothing.[13] The Pundit Duleep Ram had often told me—'My son, put not your trust in the counsels of women, for they are like ice—firm in the morning, but melt away as the sun rises'. However, he had never met an English *memsahib*. If the officers had taken counsel from some of their wives the calamities that afterwards befell the English army would never have occurred.

A garrison was left at Ghazni and our army marched on to Kabul. We received the news during the march of Maharajah Runjeet Singh's death[14] and the officers were anxious concerning the outcome of this event. It was said that the Sikhs would now make friends with the Afghans and help them against the *Sirkar*; they would cut off the English forces marching through their territory. Other reports said that the *Sirkar's* resources were limitless, and that it possessed more money in one of its towns than the Afghans did in their entire country. All kinds of rumours were flying around. First, the English had been driven out of Kandahar and their army had been destroyed in the Bolan Pass. Then, again, that the English were coming through the Bolan Pass with 100,000 soldiers. These rumours were incessant and at variance with each other. The *sahibs* did not know the real state of affairs and therefore were unable to contradict this bazaar gossip.

Messengers now arrived in our camp and the General *sahib* told us that two large armies would soon be arriving in Afghanis-

---

[11] Sita Ram has again mixed up his chronology. Some months after Shah Shujah was restored to his throne in Kabul, his harem was escorted from India across the Punjab and through the Khyber Pass. With them went the wives of several officers serving in Afghanistan, including Lady Macnaghten, wife of the British Envoy, and Lady Sale and her daughter, Mrs Sturt, whose husband was also serving in Kabul.

[12] Sita Ram is referring to Lady Sale.

[13] The reference is again to Lady Sale during the retreat from Kabul. She actually shouldered a musket and went through the motions of firing it in order to shame those soldiers who were hanging back.

[14] Maharajah Runjeet Singh (1780–1839) rose from comparative obscurity to become ruler of the Punjab. He was known as the 'lion of the Punjab' and made the Sikhs the most formidable power in India after the British. He added Multan, Kashmir, Peshawar and Ladakh to his kingdom, but avoided any conflict with the Company by signing a treaty with the British at Amritsar in 1809. His army was modelled on the Company's, and was particularly strong in artillery. He employed Europeans of various nationalities to train it. He was one of the ablest Indians of the century.

tan.[15] This encouraged our small force, and our commanders were keen to advance before the other armies arrived, since they might take all the prizes out of our hands. Kabul was eight marches north of Ghazni, and during this march emissaries from Dost Mahommed came into our camp. Among them was the Nawab Jubar Khan, a brother of Dost Mahommed. He requested that the English army should leave Afghanistan but he departed without having persuaded the political officers to agree. It was curious to see the way agents continually came to the English camp with the most foolish demands. They showed no fear and relied on the honour of the English.

About three days after the Nawab had left, we received news that Dost Mahommed had been deserted by nearly all his followers, and a light column was prepared in order to pursue him. The officers were certain that he would be captured. This column was accompanied by an Afghan called Hadji Khan Khaukar who said he was well acquainted with all the movements and intentions of the Amir Dost Mahommed. He offered to lead the column by a short cut to the Amir's hiding place, but after several forced marches and halts, these latter always on the advice of Khaukar, the Amir managed to escape over the hills into the country beyond Kabul. However, all his camp equipment and guns were captured. When Shah Shujah learned that Dost Mahommed had escaped, he demanded Khaukar's head since he had discovered him to be a traitor. The English refused to give him up; they made him a prisoner and sent him to Hindustan.[16]

The army entered Kabul without any fighting and the Shah was proclaimed king. But here, as at Kandahar, the people took no part in the rejoicings; these were all made by the Shah's own soldiers and his court. The hearts of the people were with the Amir, and not with Shah Shujah.[17]

[15] This must refer to the force under Colonel Wade which escorted Shahzada Timur, Shah Shujah's eldest son, from India and which entered Afghanistan through the Khyber Pass during August 1839.

[16] In a land where, according to Sir William Kaye, 'It is a moot point whether revenge or avarice is the stronger feeling,' Hadji Khan Khaukar was probably one of the most faithless of traitors. However, in this instance he served his master well. Dost Mahommed, who had ridden out from Kabul to oppose the advancing British, but whose nerve seems to have failed him at the last moment, managed to escape across the mountains into Kohistan. Later he took refuge with the Amir of Bokhara, where he was badly treated, and escaped to raise the flag of revolt against the British.

[17] 'At 4 p.m. on 7 August (1839) Shah Shujah . . . made a state entry into his capital. He was mounted on a white Persian horse, splendidly dressed in black velvet with a magnificent glittering sword belt, and looked every inch a king. The ominous thing was that this magnificent apparition raised hardly a cheer from the spectators, and the silence hung like a storm cloud as he rode into the ancient fortress-palace of the Kings of Afghanistan, the Bala Hissar.'

The Shah had murdered in open *durbar* a number of the prisoners taken at Ghazni, among whom were some of the leading Afghan chiefs. This act greatly disgusted the English officers and incensed the people of Afghanistan. 'Lad Macnaten' *sahib*[18] was also very angry and he told Shah Shujah that the English army would be withdrawn if ever anything of this kind occurred again.[19] It would have been well if the army had then left that wretched country. Shah Shujah had been placed on the throne, and Dost Mahommed had been driven out. However, it was common knowledge that a rebellion would break out the moment the foreign troops left. Shah Shujah and all his party dreaded this, and I believe that it was on account of their earnest entreaties that the *Sirkar* allowed its army to remain.[20] The people of Kabul talked openly in the bazaars that the Shah would remain king only so long as the red coats stayed to protect him.

The army went into quarters at Kabul. Some officers took over Afghan houses, while others occupied buildings in the outskirts of the city. Life was much the same as it was in Hindustan. Soon it became very cold—such cold as can never be experienced in our country. The *sepoys* suffered terribly; they lost the use of their limbs and their blood froze in their veins. The English soldiers who came from Europe did not suffer so much, but many of them became frost-bitten and affected with sores caused by the cold. Snow fell as deep as a man was high. Provisions were very expensive. We Hindus never dared bathe, since it was almost certain death.[21] We had no comfort nor ease, and we never received any of the lavish presents promised so profusely by Shah Shujah in order to persuade us to come to his accursed country. Before the cold weather set in several regiments of the Bombay army were sent back to Baluchistan. I believe this force went by Jagdalak and the Khyber Passes—much the nearest

[18] Sir William Hay Macnaghten (1793–1841), British Envoy to Shah Shujah, and contemptuously described by the Duke of Wellington as 'the gentleman employed to command the Army'. Miss Eden, sister of Lord Auckland, the Governor-General, called Macnaghten, '*our* Lord Palmerston, a dry sensible man, who wears an enormous pair of blue spectacles, and speaks Persian, Arabic and Hindustani more fluently than English'. He was an able, hard working, but opinionated civil servant who failed to see, or did not wish to see, the realities of the situation in Afghanistan. He paid for his obstinacy with his life. He was murdered by Akbar Khan, Dost Mahommed's son, on 23 December 1841, and his policy collapsed in ruins.

[19] The massacre took place in cold blood, and in full view of many British officers. It aroused great indignation.

[20] Shah Shujah's pleas would not have received so much consideration had it not been for Macnaghten who continued to support Shah Shujah despite the advice of most of his assistants.

[21] Scrupulous bodily cleanliness is one of the tenets of the Hindu religion, particularly among the higher castes. It often surprises foreign visitors to India when they see men bathing under a cold-water tap in freezing weather. This inability to bathe daily must have been the cause of much discontent among Hindu *sepoys*.

route and with no deserts to be traversed. However, there was some fear of meeting the Sikh troops, who would have been delighted to attack the foreigners, despite the fact that their government was supposed to be at peace with *Sirkar*. Our army was much reduced in strength, but for some time everything remained peaceful.[22]

Soon, however, the Afghans began to chafe at the occupation of their country by the English. They complained that the English were not adhering to 'Lad Macnaten' *sahib*'s promise that the army would return to Hindustan as soon as Shah Shujah was secured on his throne. They pointed out that the king had been restored, and yet the foreigners still remained. 'Macnaten' *sahib* explained that a great part of the army had been sent back to Hindustan, but the chiefs complained that everyone had not departed and that, in reality, the English held possession of their country. The Envoy said that the *Sirkar* did not consider the Afghans as enemies —only those who resisted Shah Shujah, the rightful heir to the throne. But the Afghans replied that they had a right to have whatever king they chose. There were therefore endless disputes between the *Sirdars* and the English.

Despite all this discontent, many Afghan gentlemen apparently became great friends of the *sahibs*. High-born Afghan ladies used to visit the *sahibs* secretly. The women in this country are allowed to walk about under a thick veil,[23] through which they can see without being seen, and the fact that the *sahibs* were living in houses in the city gave great opportunity for intrigue.[24] The women liked the foreigners because they were fair; they pride themselves in Kabul on being fair, and the whiter a woman is, the more beautiful she is considered to be. These proceedings gave rise to great jealousies, and more than one officer was stabbed or fired at. How true it is that women are the cause of all evil! Several ladies of rank used to visit the political officers. Some said they were sent by their

[22] There were reductions in both the Bombay and the Bengal contingents after the capture of Kabul. The Bombay Division left Kabul on 18 September 1839 and marched to Quetta via Ghazni and Kandahar. The Bengal Division was reduced in strength but remained in Afghanistan under the command of Major-General Willoughby Cotton. Sir John Keane returned to India, accompanied by the 16th Lancers, and other regiments; the Lancers took their pack of fox hounds with them. They had travelled 1,500 miles since leaving Ferozepore in November 1838. The 'Army of the Indus' was formally broken up on 1 January 1840, at Ferozepore.

[23] The *burqha* as worn by women in Moslem countries is a tent-like garment worn over the clothes whenever outside the home. It is designed to conceal not only the face, but also the shape of the body. Lattice-work over the face allows for vision.

[24] So many eyewitnesses have referred to affairs between the British officers and Afghan ladies that there must have been many of them. Sir Alexander Burnes, Macnaghten's able young assistant, undoubtedly conducted intrigues with Afghan women, and there probably were several others who followed his example. One British officer, who later achieved high rank, married the daughter of an Afghan chief whom he met while a prisoner in Kabul after the retreat.

husbands for political reasons, while others declared that business of another kind took them there. However, it is certain that their husbands must
have known they were in the habit of visiting the officers' houses, since
latterly there was very little attempt at concealment. It was a matter of
wonder to us how this could go on when the foreigners were regarded by
the whole population in the bazaars with great contempt, and were always
referred to as 'cursed kaffirs'. There is no comprehending the fancies of a
woman. They may have been sent in the first place to try and gain some
knowledge of the designs of the *Sirkar*, but it was common gossip that
they preferred the *sahibs* to their own husbands. Shri Sukhdeoji says:
'Women of low degree leave their husbands. This is the custom all over
the world, and has been so for ever.' But these were not women of low
caste; some were the wives of the *Sirdars* themselves, and they did not
desert their husbands.

'*High-born Afghan ladies used to visit the* sahibs *secretly*'

'*The Afghans wore sheepskin coats, called nimchees or poshteens, and these often turned sword cuts and even musket balls*'

10   *The Retreat from Kabul: January 1842*

Conditions in Afghanistan throughout 1840 and for the first half of 1841, although hardly justifying the optimistic forecasts of Sir William Macnaghten, the British Envoy, were at least comparatively peaceful. It is true that the peace only existed where there were British bayonets to enforce it, but there were more successes than failures. Dost Mahommed, after skirmishing with the British at Parwandara in November 1840, surrendered to Macnaghten and was sent to Calcutta in exile. His son, Akbar Khan, remained in the field, but Shah Shujah's star was in the ascendant.

Unfortunately for the British, who had staked everything on Shah Shujah, the Shah had learned nothing from his long years in exile. He offended those Afghan chiefs who might have sided with him by his arrogance and conceit. He irritated the British by his refusal to allow them to occupy the Balar Hissar, by far the best defended place in Kabul, and by his choice of some of the worst rogues in Afghanistan for his ministers. But Sir William Macnaghten, a self-opinionated man who had staked his career on seeing the Afghan affair through to a successful conclusion, was quite myopic where Shah Shujah was concerned. Not only was he incapable of understanding that the Afghans preferred Dost Mahommed to Shah Shujah, but he also fiercely resented any suggestion that his (Macnaghten's) views might be wrong.

This brought him into conflict with Sir Alexander Burnes, his talented but under-employed assistant in Kabul. Burnes had made a name for himself while still a subaltern by his travels to Bokhara, in the course of which he had visited Kabul and met Dost Mahommed, but had been unimpressed by Shah Shujah whom he had met in exile in India. Later Burnes had headed a mission to Kabul with the object of countering supposed Russian designs on Afghanistan, and his acquaintance with Dost Mahommed had ripened into friendship. Burnes had done his best to persuade Lord Auckland, the Governor-General, to support Dost Mahommed, but had been overruled by Macnaghten who favoured the cause of Shah Shujah. Although Burnes had accompanied the 'Army of the Indus' to Kabul as a political officer, performing some good work in Baluchistan on the way, he was almost persona non grata with Macnaghten. He had little to do in Kabul apart from giving Macnaghten advice which was ignored, and amusing himself.

Conditions were deteriorating fast by the late summer of 1841. Burnes could see this, and so did many other political officers, but Macnaghten remained a prisoner of his own preconceived ideas. He had managed to maintain a precarious peace by a combination of force and bribery but the East India Company, alarmed at the cost of the occupation, ordered a cut in expenditure. Lord Auckland instructed Macnaghten to economize, and this resulted in a withdrawal of subsidies to the Ghilzais, the tribe which controlled the passes leading to India. Macnaghten protested, but had to carry out his instructions, and the Ghilzais rose in revolt. This uprising more or less coincided with the news of Macnaghten's appointment to be Governor of Bombay, and it was anticipated that Burnes would succeed him as British Envoy in Kabul.

However, on 2 November 1841, the mob rose in Kabul. They attacked the house of Sir Alexander Burnes and murdered him, his brother, and another British officer. They massacred his sepoy guard. They hated Burnes because they believed (mistakenly) that he was responsible for the invasion of their country, and also on account of his reputed amours with Afghan ladies. Throughout this commotion in the city, which involved the sacking of the treasury, no troops were moved from the cantonment, barely two miles away. Thus encouraged, the rebellion gathered momentum, the tribes came sweeping in from the mountains, and within a matter of days the British had lost control of the situation.

Macnaghten can hardly be blamed for this. He had the most feeble of military advisers. Major-General Sir Willoughby Cotton had returned to India at the end of 1840. He was relieved by Major-General William Elphinstone, a veteran of Waterloo, who had spent much of the intervening period on half-pay. He was well-connected but a martyr to gout. He was also prematurely senile. Even Lord Auckland, who knew him as a personal friend, was surprised when he accepted the Kabul command. Nott, who was commanding at Kandahar, would have been a better choice, but Nott was a bad diplomat who rubbed people up the wrong way. Elphinstone was therefore chosen. His Brigadier was a one-armed Peninsular War veteran called Shelton who arrived in Kabul with his regiment, the 44th Foot. Shelton was efficient but unpopular. His regiment was exhausted after a tiring campaign in the Arakan. Neither he nor the regiment were well suited for the trials that lay ahead.

Elphinstone found it hard to make up his mind. Shelton was not prepared to do so for him. Neither of them was prepared to fight it out with the Afghans. Attempts to concentrate the garrisons from Kandahar and Ghazni in Kabul failed, Macnaghten was murdered, and retreat to India was decided upon. The intense cold of the Afghan winter had reduced the fighting value of the Bengal sepoys to nil. The cantonment in Kabul was virtually indefensible, covering too large an area and lacking in proper fortifications. Supplies were short, the Afghans were in considerable strength, and the army was encumbered by large numbers of dependants and followers. Nevertheless good leadership would have helped to overcome many of the obvious difficulties, but leadership was lacking. Too much faith was placed in the promises of the Afghan chiefs to furnish safe conduct to India. They either had no control over their tribesmen or did not choose to exert any. The British army marched out of Kabul on 6 January 1842, rather less than 5,000 strong, accompanied by approximately 15,000 non-combatants. By 13 January all but one, Dr Brydon, were either killed or captured. It was a staggering disaster from which the old Bengal Native Army never really recovered.

The Retreat from Kabul

*Sita Ram tells the story as he saw it. He found it hard to
believe that the omnipotent* Sirkar *could be so foolish as to place any faith in
Afghan promises, but even harder to witness the disintegration of the army in
which he served. He was luckier than many of his unfortunate* sepoy *comrades
who died in the snow. He was taken prisoner and sold as a slave in Kabul
to an Afghan merchant.*

The English raised some Afghan regiments[1] and the
Afghans enlisted because they had heard that pay was issued regularly. One
of the captains of our (the Shah's) force was made commander of a regiment. The Amir Dost Mahommed was known to have gone towards
Bokhara and it was said that he had been made a prisoner there; but after a
while we heard that he had escaped and was advancing with an army to
fight the English. A force from our army was sent to attack him, and they
fought a battle at a town called Saighan,[2] in which the newly-raised
Afghan regiment refused to participate, and even threatened to kill their
officers if they compelled the soldiers to fight. In spite of this, however, the
English defeated the Amir, and he escaped for a second time. Nearly all his
followers dispersed and only a few remained with him. The English were
occasionally defeated in some small engagements which took place after
this, but Dost Mahommed gained no decided advantage. More of the
Sirkar's troops now arrived in Kabul, and to the Afghans' surprise, as well
as the English, Dost Mahommed came to Kabul, accompanied by his
favourite son, and surrendered. The *Sirkar* sent him to Hindustan and
confined him at Calcutta.

There were great rejoicings at Shah Shujah's court because

[1] These Afghan irregular regiments were known as '*Jan-Baz*' or
Jezailchis and were most unreliable.

[2] Sita Ram seems to be referring to the Battle of Parwandara, 2 November 1840. Dost Mohammed, having escaped from Bokhara, raised the flag of revolt in
Kohistan in August 1840. Sale was sent out to deal with him and after some inconclusive
skirmishing came up with him at Parwandara. Sale had with him Dr Lord as political
officer. On encountering the enemy, the cavalry (two squadrons of the 2nd Bengal Light
Cavalry) was ordered to charge. They changed from a trot to a walk and then halted to
watch their British officers charge the enemy unsupported. The troopers then cantered off
the field. Dr Lord and two British officers were killed. The regiment was later disbanded in
disgrace. Dost Mahommed was in the forefront of the battle, waving on his men with
turban in hand, and can probably claim to have won the day. There was much gloom
afterwards in Kabul, and this made it all the more astonishing that Dost Mahommed should
have decided to surrender. 48 hours after the battle, he rode into Kabul, accosted Macnaghten who was returning from his evening ride, and gave himself up. Shah Shujah
refused to meet him, but Macnaghten treated him well and sent him to Calcutta in exile.
Dost Mahommed charmed everyone he met and was a great favourite with the British.

all his enemies had been removed but who can govern a people when the ruler is hated? The Afghans believed that Dost Mohammed would be killed as a result of Shah Shujah's influence and that the English had taken him to Hindustan to be executed because they were afraid of executing him in Kabul. When those *Sirdars* who hated Shah Shujah heard this they feared that they too would be seized and exiled, and they therefore worked themselves up into a great state of excitement. These chiefs worked upon the feelings of the hill tribes, convincing them that they would all be made subject to the English. Several small rebellions broke out, but they were soon put down. The Afghans dreaded the deadly volleys of the 'red coats'.

About two years after the English first came to Kabul a rebellion broke out in the city itself. At the beginning only a few discontented Afghans were involved but they surrounded the house of Burnes *sahib*, the political officer, and set it on fire. As Burnes was escaping through the garden by a small door, he was cut down by his Afghan servant.[3] Two or three other English officers were also killed.[4] Once the report got around that Burnes *sahib* had been murdered the mob joined in the rioting and fighting took place all over the city. The outburst was so sudden that our officers were taken by surprise. Some of them lived in the city, and others near the king's garden, two miles away.[5] However the English still held their own, but every day tribes came to join in the rebellion, and treachery showed itself in the Shah's court.

Now came misfortune and calamity upon the English. All their stores were looted or burnt by the enemy and the spirits of the army were much depressed. The cold was so intense that it rendered the *sepoy* portion of the army next to useless. It was soon rumoured that Akbar Khan, son of Dost Mohammed, had arrived with many troops and that he commanded in person. There was fighting every day, and because there was no good food for the European soldiers, they lost spirit and did not fight as well as they used to do.[6] There were enemies on all sides. Numerous attempts were made to drive the enemy from their positions. These

---

[3] Sir Alexander Burnes (1805–1841). Soldier, diplomat, traveller, and writer. Murdered in Kabul, 2 November 1841.

[4] Burnes' brother, Charles, a subaltern in the Bombay Army, was murdered with him, and also William Broadfoot. Broadfoot's brother had been killed exactly a year previously at Parwandara when the 2nd Bengal Cavalry refused to charge.

[5] The cantonments.

[6] The British regiment in Kabul was HM 44th Foot (later the Essex Regiment). They had suffered severely from sickness in the Arakan before coming to Afghanistan and their morale was poor. Brigadier Shelton, who had been their Commanding Officer, was a brave soldier, but a martinet. He was a bad co-operator and disagreed violently with Major-General Elphinstone, the commander in Kabul, and Macnaghten, the British Envoy. Both he and the 44th behaved well during the retreat, but indifferently during the siege of the cantonments.

sometimes were successful but they were always attended by great loss to the English. My regiment was engaged at the battle of Behmeru[7] in which it was driven back with great loss and behaved in a most cowardly fashion. The *sepoys* were not accustomed to fighting and they regretted having come to Afghanistan. We were annoyed day and night in the cantonment by cannon fire. The enemy seemed to increase by thousands and their long matchlocks outranged our muskets. Although they would never withstand a regular charge, so long as they could find cover behind walls, houses, etc., their fire was very distressing. We repeatedly drove the Afghans from the hills round Kabul but they re-occupied them in even greater strength as soon as we withdrew. The Afghans wore sheepskin coats, called *nimchees* or *poshteens*, and these often turned sword cuts and even musket balls. The general opinion was that some of them were invulnerable, and especially a tribe called Bedouranis. On one occasion I saw a party of their horsemen approach within twenty paces of a ravine where a regiment of ours was concealed. The officers made their men reserve their fire and then the whole regiment sprang up and opened fire. However, not more than three or four horses went away without riders. This dispirited the *sepoy* army very much and, as the cold increased, we became helpless. Men lost the use of their fingers and toes which fell off after great suffering. The whole English army was in a miserable plight, since the men were worn out by continual fighting, guard duties, and bad food.

Our army was in two places,[8] as I have said, which much weakened its strength. The enemy had possession of the King's garden, and from it were able to annoy us very much.[9] Several attempts were made to recapture this garden but without success. The only result was great loss of men which we could ill afford. Orders were sent to Ghazni and Kandahar to hurry forward all the Shah's and the *Sirkar's* forces, but the messengers were probably murdered. After a while a Gurkha force, which was commanded by a *sahib*, tried to join us but it was cut to pieces and only two officers managed to escape to Kabul.[10] This misfortune made matters

[7] Behmeru was a village in the hills overlooking the cantonment. There were two skirmishes there, on 22 and 23 November 1841. On neither occasion did the troops distinguish themselves.

[8] Sita Ram presumably refers to the fact that the Kabul garrison was divided between guarding Shah Shujah in the Bala Hissar and defending the cantonment about two miles away. He could however be referring to the two regiments (HM 13th Foot and 35th BNI) which had left for Jellalabad under Sale during October. They were subsequently besieged in Jellalabad.

[9] The outskirts of Kabul were covered with orchards and gardens, among which the King's garden was the largest. It was situated a few hundred yards from the north-west corner of the cantonment and provided ample cover for the Afghan riflemen. Only half-hearted efforts were made to re-take it.

[10] The 4th (Gurkha) Regiment of Shah Shujah's Levy was garrisoning

worse and we began to think this would be the fate of all the *Sirkar*'s soldiers in Afghanistan.

At this time a circumstance occurred which I have never seen or heard of before. The *Sirdars* sent in messages dictating terms to the *Sirkar*'s army. They stated that the English army was in their power and that they could completely destroy it whenever they thought fit. However, they would spare it on condition that it left Afghanistan forthwith. I saw many *sahibs* shed tears of vexation when this became known and they blamed their generals and leaders for their humiliation. They said their leaders were too old and virtually useless. Fighting ceased for a few days, during which period the enemy sent more agents into our camp. All kinds of rumours were being spread. Some said an immediate retreat would be carried out, or that the entire army would lay down its arms. Others said that the army would still fight. Nothing of good seemed to come from these negotiations, and worse fighting than ever began again.

Then at last the *burra sahib*,[11] 'Macnaten', sent to say he would agree to the terms offered, and the Amir Akbar Khan himself came to a meeting. It was soon known that the *Lad sahib*[12] and the general had agreed to give up hostages. In two or three days after this the army left the Bala Hissar, and all came into the cantonment. This was done without any opposition being offered. Now was the time when the extraordinary courage of the officers' ladies came forth. They were all against giving up hostages and when, their advice not being heeded, these were given, all those *sahibs* who had wives were followed by them into captivity. The *Sirdars* promised provisions and carriage for our army but it never was forthcoming. The force remained some time longer in a wretched condition but it was not molested during this period by the Afghans other than to prevent provisions from entering our camp. The price of food was

---

Charikar, the chief town in Kohistan. Its communications with Kabul were cut on 1 November. Lieutenant Rattray, the assistant political agent, was treacherously murdered on 3 November, and the fort was then besieged. On 13 November, the water supply having failed, the force withdrew. Only Major Pottinger and Ensign Haughton, both wounded, and one Gurkha, succeeded in reaching Kabul. Those who were not killed were enslaved. All the wounded, as well as the families of the Gurkhas, were massacred.

[11] and [12] *Burra sahib*: big, or important, *sahib*. Sita Ram often uses this expression to mean political officer but here he is referring to Macnaghten, as in *Lad Sahib* below. It must be said, in fairness to Macnaghten, that at first he was strongly opposed to accepting the conditions laid down by the Afghan chiefs. He would have preferred to fight it out, or withdraw into the Bala Hissar. In this he was supported by Shah Shujah. When the latter heard that the British had accepted the terms, he commented, 'Surely the English must be mad!' However, Macnaghten could not go against the advice of his senior military advisers, and both Elphinstone and Shelton advised acceptance of the terms. They did not believe the troops had any more fight left in them, and the cantonment was incapable of withstanding a long siege in mid-winter.

perfectly absurd and everyone endured great hardship; more particularly the Europeans, for all they could get was dried fruit and parched corn.[13]

One day, when the *burra sahib* and his ADC were at a meeting with the *Sirdars*, we received a report that 'Macnaten' *sahib* had been killed by Akbar Khan's own hand.[14] Soon the shouts of the people were heard like the noise of the wind before a storm, and there was firing into our camp. The news of the *Lad sahib*'s death was correct. Both the senior political officers[15] had now been murdered. The General *sahib* was going to take vengeance on the city, but the officers represented that their men were too weak to take the offensive. Nevertheless it would have been better to have died fighting than massacred in the retreat which followed. Wisdom seemed to have departed from everyone. The usual energy of the English officers had vanished. They had suffered such severe trials that their spirits had been depressed by misfortune. There were rumours that Shah Shujah had joined the *Sirdars* against the English; now that things were going so badly, he was afraid of being thought their friend.[16]

The retreat of our army, in the middle of the winter and with the snow four feet deep, now began.[17] There was no interference by

[13] Once it was decided that the force should not withdraw into the Bala Hissar, and could not expect to defend the cantonment indefinitely, Macnaghten had no alternative other than to negotiate with the enemy. He hoped by promises and bribery to divide the Afghan leaders but he was playing a dangerous game. After the failure to take Behmeru on 23 November, Macnaghten began negotiations. He refused unconditional surrender but on 5 December the bridge over the Kabul river was destroyed. On 11 December Macnaghten agreed to meet the chiefs with a draft treaty which allowed for the restoration of Dost Mahommed, and the withdrawal of the British to India; Shah Shujah could accompany them or not, as he felt inclined. These terms were accepted and later Macnaghten agreed to provide hostages. Captain Trevor was the first to be handed over, and he was followed by others. Also the garrison in the Bala Hissar was withdrawn to the cantonment. But the chiefs temporized, because they wanted more hostages, guns, and ammunition. They kept the British on tenterhooks; while the snow fell deeper, supplies ran short, and the sick increased daily. The garrison should have marched out on 22 December, but the chiefs had not provided the necessary baggage animals and escort by that date.

[14] On 23 December, Macnaghten, accompanied by three officers met Akbar Khan a short distance from the cantonment. Ostensibly they were to discuss a plot of Akbar Khan's to permit Shah Shujah to remain on the throne, but it was intended to discredit Macnaghten. Macnaghten had no sooner handed over a horse as a present to Akbar Khan, and seated himself for the conference, than he was attacked and stabbed to death by Akbar Khan. Of his companions, Mackenzie and Lawrence were taken prisoner, and Trevor was hacked to death.

[15] Sir William Macnaghten and Sir Alexander Burnes.

[16] Shah Shujah was assassinated outside Kabul on 5 April 1842.

[17] The Kabul Force that marched out of the cantonment on the morning of 6 January 1842 consisted of 700 Europeans, 2,000 Bengal Native Infantry, 250 Bengal Cavalry, and 1,150 Irregular Horse and Shah Shujah's Levy. There were some 12 to 15,000 followers, as well as women and children. The arrangements were that the force would be escorted as far as Jellalabad (i.e. through the Khoord Kabul Pass) by Akbar Khan and other *Sirdars* but everything went awry from the outset. Hours were wasted on

the Afghans during the first day's march out of Kabul, and the second day passed quietly. But on the third day the camp followers and the baggage crowded up with the marching troops and threw everything into confusion. When the Afghans saw this they began to harass us by day and by night. They fired into us from the hills and we were as helpless as a handcuffed prisoner. Akbar Khan himself was following us. When we complained of this treachery, he swore that it was happening against his will, and that he could not control the *Ghilzais*. He demanded more officers be given up as hostages. I do not know why this was agreed, apart from the fact that sense had left the brains of everyone, as I have already said. Once the enemy had the officers in their power, our army was deprived of leaders. Every *sahib* taken away was as bad as two hundred men lost. At last the Afghans said they would only protect the English army on condition that the General was given up. To everyone's amazement, he agreed to go, but with the example of Burnes and 'Macnaten' before him, what could he expect?[18]

When the General *sahib* left all discipline fell away. As a result the Afghans were able to annoy us the more and cut off more men than ever. A number of *sepoys* and followers went over to the enemy in an effort to save their lives. My regiment had disappeared and I attached myself to the remnants of a European regiment.[19] I thought that by sticking to them I might have some chance of getting away from that detestable country. But alas! alas! Who can withstand fate? We went on fighting and losing men at every step of the road. We were attacked in front, in the rear, and from the tops of hills. In truth it was hell itself. I cannot describe

---

the first day building a bridge over the Kabul river which was easily fordable. The intense cold and deep snow destroyed morale and caused the followers and baggage train to crowd upon the fighting troops. The *sepoys* soon lost all cohesion, and only the 44th, and the Bengal Horse Artillery (Europeans) retained their discipline. Akbar Khan, either by intention or by default, lost control over the tribesmen on the flanks of the column, and within two days the Kabul Force had ceased to exist as a military organization. Its massacre thereafter was easy.

[18] Elphinstone had little option but to comply. three thousand died that day, including women and children. Lady Sale was wounded in the arm, and her son-in-law died of wounds. Her daughter, who survived the retreat, was pregnant.

[19] Major-General Elphinstone was a dying man by the time he gave himself up to Akbar Khan on 12 January 1842; Brigadier Shelton was taken prisoner with him. The General smuggled out a message to the remnants of the 44th urging them to make a run for it. The 200 remaining men did this that same night, Captain Souter, having wound the Colours round his waist, and they made their last stand at Gandamak on 13 January 1842. Only Souter and a small group of officers and men were taken prisoner; the others were killed. The only survivor to reach Sale's Brigade at Jellalabad was Dr William Brydon, who later played a heroic part in the siege of Lucknow in 1857. Elphinstone died in captivity but Shelton survived to end his life from a fall from his horse in barracks in Ireland. He remained a martinet to the end.

the horrors. At last we came upon a high wall of stones that blocked the road; in trying to force this, our whole party was destroyed.[20] The men fought like gods, not men, but numbers prevailed against them.

I was struck down by a *jezail* ball on the side of my head. After this I knew nothing until I found myself tied crossways upon a horse which was being led rapidly away from the fighting towards Kabul. I now learned that I was being taken there to be sold as a slave. I begged to be shot, or have my throat cut, and abused the Afghans in *Pushtu* and in my own language. Many a knife shook in its sheath, but my captor could not prevent me speaking, and as the fear of death had no effect on me he threatened to make me a Moslem on the spot if I did not keep quiet.[21]

What dreadful carnage I saw along the road—legs and arms protruding from the snow, Europeans and Hindustanis half buried, horses and camels all dead! It was a sight I shall never forget as long as I live. My captor, seeing that I desired death above anything else, became more merciful. I was taken from the horse and tied in a camel pannier. This, bad as it was, was better than hanging downwards from a pony. The Afghan rubbed my wound with snow which took away the pain; the ball had only ploughed up the skin where it had grazed my skull. In four or five days we reached Kabul where I was clothed in Afghan garments and sold in the market place as a slave. Rich Afghans valued Hindustanis as servants and employed many of them. I was a fine-looking, strong man, and I fetched 240 rupees. One Osman Beg purchased me. At the same time as I was sold, there were several other *sepoys*, and also a few Europeans for sale. The latter were intended to be used as instructors for the Afghan Army, and since they were supplied with some skins of Shiraz wine, they did not appear to lament their fate as we did.

I saw one *sahib* among the Europeans; he belonged to the Company *Bahadur*'s army. He spoke to me and said that the *Sirkar* would send a large army and re-conquer the country; if our lives were spared we should all be rescued. I think he said his name was Wallan.[22] I have forgotten now if I name him rightly but his words gave me some comfort. I was not treated unkindly by my new master, but the threat was held over me that if I did not obey, or tried to escape, I should be made a eunuch and sold for a large sum to attend some harem. I would have killed myself during my captivity had I not felt certain that the words of Wallan *sahib* would come true, and that it would not be long before I would be able to

[20] At Jagdalak, where the pass was blocked with a barricade, Sita Ram had attached himself to what remained of the 44th Foot.

[21] Presumably by forcible circumcision.

[22] This was probably Robert Waller of the Bengal Artillery. Both he and his wife were taken prisoner, and both survived captivity. Mrs Waller died in 1905—the last survivor of the Kabul prisoners.

escape. I was put under a *Maulvi* [23] Mahommed Suffi, who at first did nothing but revile me, calling me an idolator, but when he saw that I took pains to learn his accursed language, he changed his tune and tried every persuasion to make me become a Mahommedan.[24]

I did not become a Mahommedan but strove to bear up against my hard fate. At first I was principally employed preparing my master's tobacco, and was thankful that I did not have more degrading work to perform. However, when it became known that I could keep accounts, Osman Beg entrusted me with the keeping of his, and from this circumstance I became of more importance to his family.

[23] *Maulvi:* Mahommedan scholar or teacher, usually of religion.
[24] Sita Ram here inserted a few lines of Persian in his original manuscript. They were not relevant to his theme, and were probably intended to display his knowledge of the language. I have omitted them.

'The men fought like gods, not men'

'Osman Beg and his horsemen moved on without noticing me'

11   *Escape from Slavery*

In this chapter Sita Ram tells of his experiences while a slave in Afghanistan, and of his subsequent escape to India. He describes his reunion with his family and the troubles he suffered before he could regain his caste, defiled by the menial duties he had to perform in the household of a Mahommedan.

Lord Auckland, whose mistaken policies had led, directly or indirectly, to the disaster in Kabul early in 1842, laid down the Governor-Generalship in March of that year. One of his last acts was to concentrate a force at Peshawar under Major-General Pollock with the task of forcing the Khyber Pass and relieving Sale's brigade which was besieged in Jellalabad by Akbar Khan, Dost Mahommed's son. Lord Ellenborough, who succeeded Auckland as Governor-General, endorsed this policy, but was unwilling to commit himself any more deeply in Afghanistan.

However, there were at this time some eighty British who were prisoners of the Afghans. Lady Sale, who was one of them, recorded on 18 January: 'We number 9 ladies, 20 gentlemen, and 14 children. In the tykhana (cellar) are 17 European soldiers, 2 European women, and 1 child.' There were a few others held prisoner elsewhere in Afghanistan. It was felt very strongly in the army that these prisoners should be freed and the Afghans punished for the massacre of the Kabul force, and although Ellenborough was against further involvement in Afghanistan, he yielded to the arguments of Pollock and others. Pollock, who was a cautious but able soldier, relieved Jellalabad without much difficulty, and then advanced to Kabul where he was to be joined by Major-General Nott with the garrison from Kandahar. The route taken to Kabul lay through the valleys where Elphinstone's force had been pitilessly butchered and the way was littered with skeletons. Pollock's force became an Army of Retribution, burning villages, destroying orchards, giving little or no quarter when opposed, and finally destroying the great covered bazaar in Kabul, which was the pride of its citizens.

Pollock arrived in Kabul on 16 September 1842. Nott marched in to join him two days later, furious that he had been beaten to the post. Shah Shujah had been assassinated, his son Fath Jung had abdicated, and it was not until Dost Mahommed returned from exile in Calcutta nine months later that some kind of order and tranquillity returned to Afghanistan. Pollock's first act on arriving in Kabul was to dispatch a force under his military secretary, Sir Richmond Shakespear, to rescue the prisoners who had been taken from Kabul to Bameean. Elphinstone had died the previous April, worn out by disease and remorse for what had occurred, and his body had been taken to Jellalabad with Akbar Khan's agreement, where it was interred with military honours. Brigadier Shelton was therefore the senior officer in the party when Shakespear arrived with the rescuing force, and he rebuked Shakespear for having kissed Lady Sale without first paying his respects to Shelton as his superior officer.

The combined forces of Pollock and Nott then marched back to India, leaving Prince Shapur, another of Shah Shujah's sons, to enjoy the doubtful privilege of ruling Afghanistan. He did not last long. The Army of Retribution crossed the Sutlej into British territory by a bridge of boats during the last fortnight in December 1842, and was greeted by Ellenborough with as much pomp and circumstance as could be mustered. But not even Ellenborough's grandiloquence could conceal the fact that the British adventure in Afghanistan had been disastrous from start to finish.

Upon the news of the total destruction of the European armies (for it was reported that their forces had been destroyed at Ghazni and Kandahar as well as at Kabul) there were great rejoicings in the city. Although Shah Shujah had sided with the Amir when he saw the sudden change things had taken, he was regarded with suspicion. The people of the country hated him because he had brought ruin upon the land by persuading a foreign army to come and place him on the throne. He remained in the palace within the Bala Hissar and still seemed to be king. But his reign lasted only a short time. One day when he was going out of the palace to visit the camp of the *Sirdars*, he was fired upon by some *Barakzais* and killed on the spot. *Sirdar* Fath Jung seized the throne.[1] However Amir Akbar Khan hastened back to Kabul with a part of his force[2] and drove him from the city. It was said that he fled to the English army which was entering Afghanistan.

I made several attempts to contact some of the *sahibs* who were reported to be prisoners in Kabul, but on account of the guards round their places of confinement I only once succeeded in seeing five *sahibs* and three ladies who were kept in a small building in the city. I was unable to do them much good. I could only tell them that there was a general report of an English army having entered the country, and this seemed to give them some consolation. I promised to let them know when it approached. One officer told me they had been repeatedly threatened with being sent out of the country and sold as slaves, and he was very much afraid that this would be done before the army could reach Kabul. He complained that

---

[1] After Shah Shujah's assassination his son, Fath Jung, seized the throne. There followed the usual series of feuds between the various factions. At one stage Akbar Khan, son of Dost Mahommed, appointed himself vizier to Fath Jung. Fath Jung eventually fled to General Pollock's camp where he was received with royal honours—much to the annoyance of Lord Ellenborough. Dost Mahommed returned to Afghanistan in April 1843 and was restored to the throne from which the British had so mistakenly evicted him.

[2] He was besieging Sale's Brigade at Jellalabad at the time.

they were all much annoyed by the mob who often came and abused them. He also made searching enquiries about General Elphinstone *sahib* who was a prisoner, but this officer must have been kept outside the city since I could never discover where he was. This meeting took place late in the evening. I went pretending I had been sent by the Amir with some tobacco but I was subjected to such a severe scrutiny that I did not dare to go again. I was thankful to have escaped with my life.

The approach of the English army was now talked of daily. The reports said that the passes had been forced by the *Sirkar's* troops and that hundreds of thousands of troops were coming to take Afghanistan.[3] Everyone now became afraid and repented of the massacre, laying the chief blame for it on the *Ghazis*. Numbers of the wealthier citizens now left the city. I tried one day to interest my master in the *sahibs* who were prisoners, telling him that he would be well rewarded if he helped them in any way, but this was only met by abuse and the former threat was repeated. Although I wore Afghan dress, my accent always gave me away, and I dare not go again to look after the English officers. Since I had no money, I could not bribe anyone, but I did try to win over a young boy who brought meat to my master's house. I had heard him once express a desire to visit Calcutta and see the wonders of the foreigners, and he said he would accompany a caravan to India when he was rich enough. I wrote a small note in the Hindi language in Persian characters and entrusted it to him to give to one of the *sahibs*, but as I never saw him again I do not know whether he ever delivered it, or if he did, whether its purport was understood. It was to say that the English army was reported to be within ten days' march of Kabul. As this army approached the fear became greater and my master decided to flee from the city. I vainly tried to explain that I knew the customs of the foreigners and that he would not be molested, since he had not taken any part against them. However, he would not believe me and for this reason he left the city.

I was now watched so constantly that I had no chance to escape. My master and his family took the road for Istalif[4] and I abandoned

---

[3] Auckland ceased to be Governor-General in March 1842, and was succeeded by Lord Ellenborough (1790–1859). Before Auckland's departure orders had been given for the assembly of a force at Peshawar under Major-General George Pollock with the object of relieving Sale's force at Jellalabad. This relieving force was subsequently augmented in order that it could, after relieving Sale, march on to Kabul, join forces with General Nott's force which was advancing from Kandahar, and release the British prisoners. All this was accomplished by the 'Army of Retribution', as it became known, and among the punitive measures carried out by Pollock, perhaps the destruction of the great bazaar in Kabul—'the architectural pride of Central Asia'—was the most regrettable.

[4] Istalif was a town in Kohistan. It was attacked in September 1842 by a force under General McGaskill in order to punish Aminullah Khan who had taken refuge there. Aminullah Khan had been one of the principal instigators of the Kabul insurrection.

any hope of regaining my freedom. Istalif was on the side of a hill, surrounded by precipices, and almost unapproachable. The people defended it with thick stone walls and small towers. The Afghans thought they could defend this place against the whole world, and it is very likely that they could have done against any but English soldiers. We heard after a while that Kabul had been taken and also Ghazni and Kandahar,[5] so my master retired still farther over the mountains to Sherkudo. On the road to this place we heard that the English had driven the Afghans out of Istalif with great slaughter and had destroyed the town. I was very unhappy, not knowing which way to go if ever I did manage to escape from bondage. I had now learned to read and write Persian quite reasonably but I could never pass myself off as a native of the country because of the difference in pronunciation.

For a long time no news arrived of the English and hope began to leave my breast. I became quite reckless of my life at the idea of remaining a slave. How bitterly I regretted having left my old regiment! At last news reached this out-of-the-way place that the English had burnt Kabul to the ground and had returned to India. Several Afghan families now returned to their homes and, when my master heard from a friend that these reports were true, he also made preparations to return. We arrived in Kabul just as the snow was beginning to fall. The city had not been burnt, but the bazaar had been totally destroyed. The inhabitants had not been molested, which greatly astonished the population, since all those who had had the means to do so had left the city for fear of retribution.

It was now more than three years since I had entered this vile country, and I had never heard from my own family or from my father's during this time. I wondered who had taken care of mine, supposing they were still alive, and how they managed to exist. Many doubts filled my mind. My master was not unkind to me, but I was made to do things against my caste without any consideration for the horror this inspired in my breast. Now that the English had left the country, my chances of escape were so much reduced that I almost gave up the idea. However, within a few months, my master had occasion to go to Ghazni on business, and I was left behind. As I had not lamented my lot for a long time, nor said anything about escaping, I was not watched so closely and greater liberty was allowed me. I had become friendly with one Ahmed Shah, a leader of a caravan that used to go every year to Hindustan. Since he knew

[5] Kandahar was never recaptured by the Afghans. General Nott remained there with the garrison throughout the Kabul insurrection and only left in order to join forces with Pollock in Kabul on 18 September 1842. He destroyed Ghazni *en route* and brought with him the gates of the Temple of Somnath (as ordered by Lord Ellenborough). These gates were reputed to be the ones looted from Somnath in Western India by Mahmud of Ghazni (who reigned from 998 to 1030) but this is unlikely.

every town in my own country, as well as being known to many merchants in Oudh, I opened my heart to him about my desire to be free. I told him that if he would connive at my escape, I would be able to pay him a handsome sum on reaching India.

After a great deal of haggling he agreed to let me go with him as his servant, on condition I promised to pay him 500 rupees on reaching India, and this agreement he made me write down on paper. I was much afraid after I had done this that he would disclose my secret, but I comforted myself with the thought that he would not gain so much by betraying me as he would by helping me. In a few days his camels were ready to depart. I bought a dirty set of clothes, pulled my hair down over my face and burnt the ends with lime, in order to make it look as much like a Pathan's[6] as possible. I entered up all my master's accounts, and left even the clothes he had given me. The only thing I took was a long knife. Early one morning I left Kabul with a caravan of 175 camels, but I soon discovered that my situation as a servant, although only assumed, was in reality a hard one. Ahmed Shah was very hot-tempered and used to shower me with abuse in his own language, which was hard to bear. I had to attend on the camels, lead them out to feed, and perform the other duties of a camel-man. I put up with all this, and as the caravan got farther away from Kabul my heart began to rejoice at the prospect of escape. But suddenly, from some news received by the master of the caravan that it was dangerous to attempt to pass through the Punjab by the north, on account of the disturbed state of the country and the numerous and heavy tolls that were certain to be levied, Ahmed Shah decided to go by another route by way of Dehra Ismail Khan.[7]

As we were now taking the road to Ghazni, I was afraid lest I might meet my old master and be claimed back by him. I therefore kept a sharp lookout for any party of travellers attended by horsemen as I knew my former master had hired some of them to escort him to Ghazni. About two marches distant from Ghazni Osman Beg and his party passed our caravan. I saw him from a distance and at once determined to use the pistol which I had been given, either against him or myself, rather than be taken back into slavery. It was an anxious moment, and any mistake on my part would have been certain to lead to my detection. I happened at the time to be on the same side of the string of camels as my master and therefore changed over to the other side, at the same time making loud noises that the Afghans make when driving camels, which sound quite different

[6] Pathan: the name applied to the Pushtu-speaking tribes of south-eastern Afghanistan and north-western Pakistan. They are often of an unkempt and hirsute appearance, their long locks matted like the Bedouin of Arabia.

[7] Runjeet Singh's Sikh empire was soon plunged into anarchy after his death in 1839.

from those the camel-men make in Hindustan. As the party passed us, my former master called out to know whose caravan it was and how many days we had been coming from Kabul. As luck would have it the man next to me replied, and thus saved me from speaking which might well have betrayed me. Osman Beg and his horsemen moved on without noticing me and my chances of escape were now more hopeful. I felt an even greater sense of relief when I saw the lances of his escort disappearing in the distance than I did when the Pindaris departed from the tomb in Bundelkhand.

Few people have had to endure such trials twice in a life-time. After leaving Ghazni the caravan struck off to the east. By paying tribute to the hill tribes we got through—wonderful to relate—without any annoyance and arrived at Dehra Ismail Khan which belonged to the Sikhs. Heavy duties were levied before the caravan could move on. Although I was not yet in my own country, I felt very happy for having left the vile country of the Afghans, and for having re-crossed the Indus. At Dehra Ismail Khan I heard that the English were fighting in Sind,[8] and I wanted Ahmed Shah to take the caravan that way, but he had determined to go direct to Ferozepore. After a great deal of trouble with the Sikh authorities, who constantly demanded some tax or other from the caravan, in October 1843 we approached Ferozepore.

As the buildings in the cantonment came in sight I could hear the drums and bugles of the garrison, and I was overcome with delight. However Ahmed Shah would not let me go to the cantonments until he had made his own arrangements in the *serai* and could accompany me. He would not let me out of his sight for a moment. After the camels had been unloaded and had been led out to feed, we mounted and set off for the cantonment. I went with him to the Brigade Major's bungalow, but we were ordered out of the compound because the *sahib* wanted no fruit.[9] I then spoke to the orderlies in their own language, explaining my situation and requesting to see the *sahib*. It was not much use when I did see him since he would not believe me. He also told me that even if my story was true, he was quite certain the Government would not pay as much as 500 rupees, or indeed anything, for my ransom!

I then went to the Magistrate and told him my tale. I claimed deliverance from being a slave, which Ahmed Shah, now that he saw that I was not likely to obtain any money, loudly proclaimed me to be.

[8] The British conquest of Sind began in February 1843, under Major-General Sir Charles Napier. The Amirs of Sind were defeated at Miani and Hyderabad, and Sind was annexed by the East India Company. The 22nd (Cheshire) Regiment distinguished itself during this campaign.

[9] Afghans are in the habit of going round to houses selling fruit, tobacco, etc. [Norgate's original translation].

At first the *sahib* refused to listen to me, but when he discovered that I knew all the officers in several regiments, he began to give me more attention.[10] However, he still refused to advance me any money, and he also said that the *Sirkar* would never do so. I tried one last resource and went to the Commissioner *sahib*.[11] By good fortune I saw a *subedar* of my late regiment on guard; he had been promoted into some other corps. I made myself known to him, but at first he would not credit my story until I spoke to him in Hindi and told him facts which put all doubt out of his mind. He went with me to the Commissioner *sahib* who listened attentively to my story and asked me a hundred questions about the army in Kabul; but he also said he did not think the Government would pay my ransom.

However, the *subedar* agreed to pay 250 rupees; and the *sahib*, after the *subedar* told him that my family were well-off in Oudh, advanced me the remainder. My promissory note was retained, the transaction was entered into some book, and I was free! But I did not possess a *pice*[12] and owned nothing apart from my dirty Afghan clothes. I went to the lines of one of the regiments but when I informed the *sepoys* who I was, they all declared me unclean and defiled. Some even accused me of having been made a Mahommedan. Therefore, until I could regain my caste, I could look for no affection and friendship from my own people! This greatly mortified me, and I almost wished I had stayed in Kabul where at any rate I had not been treated unkindly.

I returned to the Brigade Major much dispirited. After I told him that the Commissioner *sahib* had paid a part of my ransom, he agreed to take me to the Brigadier *sahib*, who was very kind to me. He knew my old regiment and told me it was now at Delhi.[13] He also wrote about me to the Adjutant-General[14] *sahib* in order that I could be reinstated in my old regiment. I was furnished with some money and allowed to live in his compound. I threw away my Afghan clothes which I had now been wearing for one year and seven months. Having been shaven and shorn, I now looked more like a soldier, but I was still shunned by all my brethren —in fact I was an outcaste. The Brigadier *sahib* often called me onto his veranda and asked about my adventures in Kabul. He took a great interest

[10] Sita Ram's appearance must have been against him. An unkempt, hirsute Pathan looks very different from a Hindustani from Oudh, and India has always been full of vagrants telling hard luck stories.

[11] The senior ICS officer in a district.

[12] *Pice*: the smallest Indian coin; less than a farthing.

[13] Sita Ram presumably is referring to the 63rd BNI which he left to join Shah Shujah's Levy in 1838. But the 63rd left Delhi for Ambala in November 1843 before Sita Ram could have rejoined, if his chronology is accurate.

[14] This would be the Adjutant-General of the Bengal Native Army who was the senior staff officer responsible for personnel matters. There was also an Adjutant-General for the Royal Army.

in me. It was entirely due to him that I owe my good fortune in being looked upon with favour by the *Sirkar*. After some time I received orders to join my former regiment at Delhi, and being furnished with the means by some officers who were exceedingly kind to me,[15] I marched down to Delhi and reported my arrival to my Colonel *sahib*. He was very pleased to see me and seemed to have forgotten about my court-martial. I was supernumerary to the establishment for some time, but I was restored to my former rank as *havildar* as soon as there was a vacancy in my regiment.

I had written home and now received an answer. My first wife was dead and also my mother and my old friend, the Pundit Duleep Ram. My father wished me to come home and promised to pay the 250 rupees which he would send me. All this time I was treated as an outcaste by the Brahmins. The only people who would associate with me and speak to me were the Mahommedans, and the Christian drummers and musicians.[16] The officers knew this and were very kind to me but I had no money and therefore could not pay to regain my caste at that time.

When the time for furlough came round I was permitted to take mine. What changes I found at my home! My father had become an old man and my young brother managed his affairs. The news that I had been made a slave had reached my village and I was not allowed to remain in my father's house. I discovered that my brother was my enemy. He had long supposed me to be dead and looked forward to succeeding to the estate. My father paid for my regaining my caste which I proved had been taken away forcibly. It did not cost as much this time as on the last occasion but I was unhappy because I could obtain no news about my *Thakurin* wife. Some said she had returned to her own country, while others hinted that she had gone off with some *sepoy*. My son had been transferred to another regiment, which had gone down to Sind, and nothing had been heard of him for two years. I had inherited a small sum of money from my first wife, and with this I paid off the 250 rupees lent to me by *subedar* Kushal Dubey [in Ferozepore].

My father did all that he could to persuade me to leave the army and live with him, but my heart yearned for my son and my wife and I knew I should never find them by remaining at home. I therefore decided to set off for Bundelkhand in search of my wife and went straight to the village where her brother was living. When I arrived there, and

[15] It would probably have taken Sita Ram two weeks or more to travel from Ferozepore to Delhi in those days. He would have had to equip himself, and feed himself on the way, and these expenses appear to have been met by some of his British officers.

[16] Musicians were of low caste in India at that time, and bandsmen and drummers were often Christians.

when I discovered that her brother was a proud Rajput owning a considerable property, who was greatly superior to me in position if not in caste, my heart began to fail me. I did not know what kind of reception I would experience. However, I made up my mind and boldly said that I had come to claim my wife. To my great delight I found that she was living under her brother's protection. I was permitted to take her away to my home, where I left her in the care of my father, and set off to rejoin my regiment at Delhi.

But I now lacked spirit and was almost tired of life. When I was in Kabul the hope of escape kept up my spirits; every day I dreamed of becoming free. Now I was free but what had I gained? I had obtained neither promotion nor reward for all I had endured. Six months' pay was owing to me but I had little prospect of getting it. I had spent a lot of money to regain my liberty and my caste, and also owed a considerable sum to a *sahib*. I became ill and spent a long time on sick report. During this time I had requested my Colonel *sahib* to present my petition to the *Sirkar* which he had promised to do. In it I had stated how long I had served the *Sirkar*, in how many battles I had participated, how I had been wounded, etc., etc., and that I had entered Shah Shujah's army by the express desire of an officer, and with the promise of promotion and better

'. . . I could hear the drums and bugles of the garrison, and I was overcome with delight'

pay. I then mentioned that I had received no promotion, was owed six months' pay, had been captured when wounded, and had been sold as a slave. I had made my escape by promising to give 500 rupees, had forfeited one year and seven months service towards my pension, and I begged the *Sirkar* in mercy to listen to my prayer.

'. . . we next heard the roaring noise of cavalry'

12   *The First Sikh War:*
1845-1846

The two Sikh Wars of 1845–6 and 1848–9 were the last serious trials of strength for the British in India—except, of course, for the Mutiny[1]—until the Independence Movement gathered momentum from 1919 onwards. Of all the many tribes and people with whom the British fought in order to establish their rule in India, the Sikhs were probably the most formidable, and Sita Ram makes it clear that the sepoys of the Bengal Army were most reluctant to cross swords with them. A Hindu sect founded by the first guru, or teacher, Nanak (1469–1539), the Sikhs were distinguishable by their beards and long hair, which they were forbidden to cut, martial characteristics and fine physique. Their home was in the Punjab and they suffered centuries of persecution by the Mughuls until, at the beginning of the nineteenth century, their numerous warring clans were united as a result of the genius of Maharajah Runjeet Singh (1787–1839).

As good a clue as any to Runjeet's character can be obtained from the Punjabi couplet he was fond of quoting:

Four things greater than all things are,
Women, and Horses, and Power, and War.

(Kushwant Singh)

By a combination of cajolery and force he united the Sikhs and pacified the Punjab, and then looked for farther fields to conquer. He fought the Afghans and took from them the fertile provinces of Kashmir and Peshawar. He extended his rule southwards to Multan and had ambitions in Sind. He dearly wished to bring under his control the Sikh clans who lived to the south and east of the River Sutlei, but that river formed the boundary between the Sikh empire and that of the East India Company. Runjeet Singh was determined not to antagonize the powerful British; he signed a treaty with them at Amritsar in 1809 and faithfully adhered to it thereafter.

The British plenipotentiary who negotiated this treaty was Charles Metcalfe and he was accompanied to Amritsar by an escort of Bengal sepoys. Runjeet Singh was greatly impressed by their discipline and appearance and decided to train his own soldiers along the same lines. He obtained the services of numerous European mercenaries, paid them well, and gave them a free hand to produce an army as good as the Company's. He was particularly interested in artillery and established an arsenal in Lahore which produced excellent guns. Within a comparatively few years the Sikh army was probably capable of taking on the Bengal Army on equal terms, apart from the stiffening of European troops which always seems to have been an

[1] The Mutiny of the Bengal Native Army in 1857 is described by certain Indian historians as the 'First War of Liberation'. The accuracy of this is disputed by other Indian historians, notably Kushwant Singh, but it contains an element of truth. Although the mutineers may have failed in their efforts to inspire a general uprising, it is probably true to say that they had the sympathy of a great many of their fellow-countrymen.

encouragement to the sepoys. Fortunately for the British, Runjeet Singh never put matters to the test, and died at the early age of fifty-two. Even his iron constitution had to yield in the end to the strains he put upon it.

His death was followed by the usual struggle for power which was bitter, protracted, and bloody. The Sikh army, which had frequently resorted to mutiny even under Runjeet Singh, became the main power in the land. The court at Lahore was divided against itself, and realized that it could not stand out against the army which was clamouring for war with the British. It was therefore decided, according to Sir Henry Lawrence, 'to fling the soldiery upon British India, supplying them with every means of success, taking, if unsuccessful, the chance of clemency and forgiveness, and, if victorious, the merit and profit of repelling the English from Hindustan'. The Sikh army accordingly crossed the River Sutlej on 11 December 1845, and war with the British was inevitable.

Sita Ram's regiment was stationed at Ferozepore on the Sutlej frontier and formed part of the Division under Major-General Littler. Sita Ram was not present at the first battle, Mudki, but seems to have taken part in the battles of Ferozeshah and Sobraon which followed, although his regiment was not at Ferozeshah, and he may have been reporting the battle from hearsay. A large British force had been collected on the Punjab frontier under the command of Sir Hugh Gough, the Commander-in-Chief, with whom the Governor-General, Sir Henry Hardinge, was serving as second-in-command. This force, 'The Army of the Sutlej', took some hard knocks from the Sikhs at Mudki and Ferozeshah before finally driving them from the field at Sobraon. Gough was a much respected commander, especially among the British troops, but he was no tactician; he preferred the bludgeon to the rapier and came near to defeat on more than one occasion. He was saved by the superior discipline of his troops, although the sepoy regiments came under criticism at Ferozeshah. However, they redeemed themselves at Sobraon where they fought well.

Sita Ram admired the courage of the Sikhs and the handling of their artillery. He was, however, critical of their leadership, and with good reason, for treachery and divided counsel on the part of the Sikh leaders weighted the scales against their own forces. The Company's army occupied Lahore on 20 February 1846, and the First Sikh War was over. Much to everyone's surprise, including the Sikhs, the British did not annex the Punjab. The frontier was advanced from the Sutlej to the Beas incorporating the fertile district of Jullundur in the Company's dominions, and a British Resident was established in Lahore. An indemnity of £500,000 was demanded and, since the bankrupt treasury of Lahore could not produce this sum, a transaction was entered into with the Dogra Rajah of Jammu, Gulab Singh, who had been a feudatory of the Sikhs. The fertile valley of Kashmir was taken from the Sikhs and handed over to the Jammu ruler in return for £1,000,000.

Sita Ram has a lot to say in this chapter about the poor spirit
he found in the Bengal Army when he returned from his captivity in
Afghanistan. All authorities are agreed that there was a significant and
progressive deterioration in discipline among the Bengal regiments from about
1830 onwards. Some of the cause for this was attributed to the abolition of
flogging, which was in fact reinstituted in 1845, but probably more was due to
the loss of prestige suffered by the British as a consequence of the First Afghan
War. The war in Sind (1843) had also been unpopular, and the sepoys
resented having to serve beyond what they considered to be the confines of
Hindustan without adequate compensation in the form of extra batta, or field
allowance. This short-sighted cheeseparing by the Company's financial
authorities caused great resentment, and was felt as keenly by the British officers
as it was by the sepoys they commanded. However, much of the blame for the
malaise that was afflicting the Bengal Native Army must be laid on the shoulders
of the British officers. The young and ambitious among them soon tired of
regimental duty and found more profitable, or more interesting, employment
with the civil government. Those who remained at regimental duty, and who
wanted to be efficient, found themselves frustrated by regulations of every kind
and description, and by senior officers who were worn out by the climate and
waiting for promotion. Colonels of sixty-five, and generals of over seventy, who
clung to the regulations and seldom if ever went on parade, were completely out
of touch with their men. A wishy-washy paternalism took the place of the
ordered discipline to which the Bengal sepoy had been for so long accustomed.
Undue attention to the sepoy's susceptibilities, reluctance to punish when
punishment was essential, and a failure on the part of the Higher Command to
support Commanding Officers, began to sap the morale of the Bengal Native
Army. It could only be a matter of time before discipline collapsed altogether,
and that time was fast approaching.

After waiting six months the Colonel *sahib* informed me
that the *Sirkar* would pay my ransom; but, as there were no accounts to
show how many months' arrears of pay were due to me, or to any others
of Shah Shujah's Levy, the money could not be given unless I could find
some officer of my late regiment to certify how many months' pay was due
to me at the time of the retreat from Kabul.[2] Since the day on which I
joined the remnants of the European regiment at Kabul was the last day on
which I saw any of my own regiment, I imagined that all the officers must

[2] Sita Ram's complaint will have a familiar ring for those readers who
have ever come into contact with the Military Accounts Department.

have been killed. I repeated all the officers' names I could remember to the Colonel *sahib*, but he was unable to tell me where a single one of them was. However, I was extremely fortunate to get even my ransom paid, and all this was due to the Colonel *sahib*. I should never have succeeded had he not been as a father to me. Although I had regained my caste, and was made a good deal of by the officers, I was nevertheless regarded with jealousy by the men of my regiment. I had prevented a *naik* and a *sepoy* from being promoted by my return, and I was constantly taunted with having been circumcized [i.e. being made a Mahommedan], and also with having eaten beef[3] while with the European soldiers in Kabul.

The Government's disasters in Afghanistan had become a common topic of conversation all over India. Many declared that the English were not invincible, and this was particularly the case in Delhi. I imagine it was from this time that the Mahommedans began to feel that one day they would be able to drive the *Sirkar* out of the country. The *sepoys* were discontented, for they found they were liable to be sent across the Indus at any time. They complained that the *Sirkar* had not fulfilled the promises made to induce the *sepoys* to go to Afghanistan; and now they had returned without gaining anything, neither promotion nor reward. The Mahommedans boasted that they all came originally from Kabul and Persia and could fight the English just as well as the Afghans. Several emissaries from the court of the *Badshah*[4] at Delhi came into our lines and tried to discover the temper and general feeling of the army. When the *sepoys* pointed out that the *Sirkar* had easily recaptured Kabul, these people replied that had not the foreign army returned so quickly on the onset of the winter, it would have been as easily destroyed as the first army had been.

As I have mentioned previously, I was always regarded with some degree of suspicion in my regiment. I was not myself spoken to on the subject but I still heard the matter openly discussed. I reported all this to the Quarter-Master *sahib*, who only laughed at me, and I went to the Colonel *sahib* who listened to me very attentively. However, he said he was afraid that I had brought an accusation against the regiment out of

---

[3] The cow is of course a sacred animal for all Hindus. Sita Ram, as a Brahmin, would have been a strict vegetarian, and would probably have starved rather than eat meat of any kind.

[4] *Badshah*: The Mughul emperor in Delhi. At this time he was Bahadur Shah, the last of the Mughuls, who ended his days in Rangoon where he was exiled after the Mutiny. The British after 1805 had continued the process begun by the Mahrattas and had stripped the Mughul emperor of all power. He was permitted to reside in the palace within the Red Fort in Delhi but exercised no influence. Alexander Burnes visited the court in 1831, and wrote: 'The mummery of the ceremony was absurd, and I could not suppress a smile as the officers mouthed in loud and sonorous solemnity, the titles of king of the world, the ruler of the earth, to a monarch now realmless and a prince without the shadow of power.'

spite, and he warned me not to talk to him again on such a subject. He considered it was all idle gossip from the bazaars. Of course, after this reprimand, I did not report anything again to a *sahib* as it only got me into trouble. After the Kabul war and the campaign in Sind most of the *Sirkar's* regiments between Delhi and Ferozepore were ripe for mutiny, and it was only the incredible good luck of the *Sirkar* that prevented a general uprising. The *sepoys* complained that additional field allowances had been promised in order to persuade them to go down to Sind, but after they had arrived there they were told that it had been a mistake and had never been authorized—although their commanding officers had said they would certainly receive it.

You, my Lord, were in India then, and know that several regiments were in mutiny.[5] In only four or five regiments did this show itself very openly, but discontent was deeply seated throughout. Many people expected a general mutiny throughout the army. Mahommedan agents were at work in every station and numbers of Afghan, Persian, and other spies, who promised that if the army would rise, their countries would join in against the foreigners and wipe out the disgrace they had suffered in Kabul when their bazaar was destroyed. They also said they would restore the throne of Hindustan to the Delhi *Badshah*. Every Rajah and Nawab was sounded; if friendly to the scheme, proposals were put forward to them to help in getting rid of the English. It is true that many had just cause for complaint. I myself had been promised promotion and extra pay, but had obtained neither the one nor the other. The *Sirkar* had, however, paid my ransom, and I was a free man instead of being a slave. The recollection of this was never absent from my mind. The year passed without any further signs of disaffection. It was well known in Delhi that during the Afghan War the *Sirkar* itself had been afraid. It had ordered the artillery to fire more than usual that year in order to remind the people of Delhi of its power. But the disasters in Kabul went a long way towards showing that the *Sirkar* was not so invincible as had always been supposed. It was certainly not feared as much now as had been the case formerly.

[5] Much of this discontent sprang from the events in Afghanistan, but as much, or more, was due to the *sepoys'* dislike for service in Sind, where the climate was abominable and the inhabitants treacherous. Moreover *batta*, or full field allowance, was not issued for service in Sind, although service there was as foreign for the Hindustani *sepoy* as Afghanistan. Nearly 300 men from the 4th and 69th BNI applied for their discharge rather than march to Sind, and, surprisingly, obtained it. The 34th BNI mutinied when ordered to Sind in 1844. The 64th BNI, already disaffected, was sent to Sind in the 34th's place, entirely as a result of the representations of its Commanding Officer. It mutinied on arrival at Sukkur, and its Commanding Officer was cashiered for misleading the authorities as to the state of his battalion. There was a deep-seated malaise in the Bengal Native Army, marked by the trebling of courts martial in the last twenty years, and flogging was reintroduced as a counter-measure.

Another year passed and then the murmurs of discontent, together with the excitement, subsided. At this time it was said that the Sikhs were anxious to try their strength against the Government. Their army was very large, well drilled, and was confident of beating the English army. The *Sirkar* now began to move up regiments to Ambala and Ludhiana.[6] We arrived at Ludhiana and remained there for some time. I think the English officers imagined the Sikhs would confine themselves to blustering on the far side of the river and would never dare to cross it. Large numbers of them were seen on the banks of the Sutlej but none had yet crossed. Eventually a party of Sikh horsemen crossed the river at Hurreeputtun[7] and cut up a number of grasscutters, as well as looting some stores belonging to the *Sirkar*. This was the first evidence of their intentions. Nevertheless the British officers thought the Sikhs would never invade Hindustan, but more troops were moved up to Ferozepore. Orders soon came for my regiment to proceed there, which we did by forced marches in four days.

The *Khalsa*[8] army had a great name because they had been drilled by French *sahibs*[9] and had muskets like the *Sirkar*'s army. Their guns were innumerable. Most of the *sepoy* regiments were afraid of fighting the Sikhs, but there were several European regiments in the force and this gave the *sepoys* more confidence. After a few days some horsemen came galloping into Ferozepore with the news that the *Khalsa* army had actually crossed the Sutlej—at least 500,000—and were intending to attack the station. Officers were sent to see, and they reported it was true but that their numbers were about 20,000.[10] There were only seven or eight regiments at Ferozepore; however General Littler *sahib*[11] moved out against

[6] Up to 1838 the troops on the frontier amounted to one regiment at Sabathu (Simla Hills) and two at Ludhiana, with six pieces of artillery. Lord Auckland increased the strength at Ludhiana and created a new garrison at Ferozepore. Lord Ellenborough formed further new stations at Ambala, Kasauli, and Simla, but closed Karnal. The frontier garrisons had therefore been increased from 2,500 to around 40,000 by the time the Sikh Wars took place.

[7] I have been unable to locate this village on the map.

[8] *Khalsa* means literally, the saved, liberated, or chosen. Guru Gobind Singh (the tenth guru) assembled his followers and told them a new faith had been declared, and henceforth the *Khalsa* should alone prevail. The Sikhs therefore called themselves the *Khalsa*, or the chosen people, and Sita Ram always calls them *Khalsaji*, and never Sikhs, in his manuscript.

[9] Notably Messieurs Allard and Court, but there were lesser fry as well as Spaniards, British, Italians, and at least one American.

[10] The Sikh army consisted of about 50,000 men, but by no means all were Sikhs. Sikh feudatories, such as the Dogra Maharajah Gulab Singh of Jammu, supplied contingents to the *Khalsa* army.

[11] Major-General Sir John Littler commanded the Ferozepore garrison. The Sikhs crossed the Sutlej on 11 December 1845. Part of their army threatened the isolated garrison in Ferozepore, which numbered no more than 7,000, but did not attack, supposedly

the Sikhs, but to everyone's surprise the Sikh army retired and did not come to Ferozepore. It was said later that they thought the entire cantonment had been mined, and therefore they wished to fight it out in the plain.

A few days after this we heard heavy firing at some distance from Ferozepore. News came in the evening that a battle had been fought. Some said that the *Sirkar*'s army had been defeated and was retreating to our station, while others reported that the Sikhs had been worsted and their army routed. There was another rumour that neither army had won the day but were occupying the same ground on which the battle had been fought.[12] However, several officers arrived during the evening and it then became known that the *Sirkar* had been victorious and many Sikh guns had been taken. All the troops were ordered from Ferozepore to join forthwith with the army.[13] We marched by night and went by a circuitous route in order to avoid the Sikhs who were reported to be ready on the road to cut us off. Next day, at 12 o'clock, we joined the other large division of the *Sirkar*'s army, but we were in great want of water, very tired, and unfit for fighting. Despite this, the order was immediately given to prepare for battle.

Owing to some movement of the Sikhs the fight was delayed until the sun was nearly down and night was closing in on us. This was fighting indeed—I had never seen anything like it before![14] Volleys of

---

owing to the treachery of one of the Sikh commanders, Lal Singh, who was in correspondence with the British political officer in Ferozepore, Captain John Nicholson (of Mutiny fame).

[12] The battle of Mudki, 18 December 1845. It was known as 'Midnight Mudki' because the fighting continued far into the night. The Sikhs were defeated but at considerable cost. Among those killed was Major-General Sir Robert Sale whom we have met previously at Ghazni and Jellalabad. HM 3rd Light Dragoons (later 3rd The King's Own Hussars, and today, after amalgamation with the 7th Hussars, The Queen's Own Hussars) greatly distinguished themselves by their charges at Mudki. They were nicknamed the 'Moodki-Wallahs' in the British Army, but the Sikhs called them the 'Devil's Children' because they came upon them 'like a flash of lightning'.

[13] The force concentrated against the Sikhs was called the 'Army of the Sutlej'.

[14] The Battle of Ferozeshah, or more correctly P'heerooshuhur, fought on 21 and 22 December 1845, has been described as 'certainly the hardest fought-out of the battles engaged in by the British in India'. The Sikhs lost 73 guns, and between two and three thousand killed. British casualties were 2,877, of whom 720 were killed. The British assault did not begin until an hour before sunset and the Sikh resistance took everyone by surprise—not least the Commander-in-Chief, Gough' and the Governor-General, Hardinge, who was present in a supernumerary capacity. 'The resistance met was wholly unexpected. . . . Guns were dismounted, and their ammunition was blown into the air; squadrons were checked in mid-career; battalion after battalion was hurled back with shattered ranks; and it was not until after sunset that portions of the enemy's position were finally carried.' (*History of the Sikhs* by J. D. Cunningham, Oxford University Press.) HM 3rd Dragoons again distinguished themselves but with a loss of 148 men and 197 horses. They lost half their strength at Mudki and Ferozeshah.

musketry were delivered by us at close quarters, and were returned just as steadily by the enemy. In all the previous actions in which I had taken part one or two volleys at short range were as much as the *Sirkar*'s enemies could stand; but these Sikhs gave volley for volley, and never gave way until nearly decimated. They had their infantry placed between, and behind, their artillery, and their fire was terrible, such as no *sepoy* has ever had to endure. The *Sirkar*'s guns were almost silenced and the ammunition wagons exploded. I saw two or three European regiments driven back by the weight of artillery fire which rained down on us like a monsoon downpour. They fell into confusion, and several *sepoy* regiments did the same. One European regiment[15] was annihilated—totally swept away—and I now thought the *Sirkar*'s army would be overpowered. Fear filled the minds of many of us.

When it was almost dark a loud shout was heard. This did not sound like the Sikhs, and we next heard the roaring noise of cavalry. The 3rd Dragoons rushed right through the enemy's entrenchment and rode over and cut down their gunners. This charge was so sudden, and cavalry charging right into artillery batteries so unheard of, that the Sikhs in perfect amazement left their guns for a short space. It now became quite dark and the *Sirkar*'s army left off fighting, but the Sikhs continued firing whenever they saw a light. The force I was with under General Littler *sahib* lost its way in the darkness. For fear of marching straight into the Sikh camp we were ordered to lie down. This night was nearly as bad as some of those in Kabul. We dare not light a fire, for fear of the enemy's round shot, there was no water, and we had nothing to eat except the few *chapattis* some men had put in their haversacks. The *sahibs* said this was real fighting and the Sikhs were noble enemies but they nevertheless looked anxious and wondered what the morning would bring forth. The weather was bitterly cold and nothing was heard among us but the chattering of teeth on empty stomachs.[16] I remember on this night a *sahib* from a regiment next to mine kept walking up and down singing; he was checked by the other officers but he still continued. The *sahib* was not drunk but was trying to solace himself for the absence of the officers' mess tent.[17] It was a dreadful night. The English had not abandoned the field, nor had the Sikhs been driven from their breastworks. It was a drawn game.

[15] HM 62nd Regiment (later 1st Battalion The Wiltshire Regiment, and now the Duke of Edinburgh's Royal Regiment) lost 260 men in ten minutes.

[16] For those who have not experienced one, the cold of a Punjab night during the winter months is hard to imagine. I well recall my first night on manoeuvres shortly after I joined my regiment in India as a Second Lieutenant in 1938. It was near Multan, not all that far from Ferozeshah, and I have never been so cold, before or since. The warm, sunny days of the northern Indian winter seem to accentuate the cold at night.

[17] Sita Ram may be right, but it would seem more likely that he was whistling in the dark to keep up his spirits!

When morning dawned the English army got into shape again and we were ordered to storm the Sikh entrenchments. My column joined up with the division from which we had become separated the previous night. The Governor-General *sahib* himself rode about the field, speaking to the European soldiers, and telling his *aides-de-camp* to bid us fight like men, and victory was certain. I do not understand how it was, but some said that the Governor-General *sahib* was serving under the command of the Commander-in-Chief.[18] It was said that the former had been a great general in England, and had fought many battles, in one of which he had lost an arm. 'Lad Guff' *sahib* was a great favourite with the European soldiers, for whenever he came near a regiment they began cheering him.[19] The Europeans rushed the batteries and the Sikhs fled. Then the horse artillery came up quite close and poured grapeshot into the enemy ranks, but the English army was too tired and faint from lack of food to be able to pursue the enemy. The Sikhs got to the ford and crossed the river. The whole of their camp was captured and 100 guns,[20] but they had set fire to their tents, and powder was continually exploding. Several men were killed as a result while engaged in looting. However, much booty was captured, such as tents lined with silk and shawls, belonging to the Sikh *sirdars*, and arms of every description. Many men were severely burnt while trying to save these tents.

After this great battle, while the whole of the English army was cooking its food, the bugles sounded the alarm, and it was reported that all the Sikh cavalry was coming down on us. The fight began again, but the *Sirkar's* guns were unable to fire since their guns had expended all their ammunition. The luck of the *Sirkar* was indeed great—

[18] Field-Marshal Sir Henry (later First Viscount) Hardinge (1785–1856) succeeded his brother-in-law, Lord Ellenborough, as Governor-General in 1844. He had served throughout the Peninsular War and was Wellington's representative at Marshal Blucher's headquarters during the Waterloo campaign, losing his left hand at Ligny. He became an MP and was Secretary at War from 1828–30, and again from 1841 to 44. He was present at some of the battles of the Sikh War, waiving his right to command in the field, and serving as second-in-command to Lord Gough. However, at Ferozeshah, he temporarily asserted his civil rank to restrain Gough from attacking until Littler's division had arrived from Ferozepore. He was created Viscount Hardinge of Lahore after the Sikh War, and later succeeded Wellington as Commander-in-Chief at the Horse Guards.

[19] Field-Marshal Sir Hugh (later First Viscount) Gough (1779–1869) was of Anglo-Irish stock. He was adjutant of an infantry battalion at the age of 15 and commanded the 87th Foot at Talavera in 1809. He held the chief command in the China War (1841–42) and was appointed Commander-in-Chief in India in 1843 at the age of 64. Gough was not a scientific soldier and his head-on tactics cost many lives, but he was immensely popular with British soldiers. His own bravery, emphasized by the white coat he invariably wore in action, which made him an obvious target, made them forgive his many obvious blunders. He had a fine presence and was the soul of Chivalry. It is said that he commanded in more general actions than any other British soldier in the nineteenth century.

[20] 73 guns were captured.

without any apparent cause the Sikh army retreated! Everyone was astonished since the Sikhs were all fresh troops. Some said they suddenly heard that another army of the *Sirkar* was in the rear, but whatever the reason they fired only a few rounds and then withdrew. They were not attacked by the English army since they never came within musket range. It was reckoned that they possessed about 100,000 cavalry, which was quite enough to have surrounded our force and totally destroy it. Some said that *Sirdar* Tej Singh was afraid to fight.[21] The *sahibs* were as surprised as everyone else, and the retreat of the *Khalsa* gave the *sepoys* great confidence as they thought the Sikhs dare not fight the *Sirkar* again.

Our army halted some days, throwing up entrenchments, and waited for the big guns to arrive. An English army was in rear of the Sikhs, but it must have been a long way off as it did not arrive for ten days or more afterwards. We then heard that there had been an engagement near Ludhiana and that some of the *Sirkar*'s guns had been captured, and also all the baggage. Then news came that there had been another battle in which the enemy had been defeated and all the lost baggage recaptured. This was true.[22]

At the beginning of the month [February 1846] all the armies of the *Sirkar* had been assembled, as well as the siege artillery. It was now a very large force, such as had never before been seen in India, but the Sikh army was reported to be at least 60,000 strong, with 400 guns. The Sikh army had marched to Sobraon[23] and had defended the position with

---

[21] 'On that memorable night,' writes Cunningham, of Ferozeshah' 'the English were hardly masters of the ground on which they stood, while the enemy had fallen back on a second army, and could renew the fight with increased numbers.' Gough considered falling back on Ferozepore, but was overruled by Hardinge. On the morning of 22 December, the Sikhs were driven from their entrenchments, but later in the day a fresh Sikh army appeared on the battlefield. This force was commanded by Tej Singh, whose troops were clamouring for a fight, but he was more concerned that the other wing of the Sikh army under Lal Singh should be defeated than the Punjab should be freed from the foreigners. He merely skirmished with the British and then left the field, leaving his subordinates without orders. The British won at Ferozeshah more by default on the part of the Sikh leaders than by any skill on the part of Gough.

[22] A subsidiary force under Major-General Sir Harry Smith was operating against Ranjor Singh who was threatening the important garrison town of Ludhiana. Smith relieved Ludhiana but lost his baggage train during a running fight with the Sikhs at Badowal on 21 January 1846. He later came up with the Sikhs at Aliwal on 28 January and won a resounding victory, driving Ranjor Singh back across the Sutlej, capturing all his artillery, and recovering most of the lost baggage. Smith described this action as 'a stand-up gentlemanlike battle', and HM 16th Lancers distinguished themselves by their charges which broke the Sikh squares. However, the 16th did not recover *their* baggage, losing all their mess silver, but Aliwal remains their most-cherished battle honour.

[23] The Battle of Sobraon, 10 February 1846, takes its name from two small villages called Subrahun on the south bank of the river Sutlej. The battle was described

100 guns. The English force moved at night and came upon the enemy's camp early in the morning. It was clear that the Sikhs had not learnt of its approach; there was great commotion in their camp and their bugles sounded the alarm. The fight was commenced by the artillery and the fire was terrible. One part of the Sikh army was on the other side of the river Sutlej, and the other inside British territory, with a bridge of boats across the river. After three hours' cannonading orders were given to charge the batteries. If it were possible, the fire on this occasion was more severe than at Ferozeshah. Sections of the English army were destroyed by the guns of the *Khalsa*, but it still stood firm. Several European regiments rushed on the guns,[24] followed by some *sepoy* regiments. It is well known that the *sepoys* dreaded the Sikhs as they were very strong men,[25] but in spite of everything their officers led them on. Through the smoke the flashing swords and helmets of that wonderful regiment the 3rd Dragoons were again seen[26]—they charged into the batteries a second time. Never was there such fighting in India ever before. At last there was a tremendous shout, which was taken up by the whole of the *Sirkar*'s army, that the Sikhs were retreating over their bridge.

Both sides of this bridge were defended with guns, but the enemy dared not fire from the other side of the river for fear of killing their own men. They marched down to the bridge in sections and many regiments managed to get across. The *Sirkar*'s artillery moved close up and poured in grapeshot at close range, mowing down hundreds. Infantry advanced and fired volley after volley. But the Sikhs marched on and seldom now answered the fire. Not one of them asked for mercy. Thousands of the Sikhs fell into the river which was very deep. Hundreds jumped

---

by Sir Harry Smith as 'a brutal bulldog fight'. It was first a duel of artillery against artillery, and then of infantry against infantry. Gough attacked the Sikh entrenchments frontally and won the day at the cost of nearly 2,500 casualties.

[24] HM 10th Foot (later Royal Lincolnshire Regiment) and 53rd Foot (later King's Shropshire Light Infantry) lost heavily, but greatly distinguished themselves; and so did the Company's Bengal European Regiment (later 101st Royal Munster Fusiliers) whose reputation is second to none in the history of British India.

[25] The Sikhs are big men compared with the average Indian. Conspicuous by their beards and turbans, their diet of wheaten bread, buttermilk, and meat gives them a splendid physique. They made the *sepoys* from Oudh look like pygmies. I have never seen such a splendid-looking body of men as the soldiers of the Sikh Regiment paraded at Meerut to receive their Colours from the President of India in March, 1968.

[26] Two squadrons of the 3rd Light Dragoons, followed by the 4th and 5th Bengal Native Cavalry, were led into the enemy position by the cavalry commander (Major-General Thackwell). The Sikh guns were so sunk in sand that the gunners could not depress their muzzles sufficiently and their fire went mostly over the cavalry's heads, and they drove the Sikhs from their guns. The 3rd Light Dragoons lost 289 men and 364 horses in the First Sikh War, and Fortescue wrote of them that 'few regiments of horse in the world can show a finer record of hardihood and endurance'.

into the water in order to avoid being carried to the bank where the English forces were lined up. The slaughter was frightful. I have seen nothing like it. The river was full of masses of struggling men, who clung to each other in their despair, and who were swept away by the current to rise no more alive.

I narrowly escaped with my life near this bridge. I saw a large round shot bounding straight into the leading files of my company and called out to my comrades. However, the cannon ball turned in some fashion and went straight for the place where we had opened out in order to avoid it. Five *sepoys* and one *Havildar* were swept away. The *Havildar* was thrown many paces by the force of the cannon ball. One of the *sepoy*'s muskets was dashed against my chest and I fell down unconscious. When I came to, I found my regiment had moved on. I was unable to move, but by good fortune was picked up later by parties sent out to search for the wounded, and was sent to hospital.

The losses of the *Sirkar*'s army in this action must have been very heavy.[27] One General *sahib* was killed, and I heard that 100 officers were killed or wounded.[28] Everything belonging to the Sikh army was captured, and the plunder was very great. Some of our *sepoys* got as much as 100 *Nanukshaee* rupees[29] from one dead body. If the river had not been so swollen, the *Sirkar*'s cavalry would have cut up hundreds of the enemy, as the river was not usually so difficult to cross at this time of year.[30] However, the boats from which the bridge was made were carried miles downstream when the bridge broke, and all the other boats near at hand had been destroyed by fire. More boats were collected after a few days and our army crossed the Sutlej into the Punjab.[31]

It was always said that the Sikh troops had been drilled by French officers, but all of these had left before the war began. They had either refused to fight against the *Sirkar*, or else the Sikh *Sirdars*, jealous of their influence, had used their influence to have them dismissed. It is certainly true that I never saw any European officers among the Sikh troops,

[27] The British losses at Sobraon were 320 killed and 2,063 wounded, of whom a considerable number died later.

[28] Major-General Sir Robert Dick (1785?–1846) was killed at the head of his Division.

[29] These were rupees coined by the Sikhs and worth rather more than the Company's.

[30] The Sutlej would normally have been low at this time of year, but rose seven feet on the day of the battle. This was thought by the *sepoys* to be the favour of God towards the British.

[31] The battle of Sobraon effectively ended the First Sikh War. The *Khalsa* was humbled, its powerful artillery captured, and its army dispersed. It would have saved much blood and treasure if the Company had annexed the Punjab after Sobraon, but Hardinge did not recommend this.

nor did I ever hear of any being seen.[32] The Sikhs fought as no men had ever fought in India before, but it was clear that their leaders did not know how to command an army. When they had decided advantages in their favour, they failed to make use of them. Their cavalry never came near any battlefield so far as I could make out, and when I was in Lahore I heard many Sikhs loudly proclaim that *Sirdar* Tej Singh was a traitor, and that he well knew, at the time he gave out that an English army was in his rear (after the feint attack at Ferozeshah which I have already mentioned), that the said army was miles away.[33]

I remember, when I was close by the head of the bridge [at Sobraon], seeing an English soldier about to bayonet what I thought to be a wounded Sikh. To my surprise, the man begged for mercy, a thing no Sikh had ever been known to do during the war, and he also called out in English. The soldier then pulled off the man's turban and jacket, and after

[32] The Spaniard, Hurbon, and the Frenchman, Moulton, were at Sobraon, and there almost certainly were other Europeans fighting for the Sikhs, but they had little or no influence.

[33] The Sikh leaders were at loggerheads among themselves, each seeking to improve his own position among the Sikhs. Tej Singh, the Commander-in-Chief, was probably a self-seeker, as was Lal Singh, the *wazir*, or chief minister.

'. . . a sahib *from a regiment next to mine kept walking up and down singing*'

this I saw him kick the prostrate man and run him through several times with his bayonet. Several other soldiers kicked the body with great contempt and ran their bayonets through it. I was told later that this was a deserter from some European regiment who had been fighting for the Sikhs against his comrades.

The *Sirkar's* army marched on Lahore a few days later and the whole of the Punjab lay at the feet of the mighty Company *Bahadur*, whose power none could withstand, and against whom it was useless to resist. All this happened towards the end of February 1846. The *Sirdars* had a meeting with the Governor-General *Sahib*, Lahore was occupied by an English force, and the pride of the mighty *Khalsa* was trampled in the dust. Large numbers of the Sikh army came to lay down their arms and it was curious to see these men. They freely admitted that they had been defeated by the *Sirkar*, but they said their time would come another day. It was general opinion in the Punjab that the English would take possession of it, as had been the case elsewhere in Hindustan. However a treaty was made, by which Rajah Lal Singh became the chief minister, and the country of Kashmir was sold to Maharajah Gulab Singh.[34] The *Sirkar* then retired over the river to its own territories, leaving the Punjab to itself and its interminable disputes.

[34] Lal Singh benefited temporarily from his double-dealing, but he had little prospect of retaining power unless the British garrison remained in Lahore to bolster his authority. Since the Lahore treasury could not pay more than a third of the indemnity demanded by the British, the Sikh territory in Kashmir was sold to Maharajah Gulab Singh of Jammu, who was a Dogra, not a Sikh, for one million pounds.

'The Sikh horsemen used to come out and challenge the English army to single combat'

13 The Second Sikh War: 1848-1849

The Second Sikh War, in which Sita Ram took part, was a direct consequence of the British reluctance to annex the Punjab after their victory in 1846. The Sikhs, humiliated by their defeat and the wresting from them of the fair province of Kashmir and the Jullundur Doab, became more discontented on account of the reforming activities of Sir Henry Lawrence, the British Resident in Lahore. His crusade against female infanticide, widow burning, cruel punishments and unjust taxation was hardly calculated to endear him to those Sikh sirdars who had a vested interest in a continuance of the old ways. Moreover the Sikh soldiers, under-paid and under-employed, were in a state of semi-mutiny for most of the time, and hoped longingly for the time when they would be able to settle scores with the hated Company.

Multan was the capital of the southernmost Sikh province. It was ruled by Mulraj, a Hindu governor, who had once found favour in the eyes of Maharajah Runjeet Singh. A minor revolt there in April 1848, resulting in the murder of two of the Company's officers, soon developed into outright rebellion. Multan is fiendishly hot during the summer and it was some time before a force could be assembled to deal with Mulraj. This force, commanded by Major-General Whish, was joined by a Sikh army under Sirdar Sher Singh, but they proved to be unreliable allies. Abruptly abandoning the siege, Sher Singh marched north to join forces with other Sikh armies that had risen in rebellion. The Punjab was soon in flames.

The Governor-General was the Earl of Dalhousie, one of the most dynamic men ever to have held that office. He had the reputation of being an 'annexationist' but he was reluctant to become embroiled with the Sikhs. It was several months before he yielded to the arguments of Lord Gough, the Commander-in-Chief, and assembled an army to deal with the Sikhs once and for all. This army, the 'Army of the Punjab', assembled at Ferozepore and crossed the Sutlej in late November 1848. The Sikhs had concentrated their forces on the river Chenab, and there followed some skirmishing along the banks of that river before Gough launched his troops against the Sikhs at Chillianwallah on 13 January 1849. It was a battle in the best Gough tradition —fought without clear orders against an enemy concealed in thick jungle and whose bravery was in no way inferior to that of their opponents. Gough's troops remained on the field when night fell but their losses were considerable. When the news of them reached London there was consternation at yet another pyrrhic victory à la Gough.

However, years of intrigue and mutiny had taken their toll of the Sikh army. The men were as brave as ever but they were no longer a disciplined army. As soon as Multan had been captured in February 1849, and the troops involved in that operation were free to rejoin Gough, he brought the Sikhs to battle at Gujerat on 21 February 1849. On this occasion Gough retrieved his reputation by signally defeating the Sikhs, largely because of the *intelligent handling of his artillery and cavalry. The Sikhs and their Afghan allies fled the field and were pursued until they were no longer an effective fighting force.*

In the words of Lieutenant F. G. Cardew, historian of the Bengal Native Army, 'Thus ended the second Sikh War, which, commencing with the treacherous revolt of Mulraj, terminated with a great victory over one of the bravest of the peoples of India, gave a fine kingdom to the British Empire, and some of the best of its soldiers to the Indian Army.' The Punjab and Peshawar passed into the possession of the East India Company whose frontier now marched with the Afghans.

Sita Ram was present at Chillianwallah, as hard a battle as ever he fought, but he was only on the fringes of Gujerat since his regiment was employed in guarding the baggage train. He had now been promoted to jemadar, and was an officer, but not it seems a very contented one. He was ageing rapidly and feeling the effects of wounds and previous hardships, but he continued to give loyal service. I suspect the old man was longing for his pension, and his seat under the pipal tree in his ancestral village, where his age and his rank would ensure him a respectful hearing among the village elders; but there were still some years to pass before he would attain this, and those years were destined to be the most difficult of all his service.

The fortune of the *Sirkar* was very high at this time. All ideas of resisting it had ceased, and the mutinous feeling in the army, which I have mentioned as having existed previously, seemed to have disappeared. All that was now talked about was the good luck of the Company *Bahadur*, and since the *Khalsa* troops, who had always been supposed a match for the English army, had now been beaten, even the Mahommedans held their peace and for a time considered it folly to go against fate. But fortune does not always remain the same, and who can tell where the seeds of the dandelion will alight?

My regiment was stationed at Ambala after this war, and after the end of the second year of its stay there I was promoted to *Jemadar*. I had now been some thirty-five years as a servant of the government.[1] True, I was a *Jemadar*, but where were the visions of wealth I had indulged in when first I took service? I had nothing to show, other than some seven wounds and four medals. I was becoming an old man, but I wore a sword

---

[1] Sita Ram was a stripling compared with *Subedar-Major* Mir Sher Ali who was killed while charging with the 8th Bengal Light Cavalry at Ramnagar on 22 November 1848. He had sixty years' service and was *seventy-eight* years old.

and was an officer. My eldest son, who had formerly served with me in the same regiment before I entered Shah Shujah's service, was somewhere in Sind and I had not heard of him for two years. Numbers of native soldiers had been carried off by the terrible fever of that country, and it had such a bad reputation that the native regiments were with great difficulty persuaded to go there. The heat was greater than in any other part of India. Those *sepoys* who escaped death from the effects of the fever were so affected by it that they were seldom any use afterwards. They were subject to attacks of the disease long after they had returned to their native country. In the last letter I had received from my son he said that 750 men of his regiment were ill with it, and that half a European regiment had died.[2] He also was in hospital and had little hope of escaping death; for four weeks before he wrote he had been unable to move.

In 1847 two English officers were killed at Multan. The *Sirkar*, to avenge this insult, went to war with Dewan Mulraj of Multan and laid siege to the place.[3] This inflamed the Sikhs. They began to collect troops and their warlike ardour seemed to revive. The prospects of yet another Sikh War were now debated. The government began to assemble troops and moved them up towards Ferozepore. My regiment was again ordered to form part of this army.[4] The siege of Multan progressed very slowly and this gave great confidence to the Sikhs who boasted that they would beat the foreigners this time. Regiments now came in every day from Delhi, Meerut, Ambala, etc., and then they were all pushed on towards Ferozepore. A large English force crossed the Sutlej and entered the Punjab, while the Sikhs were reported to have collected on the banks of the river Jhelum under the command of *Sirdar* Sher Singh.

After two or three rather serious skirmishes on the banks of the river, and towards the end of the year, we came up with the Sikh army. They were all encamped in very thick jungle and only their advance pickets were visible. No-one could estimate their strength but spies brought in word that there were 50,000 of them, and that their strength was increasing every day. They also had a vast number of guns. The enemy kept to the jungle and displayed no inclination to begin the fight. However, our suspense was soon ended for the Sikhs fired with some heavy guns on the

[2] The disease was malaria. The European regiment was the 78th Highlanders [now the Queen's Own Highlanders].

[3] On 20 April 1848, Mr Vans-Agnew and Lieutenant Anderson were murdered at Multan, probably at the instigation of Mulraj, the *dewan* or governor of the province. What began as an isolated revolt rapidly spread throughout the Punjab and resulted in the Second Sikh War.

[4] A General Order was published on 13 October 1848, for the formation of the 'Army of the Punjab' under the Commander-in-Chief, Lord Gough. It numbered about 20,000 officers and men, of which 5,000 were besieging Multan, over 100 miles to the south.

Commander-in-Chief *sahib* when he was out riding with his staff. The *Lad sahib* became enraged because someone was killed beside him and the order was given for immediate engagement with the enemy.[5] This was just as the gongs were sounding mid-day, but the jungle was so thick that it was like fighting in the dark. Regiments became disorganized—rifle company number ten of my regiment was in advance of the grenadier company. Our own regiments mistook each other for Sikhs and volleys were exchanged before the mistake was discovered. The commanding officer of my regiment suffered greatly from fever and was compelled to go away very sick only a few days before the battle. Another Colonel *sahib* was sent to us just as we were going into action. The firing had actually begun. He saw the red coats of the enemy and imagined them to be one of our regiments. He immediately stopped us firing, saying he was certain we were firing on our friends. Some of the officers then said they could see the black belts of the men of the other regiment and were certain they were Sikhs [the Sikh army wore black belts, or very brown ones, and the English *sepoys* wore white].

The Colonel then rode at full gallop up to this dubious regiment which was about 200 yards away and half hidden by the jungle. He was received with a volley full in his face but, wonderful to relate, he escaped without a scratch. He returned among us and called out, 'All right, fire away, *sepoys*!' He was a brave officer, and fearless but none of us knew him in the regiment, or his word of command,[6] which is great drawback for a regiment in action. Fighting continued all day and neither side seemed to be gaining a victory. The Sikhs lost guns, and the *Sirkar* had some captured by the Sikhs. Their batteries were so well concealed by the thick jungle that it was impossible to tell the number of the guns. One regiment, the 24th Europeans, charged a battery; the terrible fire of the guns and from a Sikh regiment concealed behind the battery forced them to retire. This corps lost nearly half its strength, and more than twenty officers were killed or wounded.[7] A native regiment was with them and

[5] The Battle of Chillianwallah took place on 13 January 1849. The Sikhs were drawn up in thick jungle with the river Jhelum to their rear. Gough's original intention seems to have been to make a reconnaissance in force with a view to attacking the next day. However, it soon became apparent that the Sikhs had advanced from their entrenchments to the edge of the jungle, and Gough decided to give battle despite the lateness of the hour (not much before 2 p.m. and darkness comes early in the Punjab winter). Sita Ram's explanation for Gough's decision to attack is also repeated in the memoirs of Sergeant Pearman who was present at Chillianwallah. Pearman says that a near miss by Sikh guns 'got the old man's [Gough's] Irish out', and orders for general action followed.

[6] It always took the *sepoys* some time to accustom themselves to the pronunciation of their language by their British officers.

[7] HM 24th Foot (later South Wales Borderers and now 1st battalion Royal Regiment of Wales). They advanced with such dash that they outstripped the other

was beaten back with great loss. How could they stand if the Europeans could not?

In the evening the Sikhs retired to a village called Rasul and threw up entrenchments. This battle was called Chillianmoosa [Chillianwallah] and took place on the thirteenth day of the first month of the year. The *Sirkar*'s army remained on the ground all night but it was not much of a victory. It also began to rain, which made the place a perfect swamp. Not far from the thick jungle in which this bloody battle was fought were plains free from any jungle; these would have been much better for fighting on. This battle was not managed with the usual splendid arrangement of the *Sirkar*, but it was fought in haste and before the orders could have been properly explained to our whole force. Besides which, the ground was not known at all by the English officers, which is always a disadvantage in war. But then in this battle, the *Sirkar* had nothing but disadvantages.[8] The Sikhs fought well but the fire was not as heavy as at Ferozeshah. It was evident that the Sikh army had not improved since its last war with the *Sirkar*, and there was not the same reluctance or dread to meet the Sikhs as had been shown by the *sepoy* regiments during the first [Sikh] war.

Rasul was a small village surrounded by deep ravines with a steep bank on its near side and the river Jhelum not far away. This place might have been shelled if its position had been accurately known, but the Sikhs were allowed to retain it unmolested by us. However, they had very heavy artillery in position all around the village and a close approach was never practicable. During this time of inactivity we used to go down to the river to bathe and drink water. We repeatedly met the Sikh soldiers who seemed to think that the English army had suffered a severe blow, so that it was stunned like a snake, or else, they said, why did it not attack them? To be honest there was some measure of truth in this but the Sikhs had had enough of fighting to prevent them from annoying our army.

One day a *sepoy* of my company, rather celebrated for boasting of his deeds of valour, came into the camp with his head nearly severed and his face dreadfully gashed. The story he told was that he was

---

two regiments in their brigade, 25 and 45 BNI, and were mowed down by grapeshot as they emerged from the jungle. They lost twenty-two officers killed or wounded, half their strength, and one of their Colours. Brigadier Pennycuick, commanding the brigade, was cut down by a Sikh horseman, and his son, an ensign in the 24th, was killed trying to defend his father as the Brigadier lay mortally wounded.

[8] The total British casualties were 602 killed, 1,651 wounded, and 104 missing. The majority of the wounded eventually returned to duty but the casualty figures horrified contemporary British opinion. Sir Charles Napier, grumbling and protesting, was hurried off to India to relieve Gough but Gough managed to retrieve his reputation at the Battle of Gujerat before Napier could reach India.

drawing some water from a small *nullah*, or arm of the river, when one of the enemy came down and attacked him. This *sepoy* made out that he had shot the man but I, knowing he was always making cats into tigers,[9] received his statement with some little doubt. Afterwards, when the Sikhs laid down their arms, a Hindustani in the Sikh service told me that he saw the *sepoy* drinking at the *nullah*, and warned him to go away as the Sikhs would certainly kill him if they saw him. But instead of taking this advice in a friendly way, the *sepoy* deliberately fired at him when quite close and missed him. The Hindustani became so angry at his countryman's ingratitude that he attacked him with his sword and left him for dead, as he thought; or at any rate with such scars as he would never get rid of for the rest of his life. After this was made known in the man's presence, boasting left his lips for ever.

The Sikh horsemen used to come out and challenge the English army to single combat. One day a *sirdar* came forth and the challenge was accepted by an English soldier in the Lancer regiment, and one out of the Dragoons.[10] One of these men was killed and the other severely wounded. The Europeans were angry at their defeat and some of them fired at the Sikh and killed him. These men went without the orders of their officers who were very angry and annoyed at their being beaten. I was here struck with the difference between the European and the *sepoy* when wounded in action. The former would shake his fist at the enemy and call down vengeance on their heads, but would never utter a cry of pain. The latter, if hit in the legs or arms, would dance round hugging the limb and crying out, 'Pity! Take Pity! Mighty Company *Bahadur*!'[11]

One morning it was reported that the Sikhs had left their position and moved up the bank of the river. The English were now expecting the force that had been engaged in the siege of Multan to join forces, since Multan had fallen into the hands of the *Sirkar*.[12] This force did arrive some time in February and our army pursued the Sikhs who had determined to make a stand at a place called Gujerat, where their religious leaders had promised them victory. The Sikhs had also been joined by *Sirdar* Chattar Singh who had managed to get away from Multan without

---

[9] The same meaning as geese into swans, or mountains out of molehills. [Note by translator.]

[10] Presumably from HM 9th Lancers and 3rd King's Light Dragoons. (now 9th/12th Royal Lancers and Queen's Own Hussars).

[11] This surprises me. I have always been struck by the stoicism of the Indian soldier when wounded.

[12] Multan was finally captured by Major-General W. S. Whish on 22 January 1849. Whish's force joined Gough on 20 February but this reinforcement was offset by the junction of Chattar Singh's force, from Multan, with Sher Singh's. In addition 1,500 Afghan horse under Akram Khan, a son of Dost Mahommed, had joined the Sikhs.

being molested. An action was fought at this place, Gujerat, and it was almost entirely a fight between the heavy artillery. My regiment was on guard over the baggage, and therefore a good way in the rear, and I do not know much about this battle from actual eyesight. The Sikh guns were dismounted, their lines broken, the village carried at the point of the bayonet, and the whole of the Sikh army fled towards Rawal Pindi.[13] After this battle some Europeans were walking about the field with lighted pipes when some *dubahs* [skin containers in the shape of a jar] exploded, being filled with powder, and burnt five or six Europeans and several *sepoys* so severely that they all died in dreadful agony. The unfortunate men ran towards their comrades, begging they would put a bullet into their heads and put them out of unbearable torment. I saw one or two *sepoys*—I think

[13] The Battle of Gujerat was fought on 21 February 1849. Gough had some 20,000 men and 88 guns, of which 18 were heavies. The Sikhs probably amounted to 50,000, but they had only 59 guns. It was mainly an artillery battle, but the 3rd Light Dragoons again distinguished themselves. 'Thank you, 3rd Light,' said Gough, 'a glorious victory, men!' The Scinde Horse also distinguished themselves.

'*They were allowed to depart to their homes, after laying down their arms*'

they belonged to the 72nd BNI. They were burnt from head to foot and the flesh fell off in charred lumps. I have often seen Sikhs fearfully burnt by their matches setting fire to their cotton-wadded coats when wounded, and then exploding their powder pouches, but I never saw such a frightful sight as these *sepoys*. What a wonderful thing is fate! These men, Europeans and *sepoys*, had survived both battles without a scratch and yet, when taking a stroll after the battle, for mere amusement, they met their death. The God of War was not satisfied with the slain!

After this battle of Gujerat the Sikhs fled across the river Jhelum and were followed by a light column of our army. They came up with them near an old fort on the road to Rawal Pindi, where the remainder of the Sikhs, finding they had no chance of escape from the *Sirkar* and having lost nearly all their guns, surrendered to the English general *sahib*. They were allowed to depart to their homes, after laying down their arms, and every man was offered a rupee to help him on the way home. Some took this but many refused it with contempt. There was a body of Afghan horse with the Sikhs, sent by Dost Mahommed to do mighty deeds against the foreigners, but these all escaped on account of the quality of their horses and fled through the passes by Peshawar without being attacked.[14] I have heard that they made an attempt at attack at Chillianwallah but I never saw any of them. I am inclined to think that they took good care to keep well clear of shot or shell, and confined their mighty deeds to vainglorious boasting.

[14] A force led by Major-General Sir W. R. Gilbert pursued the Sikhs so closely that they had no alternative but to lay down their arms on 4 March 1849. Gilbert subsequently chased the Afghans back over the Khyber Pass.

'*Agents of the Nawab of Oudh and also of the King of Delhi*'

14   *The Wind of*
        Madness

In this chapter Sita Ram describes his experiences during the Mutiny of the Bengal Native Army which first broke out at Berhampore in Bengal in March 1857, and continued until Oudh was finally cleared of the rebels two years later. Sita Ram gives us an excellent example of the conflict of loyalties that result from an uprising of this kind and, although he chose to remain loyal to the Government he had served so long, he is honest in admitting that he feared he might well be serving a losing cause. His account of his doubts and fears reminds me of a similar situation some years ago when an Arab officer of the South Arabian Army took me into his confidence and told me of his dilemma at the time when nationalism was gathering force in Aden. He too chose to remain loyal to his salt and was, like Sita Ram, called a traitor by his compatriots.

The Indian Mutiny was basically a revolt by a conservative and traditionalist society against what seemed to be a threat to their religion and ancient customs. There were many causes for the Mutiny, but au fond it was the imagined threat to their religion that caused so many Hindu and Mahommedan sepoys to break out into revolt. However, all this did not happen in a night, as we are sometimes led to believe in novels of the Mutiny, but was a slow simmering over many years that only came to the boil in the spring of 1857. And even then many of the mutineers hurried home from their garrisons and took no further part in the proceedings, leaving it to their more politically-motivated or fanatical comrades to pursue the rebellion against the British. It is this which makes the Mutiny less a nationalist uprising than a military rebellion pure and simple but it is of course true that there were many in India, or at least in Hindustan, who sought to utilize the soldiers' mutiny to drive the British back into the sea whence they had come.

Field-Marshal Lord Roberts, one of the Indian Army's best-loved Commanders-in-Chief, fought throughout the Mutiny as an officer in the Bengal Horse Artillery. In his view the causes of the Mutiny were as follows. First, the fears of the high-caste Hindu soldiers that their religion was in danger, and this fear was in turn communicated to their Mahommedan comrades. Second, the annexation of Oudh by Lord Dalhousie, which offended local sentiment, and resulted in the loss by the sepoys of their former privileged standing in the courts: they could scarcely claim special privileges in what was now British territory. Third, the affair of the cartridges which were supposed to be smeared with a mixture of cow's fat and lard for preservative purposes, and which the sepoy had to bite before loading his weapon. Fourth, pampering of the sepoy in the Bengal Army, which gave him an undue sense of his own importance. Fifth, the dangerous disproportion in numbers between the European and Indian troops. It is astonishing to learn that in 1857, when the Mutiny broke out, there were only 21,197 British troops in India, whereas the Bengal, Madras, and Bombay Native Armies totalled 277,000 men; and this

*figure does not include the para-military forces such as the armed police.
Sixth, dissatisfaction among the sepoys over various administrative measures,
such as the withdrawal of field allowance for troops serving in the Punjab and
Sind, and the insistence, after November 1856, that sepoys must undertake on
enlistment to serve beyond the sea. Most high-caste Hindus believed that service
beyond the Kala Pani, or Black Water, would inevitably destroy their caste
and the new regulation was regarded as yet another nail in the coffin of their
religion.*

*Finally, and possibly most importantly, Lord Roberts places
much of the blame for the Mutiny on the shoulders of the British officers of the
Bengal Native Army who were too complacent, too old, and too susceptible to
the prejudices of their men to take a firm line with them. Although the
Bombay Army recruited high caste sepoys from the same areas as the Bengal
Army, these men were allowed no special privileges vis à vis the low caste and
outcaste races who supplied a most trustworthy ingredient to the Bombay Army.
At the siege of Multan the Bengal sepoys refused to dig in the earthworks
because of their caste but their co-religionists in the Bombay Army worked
without demur. In the Bombay Army promotion was by selection, whereas in
Bengal it was by seniority, which accounts for Sita Ram having to wait until he
was nearly sixty before becoming a jemadar. But the most damning indictment
of the Bengal Army is contained in a footnote in Lord Robert's Forty-One
Years in India, in which he wrote:*

*'It is curious to note how nearly every military officer who held
a command or a high position on the staff in Bengal when the Mutiny broke out,
disappeared from the scene within the first few weeks, and was never heard of
officially again. . . . Two Generals of divisions were removed from their
commands, seven Brigadiers were found wanting in the hour of need, and out of
the seventy-three regiments of Regular Cavalry and Infantry which mutinied,
only four Commanding Officers were given other commands, younger officers
being selected to raise and command the new regiments.'*

*Despite the strains to which he was subjected, Sita Ram
remained loyal, and so no doubt did many others of his kind about whom we are
never told. The mutineers considered him to be a traitor and carried him off to
Lucknow to be put to death by torture but he was rescued by a roving party of
European Moss-Troopers and eventually joined one of the new regiments
raised in the Punjab to replace the Bengal regiments. This must have been the
time he met his future Commanding Officer, Norgate, who was serving in the
12th Punjab Infantry, and who may have been the officer who relieved him of
the responsibility of commanding the firing party that executed his son as a
rebel.*

After the fall of Multan and the total defeat of the Sikhs at Gujerat, the English took possession of all the land of the Punjab, or Five Rivers. The mighty power of the Sikh nation became as dust and the mantle of rule descended upon the *Sirkar*, the great Company *Bahadur*. The *sirdars* were all taken prisoner and their troops, deprived of their weapons, were disbanded and sent to their homes. English regiments were stationed all over the Punjab—at Lahore, Wazirabad, Jhelum, Rawal Pindi, Attock, Peshawar, and many other places—without any further opposition. Truly, the English are a remarkable people; within six months barracks rose out of the ground as if by magic. The *sahibs* built houses, police were organized, and the country appeared as if it had belonged to the *Sirkar* for many years.

My regiment was now sent to Jullundur. Two regiments of old Sikh soldiers were enlisted for the *Sirkar*[1] and young Sikhs were taken into the native regiments. This annoyed the *sepoys* exceedingly, for the Sikhs were disliked by the Hindustanis who considered them to be unclean and were not permitted to associate with them. Their position was very uncomfortable for a long time but after a while this dislike to some extent disappeared. However, these men always kept to themselves and were regarded as interlopers by the older *sepoys*. They were never as smart as we were on parade and their practice of using curds to clean their long hair gave them an extremely disagreeable odour, but many of them became like Hindus after they had been away from their own country for a long time.

No wars took place for several years in Hindustan and nothing particular occurred apart from several innovations which were introduced into the Army, and into the Civil Courts, which caused great offence among the people.[2] In 1855 a small war broke out in Bengal with

[1] Sita Ram is incorrect. Two battalions of Sikhs were raised in 1846 from those Sikhs living to the east of the Sutlej in British-controlled territory. The 14th Sikhs (Regiment of Ferozepore) subsequently became the 1st (King George V's) Battalion, 11th Sikh Regiment. The 15th Sikhs (Regiment of Ludhiana) became the 2nd (Royal) Battalion, 11th Sikh Regiment. They are today the 1st and 2nd battalions of the Sikh Regiment, Indian Army.

[2] Sita Ram refers here to two events which caused great dissatisfaction in the army. The first was the withdrawal of field, or foreign service, allowance for all troops stationed in the Punjab after its annexation in 1849. Mutiny occurred in several regiments, and particularly in the 66th BNI stationed in Amritsar. This regiment was disbanded forthwith by the Commander-in-Chief, Sir Charles Napier, without waiting for the Government's sanction, and its place in the Bengal Native Army was taken by the Nasseri Gurkha battalion, which later became the senior Gurkha regiment in the Indian Army. The other event to which Sita Ram refers is probably the annexation of Oudh by Lord Dalhousie in 1856, as a result of the misgovernment of the King, or Nawab, of Oudh. This led to the *sepoys* losing their privileged position as soldiers of the Company in the Civil Courts, and was most unpopular. Moreover the disappearance of one of the last independent dynasties of India undoubtedly offended Indian sentiment.

some jungle people called Santhals,[3] and my regiment formed part of the force and was stationed near Raniganj, not far from Calcutta. It was there that I first saw the iron road and the steam monster and this was more wonderful than anything I had ever seen before. When I asked the people about it they said they believed that the English put some powerful demon into each iron box, and it was his efforts to escape which made the wheels turn round. However I saw the water put in, and the coals lighted under it, but I am so ignorant of how it works that if an officer had not told me that it was all the force of steam, I might easily have believed that this demon fed on wood, coal, or stones, and drank gallons of water.

I went down to Calcutta in the train but it went so fast that it nearly took away my senses. As it neared Calcutta all kinds of low caste people entered the train and behaved as if they were equal to everyone. This is not good and caused great annoyance to many. I was amazed by what I saw in Calcutta but what is the use of describing it to you, my Lord, who know it so well? The ships—what can I possibly say? They were a hundred times larger than I had expected. No wonder the *sahibs* can travel all over the world. Each ship could carry a regiment. The Lord *sahib*'s house[4] was very big, and if every nobleman in England lives in a house as big as that, what a wonderful country England must be! I noticed in this magnificent city that the *sahibs* seldom spoke to each other and I was told they did not know one another. But can this be possible if they all come from such a small island?

The Santhals used bows, arrows, and large sharp axes, but they always dispersed when we fired on them. At first it was reported that they used poisoned arrows, and for this reason they were much feared, but we soon discovered that this was not the case. After a good deal of marching through thick jungle, and after guarding the main road by the Sone river throughout one hot weather, the rebellion was put down and my regiment was sent to ————. I was told by some of the Santhals that they rebelled because they could obtain no justice from the Civil Courts. They had no money with which to bribe the native officials and their complaints were all against the rich landlords and moneylenders, who had managed to get these simple folk into their clutches. I cannot vouch for the truth of this but it was certainly a curious war. In one part of the jungle we were firing at them, while in another the *Sirkar* was providing them with cart-loads of rice.

There was now a rumour that the *Sirkar* was going to

[3] The Santhals were aboriginal tribesmen. They lived in the jungle-covered hills of the Santhal Parganas in Bengal and rose in revolt in 1855.
[4] Government House, Calcutta.

take Oudh from the Nawab. This led to great excitement within the army, which was largely composed of men from Oudh. Many of them did not much care whether the *Sirkar* took Oudh or not but these were men who owned no property there. Nevertheless an undefined dislike and disquiet took possession of all of us. During the year [1856] the *Sirkar* removed the Nawab to Calcutta and took over the government of the Kingdom of Oudh. Regiments of local infantry and cavalry were formed, officered by English officers, and a number of Assistant Commissioner *sahibs* were brought in. Many of these officers came from the Bombay and Madras Armies and were totally ignorant of the language, manners, and customs of the people, and the same was true of all the *sahibs* who came from Bengal from the college.[5] The occupation of the country was effected without any open resistance at the time. It took place so quickly that the people did not have time to combine against it but the minds of all the *Taluqdars*[6] and headmen were excited against the *Sirkar*, which in their view had acted dishonourably, and had been unfair to the Nawab.[7] There were plenty of interested people to keep this feeling alive. They assured everyone that the estates of the rich would soon be confiscated by the *Sirkar*, which could easily manipulate the law courts to show that the present owners had no right to these estates. The truth was that so many people in Oudh had acquired property by methods which the Government would never recognize that they began to fear an inquiry. Since all these people had large numbers of relations, retainers, and servants living with them, who were all interested parties, it explains the great excitement prevailing in Oudh at the time, and consequently throughout the *Sirkar*'s army.

It is my humble opinion that this seizing of Oudh filled the minds of the *sepoys* with distrust and led them to plot against the Government. Agents of the Nawab of Oudh and also of the King of Delhi were sent all over India to discover the temper of the army. They worked upon the feelings of the *sepoys*, telling them how treacherously the foreigners had behaved towards their king. They invented ten thousand lies and promises to persuade the soldiers to mutiny and turn against their masters, the English, with the object of restoring the Emperor of Delhi to the throne.

---

[5] Sita Ram is presumably referring to the junior officials of the Company's Civil Service who were sent to Oudh straight from their training in Calcutta.

[6] The hereditary land revenue receivers of Oudh who had become the landed gentry.

[7] Misgovernment in Oudh had been notorious for more than fifty years, but each Governor-General in succession had been chary of annexing Oudh. Even Dalhousie had advised that the best solution would be to leave the Nawab as titular ruler, and for the Company to administer Oudh in his name, but the India Board in London chose his alternative solution, which was outright annexation.

They maintained that this was wholly within the army's powers if the soldiers would only act together and do as they were advised.

It chanced that about this time the *Sirkar* sent parties of men from each regiment to different garrisons for instruction in the use of the new rifle.[8] These men performed the new drill for some time until a report got about, by some means or other, that the cartridges used for these new rifles were greased with the fat of cows and pigs. The men from our regiment wrote to others in the regiment telling them of this, and there was soon excitement in every regiment. Some men pointed out that in forty years' service nothing had ever been done by the *Sirkar* to insult their religion, but as I have already mentioned the *sepoys'* minds had been inflamed by the seizure of Oudh. Interested parties were quick to point out that the great aim of the English was to turn us all into Christians, and they had therefore introduced the cartridge in order to bring this about, since both Mahommedans and Hindus would be defiled by using it.[9]

I reported this curious story to my officer but no notice was taken. He only told me not to talk about it. Some time later an order was read out to the regiment from the Commander-in-Chief, or Governor-General *sahib*, saying that the *Sirkar* had not used any objectionable fat but that in future the men could make up their own cartridges and use their own grease. They could then be satisfied that the *Sirkar* had no intention whatsoever of hurting their feelings or breaking their caste. However the very reading out of this order was seized upon by many as proof that the *Sirkar* had broken our caste, since otherwise the order would never have been issued. What was the use of a denial if it had not been the Government's intention originally to break our caste?

It was the time of year for furlough[10]—that is the month of April—and it was my turn to go on leave. Before I went I told my Commanding Officer what I had heard, and I warned him that great madness had possessed the minds of all men. I could not say what shape the discontent would take, but I never thought the entire army would mutiny— only those men who might have suffered as a result of annexation of Oudh —and at present only a few of the really bad characters were disaffected. The Colonel *sahib* was of the opinion that the excitement, which even he

---

[8] The Brown Bess had been superseded by the Enfield rifle in 1856. Prior to loading the new rifle it was necessary to bite off the end of the cartridge.

[9] The cow is of course sacred to the Hindu, while the pig is unclean to the Mahommedan. The authorities could hardly have chosen a worse preservative for their cartridges than a mixture of cow's fat and lard, which, according to Field-Marshal Lord Roberts, were the ingredients used.

[10] Furlough, or long leave, was taken to coincide whenever possible with the harvest.

could not fail to see,[11] would pass off, as it had often done before, and he recommended me to go to my home.

I arrived at my own village without hearing anything out of the ordinary on the road, but shortly afterwards we heard that the troops of Meerut and Delhi had risen and killed their officers, and had proclaimed the King of Delhi as Emperor. They were excited to revolt because a complete regiment[12] had been cast into jail, having been loaded with irons which destroyed their honour. This was such an extraordinary story that I refused to believe it, considering it a story invented to inflame the minds of the populace, but the rumour gathered strength daily, so I went to the Deputy Commissioner to enquire whether it was true. I could not do this openly without arousing suspicion, for at this time all the office staff were on the watch for all who came to the office. I went to the Deputy Commissioner's house with a petition, but the *chaprassi*[13] refused to take it in to the *sahib*, saying the orders stated that no-one would be received except during office hours. However I managed to see the *sahib*, and I told him the tale I had heard and asked if there was any truth in it. The *sahib* said neither one thing nor the other but asked me a number of questions to discover how much I knew and what effect it was having on the minds of the people in my district. Finally the *sahib* admitted that he had heard the rumour—as I had known from the beginning by the questions he asked me—but said that the reports were very vague.

Had I asked some important Indian official, he would probably have denied any knowledge of the facts, and the more vehemently he denied any knowledge, the more I would have been certain that he knew all about it. Had I persisted, he would have attempted to discover my own feelings on the subject, and then, if I had committed myself by wishing the mutineers well, he would have informed against me, even though he himself might have been heart and soul in their favour.

By the time I returned to my village the whole place was

[11] Dissatisfaction among the *sepoys* of the Bengal Native Army was not new; indeed, it had been gathering strength over a period of thirty years. The surprising thing is that so many British officers seem to have been blind to the discontent.

[12] Eighty-five men of the 3rd Bengal Light Cavalry, stationed at Meerut, had refused to receive the offending cartridges. They were tried by court martial on 8 May 1857, publicly degraded by being stripped of their uniform and fettered in front of the entire garrison, and handed over to the civil authorities in the local jail. Two days later, on 10 May, the 3rd Cavalry broke into open mutiny, and were joined by the two Native Infantry regiments in the garrison. They released the prisoners and set off for Delhi where they proclaimed Bahadur Shah Emperor of Hindustan, and where they were joined in mutiny by the Delhi garrison. The British regiments stationed at Meerut failed to prevent the mutiny, and the local commanders were woefully dilatory in following up the mutineers on the way to Delhi.

[13] *Chaprassi*: office messenger who waits on the verandah of his master.

talking about the news. In a short time the entire country was in a fer-
ment[14] and every regiment was reported to be ripe for mutiny. Reports
came in every day that the regiments at the different stations had risen and
killed their officers. I went again to see the Deputy Commissioner and
offered to collect the furlough men of my own regiment, as well as any
pensioners who could use arms. He thanked me and promised to let me
know if I would be required to do this. Shortly afterwards the regiments
at Lucknow, Sitapore, and other stations in Oudh broke out into open
mutiny, and the country was overrun with *sepoys* from these regiments.
Many of these men returned to their homes and had nothing further to do
with the mutiny, other than having been in a regiment which had
mutinied.

I now discovered that I was being watched. I was sus-
pected of giving information to the civilian officials. One day a large party
of *sepoys* from one of the mutinied regiments came through my village,
and I tried to persuade them to go quietly to their houses. I explained to
them the folly of going against the English Government, but these men
were so intoxicated with the plunder they had taken, and by their hope of
reward from the Emperor of Delhi, that they turned on me and were
about to shoot me on the spot for having dared to speak out in favour of
the English Government. They called me a traitor, and ended by taking me
prisoner. They put heavy irons on me and a chain round my neck, declaring they would take me to Lucknow where they would receive a large
reward for having captured me, and where my punishment would be to
have molten lead poured down my throat for having dared uphold the
English rule under which I had served and eaten salt for so many years. I
was treated with every possible indignity. My captors boasted of the deeds
they had done—how the *sahibs* had been so easily killed, or terrified into
running away into the jungles like hares—and they were convinced that
the English rule had ended throughout India. I never saw men behave in
such a shameless fashion—not even during *Holi*.[15] They all believed they
would be made princes for what they had done, and debated among themselves about the offices they would be given by the King of Delhi. I could
not discover what they had done, other than that they had shot down their

[14] Sita Ram is of course referring to his own country, Oudh, or what is
now the UP. The mutiny was almost entirely confined to the Bengal Native Army. The
Madras Army was unaffected, and there was little disaffection in the Bombay Army,
despite the fact that many of its *sepoys* were recruited from Oudh.

[15] *Holi* is one of the principal Hindu festivals and takes place in the
spring. It is a kind of Hindu saturnalia, connected with the god Krishna, but must originally
have been a fertility ceremony. Few things are barred during *Holi* and most sober-minded
citizens remain indoors; those who venture out must bear their indignities with composure,
if not with a smile.

officers on the parade ground, looted the station without any resistance, and set it on fire. While we were on the march some people informed them that there was a European regiment not far behind, and their boasting was redoubled. They would immediately annihilate it! This was what they said in public but inwardly they were terrified of coming up against the English. The European regiment never materialized, nor indeed was there the slightest truth in the report. I was relieved to hear this since they had told me that I should be shot at once if any Europeans appeared on the scene.

The leader of this party was a *sepoy*, although there were two *subedars* with it. He came one day and showed me a proclamation from the King of Delhi. It called upon all the *sepoys* to rise and destroy the English, promising great rewards and promotion if the men of any regiment would mutiny and kill their officers. It stated that the English *Sirkar* intended to make all Brahmins into Christians, which had in fact been proved correct, and in proof of it one hundred Padres were about to be stationed in Oudh.[16] Caste was going to be broken by forcing everyone to eat beef and pork. The *sepoys* were exhorted not to allow this to happen, but to fight for their religion and drive the detested foreigners out of the country. It also stated that the king had received information from the Sultan of Turkey that all the English soldiers had been destroyed by the Russians;[17] there were only left the few regiments remaining in India; and these were all separated by great distances and could easily be surrounded and destroyed. This proclamation was printed on yellow paper and was said to have been issued by order of the king. Every man who heard it believed every word of it. Even I was impressed by it. I had never known the *Sirkar* to interfere with our religion or our caste in all the years since I had been a soldier, but I was nevertheless filled with doubt. I remembered the treatment of many regiments with regard to field allowance—how it had first been promised and then withheld. I could not forget that the *Sirkar* had seized Oudh without due cause.

I had also remarked the increase of Padre *sahibs* during recent years, who stood up in the streets of our cities and told the people that their cherished religion was all false, and who exhorted them to become Christians. They always maintained that they were not employed by the *Sirkar*, but how could they have acted like this without the Government's sanction? Everyone believed that they were secretly employed by

[16] There was an almost obsessive belief that the British intended to convert the population to Christianity, and the activities of missionaries in India added fuel to the flames. Moreover this was the period of the evangelical revival in Britain, and men like Havelock and Nicholson, whose religion was a burning faith, merely added to the confusion in the minds of the *sepoys*.

[17] In the Crimean War

the Government; why else should they take such trouble? Then I remembered how the *Sirkar* had been my protector, and that I had eaten its salt for over forty years, and I was determined never to betray it so long as it continued to rule but to do all that I could to support it. But, my Lord, you must not forget that I was bound with chains at this time, and to all appearance being taken to a terrible death. As each day passed and I heard that city after city, garrison after garrison, had fallen into the hands of the local population, I must confess that the thought passed through my mind that the mighty Company's rule was passing away. All its guns had been captured, and also all its arsenals—how could I help thinking otherwise? However I still had faith in the incredible good fortune of the *Sirkar*, which had always been so wonderful and marvellous. I also believe that those who had broken their word and committed such crimes could not expect to have good fortune for long.

When the party of *sepoys* with whom I was drew near to Lucknow, from some orders they pretended to have received direct from the Nana of Bithur[18] the route was changed and they marched towards Cawnpore and crossed over the river. While on the march, however, our party was surprised by a troop of mounted *sahibs*.[19] It was early morning, just before the dawn, and we were attacked so suddenly that these brave warriors, so far from attempting to fight and annihilate the Europeans, fled into the jungle. Luckily for me, they forgot to carry out their threat to shoot me. I was pulled out of the pony trap in which I was travelling and narrowly escaped being shot by one of these trooper *sahibs* who thought I was a wounded or sick *sepoy*. He had not noticed my chains and could not understand Hindustani. Luckily there was an officer nearby who came up, heard my story, and saw my chains, which were very convincing proof of my story. He gave orders for my chains to be knocked off and took me to the officer commanding who wrote down my statement, my name, and my regiment. He was also very anxious to learn of the conditions in Oudh,

[18] Dandu Pant, or the Nana Sahib, was the adopted son of the last Peshwa of Poona, head of the Mahratta confederacy. He inherited a vast fortune in 1851, but the pension paid by the Company lapsed on the Peshwa's death. This rankled with the Nana Sahib, and although outwardly friendly to the English, he was in fact thoroughly disgruntled and disloyal. He played a leading part in the Massacre at Cawnpore, his estates being in the vicinity, and became one of the principal villains of the piece so far as the British were concerned. He was never captured and his exact end remains one of the mysteries of the Mutiny.

[19] In the confusion following the outbreak of the Mutiny, individual Europeans banded themselves together as Moss-Troopers, such as Vincent Eyre's troop of twelve hog-spears. Indigo planters without plantations, Judges without courts, Officers without regiments, and District Commissioners without districts took to the sword and saddle. They did good work in restoring order in outlying districts but the justice they meted out was sometimes rough and ready. Sita Ram probably joined the Troop of Lousada Barrow of the Madras Cavalry.

and whether I had seen or heard of any *sahibs* or ladies in the jungles. The last English officer I had seen was the Deputy Commissioner of ———, who was, when I left, carrying on his work as usual but this was a month ago.

As I was not a very good horseman, the Captain *sahib* could not turn me into a trooper but when he found out that I could read and write Persian, he made me interpreter for the Troop. He also gave me a certificate of the account of my recapture etc. I went about with this *rissalah*[20] for about six weeks, during which time it destroyed several bands of mutineers and one day had a hand-to-hand fight with a party of regular cavalry. They fired off their pistols and made off as hard as they could although they were three times the size of our party. Nineteen *sowars*[21] were killed and twenty-one of the best of the Government's horses were taken. We lost five men killed and seven wounded. After this our Troop returned to Cawnpore, which had been re-taken twice by the English. Through the kindness of my Captain—may the shadow of greatness always surround him—he took me to the officer commanding a Punjab regiment,[22] and I was taken on the strength of this corps as a supernumerary *Jemadar* and attached to it. This regiment was engaged in several actions, and also before Lucknow. We pursued the mutineers right into Nepal and I passed the old place again where I had been so frightened by the elephants forty years previously. All this is so well known that I need not tell it again, but in no fight that I was in—and they were not a few—did I ever see the mutineers, be they Hindus or be they Mahommedans, ever make a good stand and fight. Usually they stood the first discharge and then took to flight—if they could not find shelter behind walls or trees. I am told it was tough work at Delhi. I was not there, but the *sepoys* could not have fought well to have allowed an English force of under 10,000 defeat 70,000, with the latter in possession of all the houses and fortifications.

One day, in one of the enclosed buildings near Lucknow, a great number of prisoners were taken. These were nearly all *sepoys*. They were all brought in after the fight to the officer commanding my regiment, and in the morning the order came that they were all to be shot. It happened that it was my turn to command the firing party. I asked the prisoners their names and their regiments. After hearing some five or six, one *sepoy* said he belonged to a certain regiment which was my son's. I naturally inquired whether he had known my son, Ananti Ram, of the

[20] *Rissalah*: a Troop of Horse, or Cavalry.
[21] *Sowar*: a horseman, or cavalry trooper.
[22] This may have been the 12th Punjab Infantry, which was commanded by Major T. C. Blagrove. The second-in-command was Captain J. T. Norgate, who later commanded the regiment.

Light Company. He answered that that was his own name. However this is a very common name, and because I had always imagined that my son must have died from the Sind fever, since I had never heard from him, it did not at first strike me. But when he told me that he came fromTilowee, my heart leapt in my mouth. Could he be my long lost son? There was no doubt about it, for he gave my name as his father, and fell down at my feet imploring my pardon. He had mutinied with the rest of his regiment and gone to Lucknow. Once the deed had been done, what else could he do? Where could he have gone, even if he had wanted to escape?

The prisoners were to be shot at four o'clock in the afternoon and I must be my son's executioner! Such is fate! I went to the Major *sahib* and requested that I might be relieved of this duty as a very great favour. He was very angry and said he would bring me before a court-martial for trying to shirk my duty. He would not believe I was a faithful servant of the English Government—he thought my real sympathies were with the mutineers—and he would not listen to me any further. At last my feelings as a father got the better of me and I burst into floods of tears. I told him that I would shoot every one of the prisoners with my own hands if he ordered me but I confessed that one of them was my own son. The Major declared that I was only making up an excuse to avoid having to shoot my own brethren but at last his heart seemed to be touched. He ordered my unfortunate son to be brought before him and questioned him very strictly.

I shall never forget this terrible scene. Not for one moment did I consider requesting that his life should be spared—that he did not deserve. Eventually the Major came to believe in the truth of my statement and ordered me to be relieved from this duty. I went to my tent bowed down with grief which was made worse by the gibes and taunts of the Sikhs[23] who declared I was a renegade. In a short time I heard a volley. My son had received the reward for mutiny! He showed no fear but I would much rather that he had been killed in battle. Through the kindness of the Major I was allowed to perform the funeral rites over my misguided son. He was the only one of the prisoners over whom it was performed, for the remainder were all thrown to the jackals and the vultures.[24]

I had not heard from my son since just after my return

[23] Sita Ram's antipathy for the Sikhs was shared by many of the old-style British officers. 'I recollect,' says Lord Roberts, 'the commanding officer of the 25th BNI, who had served all his life with clean-looking, closely-shaven Hindustanis, pointing with a look of contempt, not to say disgust, to some Sikhs, and expressing his regret that he could not get them to shave their beards and cut their hair. "They quite spoil the look of my regiment," he said.'

[24] The correct performance of the funeral ceremonies is of immense importance for all Hindus, and particularly for Brahmins.

from slavery. I had not seen him since I went to Kabul, and thus I met him again, untrue to his salt, and in open rebellion against the master who had fed his father and himself. But I have said enough—more is unnecessary. He was not the only soldier who mutinied. The Major told me later that he was much blamed by the other officers for allowing the funeral rites to be performed on a rebel but if good deeds wipe away sins, and I believe some *sahibs* believe this as we do, then *his* sins will be very white. Bad luck never waits upon the merciful! May my Major[25] soon become a General.

[25] It is more than likely that this 'merciful Major' was Norgate, translator of Sita Ram's memoirs. It is known that Sita Ram served under him during the Mutiny, and an incident such as the one described would have formed a strong bond between the two men, and may have accounted for Norgate's success in persuading Sita Ram to part with his memoirs.

'. . . *bowed down with grief which was made worse by the gibes and taunts of the Sikhs*'

'How could I double-march, or perform Light Infantry drill?'

15   *The Pensioner*

In this the last chapter of his memoirs Sita Ram covers some old ground, inveighs against the corruption of minor Indian officials, and complains of the changed attitude of British officers towards sepoys like himself. He also included some allegations against the Mahommedans but these I have omitted. India is now a secular state and there is nothing to be gained by reviving old quarrels that do no good to either side.

He does not like the new Army with its preponderance of Punjabis, considering them to be hairy and uncouth, nor is he enamoured of the new-style British officers who seem to have suffered from all the arrogance of youth. He prefers the easy-going officers of the old days, with their hookahs and interminable curry dinners, whose morals may have been questionable but who, in Sita Ram's opinion, understood India better than the new generation. Conditions could not have been easy for a Hindustani sepoy in the years immediately following the Mutiny. Memories such as the massacre of the women and children at Cawnpore died hard and repression was a more popular word than clemency. Those sepoys who had remained loyal were probably made to feel responsible for the sins of those who had mutinied.

The old Subedar has a lot to say about bribery, which was not confined to India either then or since, but India has always been a very poor country, where the margin between ease and poverty is pathetically small, and in such circumstances bribery and corruption are probably inevitable. Office of any kind under the Government was regarded as an excellent opportunity for feathering one's nest, or at least for acquiring some degree of comfort for one's family, and bribery was certainly not confined to civilian officials. Sita Ram has already told us of the trouble he had as a recruit for failing to reward his Drill Havildar and European Sergeant when he completed his recruit training.

He complains a good deal about the administration of justice and it must be remembered that Indians are among the most litigious people on this earth. There is nothing an Indian peasant enjoys more than a long-drawn-out lawsuit in which he will argue his case with more heat than skill. However, it is true that the new laws introduced by the British when they annexed Oudh bore little resemblance to traditional Hindu justice, and were utterly incomprehensible to the older generation who naturally preferred the old ways.

It is unfortunate that Sita Ram's account of his long life in the service of the Sirkar should end on rather a sour note but we must make allowances for the fact that the aftermath of the Mutiny was a particularly unhappy period in Indian history. However, in his concluding sentences, Sita Ram expresses contentment with his lot and asks to be remembered as a faithful servant of the English Government.

After my return from my second campaign in Nepal, fought this time not against the Nepalese but against those men with whom the *Sirkar* had formerly defeated the Nepalese, I was promoted to *Subedar* after forty-eight years of hard wear and tear in the *Sirkar's* service. I entered the army under the flag of the Company *Bahadur*, and I ended under the flag of the Empress of the World.[1] I was an old man of sixty-five years of age and had attained the highest rank to be gained in the Native Army,[2] but I would have been much better fitted for this position thirty years earlier. What could I do now at the head of my Company? How could I double-march, or perform Light Infantry drill? But I was expected to be as active as ever and no allowance was made for my forty-eight years' service. No one bothered to remember that I had carried a musket for thirty years and had been present in as many battles as most of the officers had lived years. I was shouted at by the Adjutant as if I was a bullock, and he a mere boy, young enough to be my grandson. I was abused by the Commanding Officer, and called a fool, a donkey, and an old woman! Finally I was taken before the Commander-in-Chief and reported on as being utterly useless—a man the Commanding Officer could do nothing with.

I was taken before the Invaliding Committee which agreed my discharge, and I acquired the pension of a *Subedar*. Had any attention been paid to my rights, I should have received this pension years before. I wanted this pension more than anything else in the world and yet I did not like to ask for it; and when I was, as it were, discharged compulsorily, of course I was not pleased. I do not doubt that the Company *Bahadur* would have wished me to have my pension earlier and the delay was not the Company's fault. It was due to the new hard regulations. The time it took to become a *Subedar* was far too long for most *sepoys* to aspire to, for this promotion was seldom given until after forty years' service. In recent years some men have become *Jemadars* and *Subedars* more quickly, and many of them were immediately promoted if they brought young men for enlistment during the Mutiny. This is a much better system. These officers were men of influence and were much more highly regarded by the *sepoys*, being looked upon as fathers of the company. But if the *Sirkar* wants men of rank and position, the pay of sixty-seven rupees a month is hardly likely to tempt them.[3] The native officers of the Irregular Cavalry are generally men of some wealth, and the younger sons of good

[1] The transfer of the Government of India from the Company to the Crown took place on 1 November 1858. Queen Victoria was proclaimed Empress of India in 1876.

[2] The highest attainable rank was in fact *subedar-major*, which was instituted in 1817.

[3] About £5 a month, but with a purchasing power that was nearer £20.

families, but then their pay is good and this enables them to keep up their position.[4]

Those native officers who became *Jemadars* and *Subedars* at once did good service during the Mutiny and led their men well. They were young and full of spirit. However, once the fighting was finished, they were found not to know their drill so well as a *sepoy*, who had spent forty years at it and was therefore much too old to perform it. They were bullied, questioned, examined, and drilled until they became quite sick of the service, and numbers of them left in disgust as they had nothing more to look for in the way of advancement. Some were sent away with gifts of land which no-one else had cultivated. The ordinary *sepoy* would be quite contented with a larger pension, and if he could obtain this after twenty-five years' service, he would not worry over becoming a *Subedar*. He could only achieve this rank when he was too old to be fit for it, unable to march, and at a time when he ought to have been at home taking his ease and preparing for death.

Our learned men had told us that the Company's rule would come to an end in 1857, since this was one hundred years after the Company's first great battle,[5] but they did not tell us that another kind of English rule would take its place. This rule was far harder and much harsher. The Company *Bahadur* and its officers were much kinder to the people of India than the present Government. If it were not for the old servants of the Company, it would be even worse than it is. In my last regiment there were five or six young *sahibs* who came to us from some European regiment. Several of these commanded companies but it was obvious that they hated the *sepoys*. They always spoke severely and sneeringly to us. In my opinion this is not calculated to endear them to the *sepoys*. Very few of these officers could speak to the men, and when they did so it was in unpleasant fashion. They may have learned how to command European soldiers but they did not know how to command *sepoys*. My Lord, *sepoys* will not fight well for those they do not like, or for a Government which is not kind to them. They used to be treated kindly, but then they turned against their master. They will never find as good a master again.

[4] The Irregular Cavalry was largely composed of the *zemindari*, or landowning, class. The soldiers provided their own horses, while the Government fed, clothed and equipped them. An officer provided recruits from his own tenants and a man's place in the regiment (*asami*) was regarded as his own property and could be farmed out by him to the highest bidder on his retirement, with the commandant's approval, until he had a son or nephew to put into the regiment. The Mutiny resulted in a great increase in the Irregular Cavalry, officers being deputed on the authority of a Commissioner or a General to raise a regiment of Horse, such as Hodson's, Wale's, Murray's, Cureton's and Lind's Horse. Many were later brought into the regular establishment.

[5] The Battle of Plassey, 23 June 1757.

The Mahommedans were the first instigators of the Mutiny, and the Hindus followed like a flock of sheep over the bank of a river.[6] The principal cause of the rebellion was the feeling of power that the *sepoys* had, and the little control the *sahibs* were allowed to exert over them. Naturally, they assumed from this that the *Sirkar* must be afraid of them, whereas it only trusted them too well. But a son is not discarded by a parent for once rebelling against his authority, and I trust that the chastisement meted out to the rebellious son for this Mutiny will have a lasting effect, and that wickedness will never again be permitted to enter into the hearts of the *sepoys*. It is obvious that all officers are now afraid to trust the *sepoy*, and this must be so for many years to come, but it is unjust to condemn everyone. There were some who remained faithful, and there were still more whose fate it was to be in a regiment that mutinied. These had no desire to rebel against the *Sirkar*, but feared that no allowance would be made for them when so many others had gone wrong. This was well understood by those who instigated the Mutiny. Their first object was to implicate an entire regiment so that everyone had to throw in their lot with them. All regiments took their Colours with them. They did not break their oath by deserting them.[7] They left the service of the English and were supposed to have entered the service of another government.

I know the *sahibs*. Nothing pleases them more than a straight answer to a plain question but the Indian does not usually understand this. He will always try to answer a question in such a fashion as will please the asker—exactly the answer he imagines the asker desires. I never could feel myself again, nor hold my head as high as formerly, after the death of my son. The fact that he had fought against the giver of his salt brought great disgrace upon me. My chief solace today is thinking over the many years of my service, during which I was never punished, except for the single instance I have already mentioned. I have given my entire life to the service of the *Sirkar*. I have one son left, by whom I send your Lordship my papers, and I have two daughters who are married and have large families.

I have not acquired any fortune but I have my paternal estate and the pension of a *Subedar*. This is enough for me. The people in my village seem to respect me, and are now fully satisfied with the ease and benefits they enjoy under English rule. The man who sows now knows that he will reap, which he never could reckon on doing in the old days.

[6] Sita Ram's religious antipathies are again coming to the fore. Both Hindus and Mahommedans were discontented and if anything the Hindus broke into mutiny first.

[7] Recruits in India take the oath of allegiance while holding the regimental Colour.

The people are still sometimes oppressed by the subordinate Indian officials but redress can often be obtained, and in any case this oppression gets less and less each year. If the District Commissioner *sahib* goes about himself and personally inquires into all complaints, as our good *sahib* does (may his office last for ever!) and takes an interest in our welfare, there will be little inclination to resist the *Sirkar*'s authority. But if everything is left to the Indian officials, as is sometimes done through the inability of the *sahib* to understand what is said to him, the people become dissatisfied, talk against the government and long for a change. My Lord, the Indian officials are all corrupt, whether they be Hindus or Mahommedans; in this respect there is no difference between them. There may be one man who would not take a bribe of five rupees, but I have never yet heard of him. The principal reason for this is the poor pay provided by the *Sirkar*, but if it was only half as much, there would still be hundreds of applicants who would make up by bribes what was deficient in their wages. This was always the case in former times—the man who could give the biggest bribe would always win his case. 'When there are those who are willing to receive, there will be found those who will give; and when there are those who will give, it is not difficult to find those who will take.'[8] The *sahibs* have tried to put down bribery but there is such a combination against them that they will never be successful.

A British official is always very angry when he learns that a petitioner has given a bribe. He asks him why he did it. Perhaps he does not know that the man firmly believes that part of the bribe went to the *sahib* himself! Therefore he does not dare to say anything, because all the officials have told him this, from the office runner to the head clerk. I have never yet heard of an office where the petty clerks did not make out somehow or other that the *sahib* was amenable to a bribe. Since they live by bribes themselves, it is of course in their interest to maintain the system. The head *Patwari*[9] in my village told me one day that it must have been my own fault that promotion was so slow in coming. When I replied that I had never done anything wrong, he laughed and said I was not wise, even though I had been so much in the world. He meant of course that I had not paid for my promotion, thinking that promotion could be bought like everything else. I have known very few cases of English officers taking bribes. I have been told that many did, but I have never believed it since I know their personal honour is very strict. However I have seen no difference where bribery is concerned between the Indian and the European soldier

[8] This is marked as a quotation in the manuscript, but there is no indication of its origin.

[9] *Patwari*: The man who keeps the village records for land revenue purposes etc.

of subordinate rank. I know the *sahibs* do not take bribes but I also know that many much better educated than I am firmly believe that the *sahibs* do so. Since this is part of their own nature, how can they believe anything different?

I remember I once had occasion to go to the Deputy Commissioner's office on some petty business of my own. I was in Hindustani dress and imagined I could walk straight in, as I had been told it was an open court of justice. Immediately two or three *chaprassis* came to me to know what my business was. I told them it was with the *sahib*, not with them. They then said it was very difficult to see the *sahib* for he was engaged, and a hundred other excuses were invented. They ended by telling me that one of them would take the petition himself and lay it before the Commissioner if I gave him five rupees. I answered that I had no petition. I was then prevented from entering the *sahib*'s presence for a long time and only because I would not produce a bribe. At last a head clerk came out and spoke to me. He told me the *sahib*'s temper was very bad that day, but if I particularly wished to see him, some other official would dare to brave his wrath by mentioning the fact to him, but this would cost me ten rupees.

Tiring of these attempts at extortion, and also not believing the man's story, I entered the office, but the *chaprassis* and clerks did their best to prevent me. They all began talking against me, saying 'what a mannerless person I was to intrude in such fashion', and they spoke out loudly in order to attract the *sahib*'s attention. I walked straight up to him, gave him a military salute, and requested permission to speak but he ordered me to be thrown out and also abused me. The office runners tried to throw me out but I would not allow them to touch me. Since the *sahib* himself had ordered me to leave, I went outside, after giving him my name, regiment, and rank. One of the *chaprassis* who had first accosted me then trumped up a case that I had resisted authority. The entire office swore that I had beaten the man dreadfully. He showed his face all covered with blood, which he must have had ready for the purpose, as I only pushed away those who were attempting to lay hands on me. I was fined ten rupees for resisting authority. When I returned to my regiment I reported the whole case, just as it had occurred, to my Commanding Officer. He was very angry and wrote about it but I never received any redress for this great insult. If a District Commissioner *sahib* is easy of access, and will take the trouble to listen to the complaints of the poor, bribery can in large measure be prevented. The subordinate officials will then be afraid that the *sahib* will hear the rights of the case and the people will then realize that there is no use offering bribes.

The *Sirkar*'s punishments for offences are considered by

many to be absurd. A low-caste man is convicted of breaking into a house and stealing jewels from the women, attended by violence. He is sent to prison for a year where he is much better fed, clothed, and looked after than he has ever been in his life. It is true that he has lost his liberty but he gets his food and laughs at the hard labour. What is hard labour to a coolie who has to work so hard for his few ounces of flour? His hand would have been chopped off under a native government. This is real punishment and one the thief would never forget. It is a punishment that has great effect upon all evil-doers, and this I conceive to be the purpose of punishment. The *Sirkar* should remember that the peasant is only a bullock. A bullock does not mind being beaten with a small stick. He requires a goad, and so it is with these criminals. The *Sirkar's* punishments have no effect on them. They are in fact a perfect laughing stock.

    The laws of the English are doubtless very wise and good for the English but the laws of the Hindu code are the best for us. We much prefer them. They are written in a language which can be understood, but

'. . . sometimes the District Commissioner is pleased to listen to my story'

few Hindus can understand the English laws which are all written in Arabic. I have often asked learned men why our laws cannot be written in a language we understand and they have told me their meaning cannot be given in Hindi. It would seem to me that crimes which cannot be described in a people's tongue do not need any laws to lay down the punishments. Who can understand why a man should not punish his wife if she is guilty of adultery? Can money satisfy his desire for revenge? Yet we are not now permitted to punish either the wife or her paramour. This is not justice and leads to great dissatisfaction. There can only be one opinion of this.

I have now written all I can remember of interest in my life, and I have given my opinion on many subjects. I should never have thought of doing this but for your Lordship's desire that I should so do. If I have said anything unseemly, my Lord must grant me a pardon. But what I have said is true—I have fired at no mice with cannon.[10] I meet very few *sahibs* in my own village but sometimes the District Commissioner is pleased to listen to my story. I go twice a year into cantonments to receive my pension and I then have a gossip about the old days. However, there are few of the old *sahibs* left now, and the new *sahibs* do not much want to listen to an old man's babbling of things and events which took place before they were born. Thanks be to God the Creator! I lack nothing thanks to the bounty of the *Sirkar*, and I have a son still left to perform my funeral ceremonies.[11] If your Lordship, when you return to your own country, will always remember that the old *Subedar* Sita Ram was a true and faithful servant of the English Government, it will be enough for me.

And now, with profound respect for one who has always been to me as a father, I make my most humble obeisance!

[10] i.e. I have not exaggerated.

[11] These ceremonies are considered among the Hindus of very great importance, and to have no one to perform them is one of the greatest misfortunes that can possibly befall a worshipper of Bramah. This accounts for their custom of adopting sons when none are born to them or have died. Every year these ceremonies are repeated. [Note by Translator.]

Glossary

A

Abdar — a butler, more properly a 'water cooler'.

Assami — an office, place, appointment (applied particularly to an appointment in Irregular Cavalry, i.e. a Sillidar Regiment).

Atta — wholemeal flour.

B

Badshah — a king.

Bahadur — a hero or champion, a title bestowed by the Moguls. Used after the names of European officers. (Can be compared with the Parliamentary courtesy, 'The gallant officer'.) A term said to have been brought down by the armies of Changiz Khan from the Mongol steppes, in 1221.

Bannia, Bania or Baniya — a trader in grain, merchant or shop-keeper, often a money lender. Always a Hindu.

Barakzais — one of the powerful clans of the Durrani tribe. With the Sudduzais provided the rulers of Afghanistan from 1747.

Batta, Bhatta — an allowance or compensation in the form of money given for war service or for being posted to certain areas.

Bhonsla — the family name of the Mahratta rulers of Nagpur.

Blayut, Billait or Wallyte — Europe, from the Arabic 'Wilayat', a kingdom or province. From this came the word 'Blighty', used by British troops to refer to Great Britain and Ireland.

Burra — big.

C

Cantonment — a military station usually a few miles from a city.

Chapatti — a flat, circular disc of unleavened bread.

Chaprassi	a peon, messenger or door-keeper.

D

Dacoit	an armed bandit.
Daffadar, Duffadar	originally a sergeant of Irregular Horse, later used by all Indian cavalry.
Diwali	festival of Light.
Doab	a tract of land between two rivers.

G

Ghazi	a Moslem fanatic, a 'fighter for the Faith' who gains much merit by killing infidels.
Guru	a Sikh priest or teacher.

H

Haji	a title of respect given to one who has made the pilgrimage to Mecca.
Havildar	a sergeant of Infantry, but also used in the old Indian Regular Cavalry.
Holi	a Hindu festival.

J

Jemadar	an Indian officer equal to a lieutenant.
Jezail	a long-barrelled musket used by Afghans and Pathans.
Jheel	a marsh, lake or pond.

K

Kala	black.
Kala Pani	'Black Water', refers to the sea.
Kali	'Dark Mother', worshipped by the Thugs.
Khalsa	the Sikh community.
Kila	a fort.
Kiladar	the commandant of a fort.

L

Lance Naik	a Lance Corporal.

M

Maulvi	a learned man, a Mahommedan scholar or teacher, usually of religion.

Mohur	a gold coin of Mogul times, but used by the Hon. East India Company.
Munshi	a secretary or interpreter. Later a teacher of languages.

N

Naik, Naigue	a corporal of Infantry. Lit. a master or landlord.
Nanukshee Rupee	a Sikh coin worth slightly more than the Company Rupee.
Nawab	a Mahommedan prince or landowner.
Nullah	a ravine or water course.

P

Padre	a priest, clergymen or minister of the Christian religion, from the Portuguese of 16th century Goa.
Paltan	a regiment of Indian infantry from the French 'peloton' and later English 'platoon'.
Pathan	a tribesman from the North-West Frontier.
Patwari	the man who keeps the village records for the Land Revenue Authorities.
Peons	Peon—from the Spanish; peon, a footman, orderly or messenger. Used in South India whereas Chaprassi used in North India.
Pice	less than a farthing.
Pipal-tree	the tree is sacred to the Hindus and often has a shrine at its base.
Poshteen	a coat or jacket of sheepskin worn on the North-West Frontier and in Afghanistan. The wool was always inside, the outside was much embroidered.
Pundit	a learned man, a Hindu religious teacher.
Punjab	from Panch-ab, land of the five rivers.

R

Raj	rule, kingdom.
Rissala, Rissalah	a body of Irregular Horse, and later a regiment of Indian Cavalry.
Rissaldar	originally the commander of a rissala. Later the Indian officer commanding a troop.
Rissaldar Major	the senior Indian officer of an Indian Cavalry regiment. A rank introduced in 1866.

S

Sahib	Sir or Mr.
Sepoy	a Private of Indian Infantry, from the Persian 'Sipahi'.
Serai	a place for the accommodation of travellers, usually in the form of a square courtyard with animals inside and cells to sleep in.
Sirdars	Sikh chiefs.
Sirkar	the Government.
Sowar	a trooper of Indian Cavalry, from the Persian 'Sawar', a horseman.
Subedar	*Lit.* the Governor of a province. An Indian officer of an Infantry regiment equal to a Captain.
Subedar-Major	the senior Indian officer of an Infantry regiment and adviser to the Commanding Officer on all matters.
Suddar Bazar	The Cantonment Bazar.

T

Taluqdars	landed gentry of Oudh.
Thakur	Rajput landholder or minor nobleman.
Thug	more properly 'Thags', meaning 'Deceivers'. Thugs worshipped the goddess Kali, the Dark Mother, and in her honour murdered and robbed travellers.
Tykhana	a cellar.

Z

Zemindar	a small landowner.

Index

'*It is finished*'